PARADIGM SHIFT

A HISTORY OF *THE THREE PRINCIPLES*

A BRIEF HISTORY
IN THREE PARTS
OF THREE PRINCIPLES UNDERSTANDING
AS UNCOVERED BY SYDNEY BANKS,
AND ITS DISSEMINATION

Compiled by
Jack Pransky

Interview with
George Pransky

Foreword by
Don Donovan

CCB Publishing
British Columbia, Canada

Paradigm Shift: A History of *The Three Principles*

Copyright © 2015 by Jack Pransky
ISBN-13   978-1-77143-228-3
First Edition

Library and Archives Canada Cataloguing in Publication
Pransky, Jack, 1946-, editor
Paradigm shift : a history of the three principles / compiled by Jack Pransky ;
interview with George Pransky ; foreword by Don Donovan. -- First edition.
Issued in print and electronic formats.
Additional cataloguing data available from Library and Archives Canada

Cover design by:
Serena Fox Design Company
2692 East Warren Road
Waitsfield, Vermont 05673 USA
Tel: 802-496-2326
Fax: 802-793-6006
Website: http://serenafoxdesign.com

Publisher: CCB Publishing
               British Columbia, Canada
               www.ccbpublishing.com

This book is dedicated to the life of Sydney Banks,
1931-2009

from one man's heart to the world*

…and to all those who have since shared
his profound wisdom with others.

---

* Thank you, Serena Fox

Contents

Foreword

I was honored but surprised when Jack asked me to pen this Foreword. I couldn't help but think I was an unlikely choice. After all, I am not a psychologist, psychiatrist, social worker, teacher or practitioner of any kind. I am just a businessman. And, though I have been on the periphery of *The Three Principles* community for a while, I am—as my Dad used to say—a "piker" compared to the people you are about to meet in this book. Then, after reading the book and learning more about the incredible things all of the wonderful people in this community have done over the last forty-plus years, I went from feeling unlikely to feeling *unfit*. But I trust Jack implicitly and I feel passionately about *The Three Principles* that Sydney Banks discovered and shared with the world and the community that has embraced his vision, so here I am.

Like I said, I'm a business guy who has worked in and run high-tech businesses for nearly thirty years. In the mid-1990s during a particularly challenging time, I was fortunate to meet Dr. George Pransky and, at the recommendation of my friend and colleague, Dick Bozoian, hired George to work with my leadership team, my employees and me. George brought with him an amazing cadre of Principles-based practitioners (all of whom are featured in this book) —and, ultimately, Syd Banks himself—to help us at a time when we were struggling and feeling we were out of ideas about how to turn our business around.

It is impossible to convey in a few paragraphs what transpired over more than a decade of sharing *The Principles* with thousands of people in our company. In short, our performance improved dramatically as we exceeded our commitments and objectives year after year. The more deeply and broadly our workforce understood *The Principles*, the more successful we became. We would often say that through our understanding of *The Principles,* our workforce became incredibly resilient—nearly 'discouragement-proof'—and I believe that our *Principles* program (that we called 'State of Mind and Business Success') was the single most important competitive advantage we had in the marketplace and a primary factor in our success. And we had a blast.

While our customers and shareholders loved the terrific performance—as did I—it paled in comparison to the profound impact that learning *The Principles* had on the personal lives of our employees. People frequently talked of how their understanding helped them to be better spouses, parents, friends, siblings, sons & daughters and members of the community. Some spoke about how it helped them deal with long-standing problems of depression, addiction, PTSD, guilt, habitual negative thinking, anxiety, OCD, ADHD or just plain-old insecurity and chronic unhappiness. Others, who felt that they were healthy and happy, were amazed at how their new understanding helped unleash their potential and took the quality of their lives to levels they had never imagined.

It was an amazing ride.

Having seen how understanding *The Three Principles* helped me, my business, my family, friends and colleagues, when I was asked to help create what is now The Three Principles Global Community (3PGC) after Syd passed away in 2009, I was happy to sign on. Since then, I have had the honor of meeting and becoming friends with so many of the incredible people in this fascinating community. They are some of the most impressive and caring people I've ever met. The book you hold in your hand tells their story—the story of how they have shared a profound truth with hundreds of thousands if not millions of people throughout the world for more than forty years. From Syd Banks' experience in 1973 through to today, the story of *The Three Principles* and its community is a compelling one. I am forever grateful to Syd Banks and George Pransky for their friendship and for all they have done to share *The Principles* with the world. I miss Syd and know he would be proud of all of the great Principles-based work that is going on all over the world. I am also grateful to Jack Pransky and the other contributors to this book for putting the time and energy into capturing all of the elements of that story and, more importantly, for creating the story in the first place.

It normally takes dozens, if not hundreds of years for a new paradigm to take hold in the world and to become a fundamental element of mainstream culture. I've read that the idea of sanitizing the medical equipment—and the *hands*—of surgeons took nearly 50 years to become doctrine and required practice *after* germ theory had been validated. It was even longer until it was seen as 'common sense' in the mainstream. *The Three Principles* is a radical new paradigm that is diametrically opposed to how most of the human race has viewed life since time began. Gaining widespread acceptance is an uphill battle to be sure. In the face of such a headwind, I am humbled and amazed by the impact Syd and the people in this book have had in the last 40-plus years. And as I watch that impact grow through technology and the passion and energy of an ever-increasing number of bright, enterprising teachers, I know this is just the beginning. I feel an evolutionary inflection point coming. It may take a while, but I believe there will be a time where most of mankind will live their lives with a solid understanding of these *Principles*. It *has to happen*—because truth cannot be constrained indefinitely. It *must* get out and the people in this book are the catalysts for its escape. So, in the end, this book may well represent one-tenth of one-percent of the story. But it is the essence. It is the piece without which there is nothing.

Thank you, Jack… And thanks to all of the people who have done their part to help realize Syd's vision for mankind.

Don Donovan
Business Executive & 3PGC Board Member
New Hampshire, USA
February 2015

Introduction and Editor's Note

This book presents a history of a new paradigm understanding, discovered in the 1970s, that very gradually and silently has crept into the consciousness of perhaps hundreds of thousands of people, touching and changing lives worldwide.

I never set out to write it.

First, to be clear, I am not so much this book's author as the interviewer and editor of, primarily, other people's contributions. It did take a great deal of time and effort to put it all together, but it all came about and evolved spontaneously, which is probably what makes it special.

This project materialized because Sydney Banks, who uncovered this understanding in a moment of spiritual enlightenment, and Roger Mills, one of the two original mental health professionals to transform this spiritual understanding into a psychology and pioneer its practical application for the fields of prevention and community mental health, both passed away within about a year of each other. Besides mourning both their losses because my own life had been so personally touched by each of them, the thought hit me like a ton of bricks that at some point perhaps in the not-too-distant future all of the originators of this understanding could be gone, and all that history would be lost with them.

So I called my cousin, George Pransky, the other original pioneer or founder of this inside-out psychology, and asked him if he would be willing to do an interview with me. He said, "Sure." We both realized this was only one person's view of this history, but it is an enormously important perspective. The interview became very extensive and detailed. I, like many others who had learned of the Three Principles, had heard the general story, but I found the details, especially of the early days, absolutely fascinating.

Perhaps even more fascinating to me was the deeper appreciation I gained for what today is often taken for granted: How difficult it was to create an entirely new psychology from nothing, from scratch, from the formless, spiritual nature, for which Syd Banks, himself, even struggled to find words. Furthermore, this was a completely new psychology—a true paradigm shift to the inside-out—which flew in the face of the traditional psychology accepted not only by the powers that be (whoever they are), but by millions of people around the world who studied it and practice it. Further still, I realized that creating something of this magnitude from nothing was like conducting experiments within a maze, where it was so easy to run into dead-ends that looked so promising at the time. Through this process of looking back I gained a much deeper appreciation and gratitude for the ability and flexibility of the original creators to regroup and begin anew, which over the years happened a number of times.

We take so much for granted now! People now coming into Three Principles understanding appear to have a much easier time grasping it than most of us did in the early days. Why is this? Because the teaching of this understanding today is a result of all the fumbling around, experimentation, mistakes made along the way, and all the learning that transpired from it throughout its history. This is partly what Syd Banks referred to as "jumping time." And this learning and communication of it continues to evolve; it is never-ending.

At one point during the interview George became fuzzy about a couple of dates, so I went into my old files to try to find them. There I bumped into a number of events in which I had been personally involved, stemming from the early 1990s when I first found this understanding. It occurred to me that to complement this interview I could compile these as an appendix of key events in the history of Three Principles understanding and dissemination. So I put it together from what I had in my own files. Looking at it, I then had the thought that I was probably missing some important events; clearly, I didn't know everything that happened. So I decided to send it out to the key figures in the development of this understanding to ask for their input.

I did this with a certain amount of trepidation. I did not know how the idea of a historical chronology would be received. Separate realities could make it a bit of a slippery slope. George felt even more strongly about it than I did; he really didn't want to have anything to do with a chronology. But something told me it would be important to have a historical record, so I decided to give it a shot.

Bless their hearts, I got deluged with information. In fact, I became so overwhelmed with the volume of important information to add that I had to set down my own new book I had started to write to only concentrate on this one. It took me a while, but I put it all together and sent it back to everyone again, asking them to review it for accuracy and whether anything was still missing. I got even more deluged the second time! I questioned what I had gotten myself into. However, any trepidation I had about how it would be received was dispelled by the wide range of acknowledgments and appreciation I received from nearly all the leaders and well respected members of the Three Principles community. During this process two things became abundantly clear to me: 1) This section now looked far too important to simply be considered an Appendix to the interview; it needed to be an entirely separate part (Part II) of this book. 2) This historical depiction had evolved far beyond the point where it could be considered only *key* events; instead, it had become a chronological depiction of the scope and sequence of many of the amazing things that occurred along the way, resulting in so many lives being touched and changed around the world.

And all this from one man's enlightenment experience in one moment of time! Do we fully grasp the significance of this?! From one moment in time it gradually rippled out, affecting one person at a time, who then affected others, who then affected others, and on and on into futures we cannot even imagine. Now I had an even greater appreciation and gratitude for how it all came about. I became even more in awe of the magnitude of what had occurred—and will keep occurring.

I am so grateful to all of those who contributed so graciously to this chronology. They are listed on the page where the chronology begins. I would be remiss if I did not give extra special thanks to a few people: Judy Banks, who ensured that all the information I had on Syd was completely accurate; Linda Quiring and Barb Aust, who spent much time enlightening me about the early days on Salt Spring Island; and Dr. Keith Blevens, who midway through this process went through the chronology with a fine-toothed comb and helped me clarify criteria for inclusion.

To my knowledge nothing like this had ever been attempted for the Three Principles. From this point on it can be used as a starting point for others who want to conduct further historical research.

But that was not all. During George's interview, when I asked George about his experience with the West Virginia University School of Medicine and got into areas he was not privy to, he said, "You'll have to talk with Judy [Sedgeman] about that." I took him literally. I wrote to Judy, and she responded with an eloquent description of her time coordinating that effort. I thought it would be a great idea to insert that as an aside into George's interview. George didn't like that idea. I could understand his reasoning. This was his own story. And, in fairness, it would mean wherever George mentioned something of which he did not have direct experience I would have to ask many others for write-ups. This could easily get out of hand. Probably all the key players should be interviewed, but this would be well beyond the scope of this book. So in that sense at least, this should not be considered *the* definitive history; it is merely a good start. However, as an alternative I suggested I could take what Judy wrote and put it in a separate section. George then had the idea that I could select five or so of the major historical efforts that resulted in major institutional change over a long period of time and put all those in a separate section. George and I agreed easily on which efforts should be chosen. I then contacted the main people involved and received written descriptions from each of them. This became Part III.

Finally, early on in the interview with George I realized it did not feel appropriate for either of us to make any money off this book; that it would be more appropriate to be offered as a public service. So I had the idea to also use this as a small fundraising opportunity in support of the Three Principles Global Community (3PGC). George readily agreed. My main publisher, CCB Publishing of British Columbia, Canada had already agreed to publish it, and when I told Paul Rabinovitch, the head of CCB Publishing, of the donated, fundraising idea we had in mind, he amazingly and graciously agreed to also contribute 80% of all proceeds from the sale of this book to the 3PGC. Paul deserves tremendous gratitude from all of us for this. I have always loved working with him; now he has earned my greatest respect. Then Serena Fox, a wonderful graphic designer who attended one of my trainings locally in Vermont and got touched, offered to design the cover—for free! And Katja Symons offered important last moment proofreading. The generosity of people who have come through in this endeavor makes me shake my head in wonderment. I am so grateful to all of you!

And that is the history of how this history book came to be—it's natural evolution. I hope you will be as fascinated by all that occurred and how it all unfolded as I have been by putting it together. And judging by the comments I received already from those who contributed, I suspect most of you will be.

And even if you aren't, you will be supporting the Three Principles Global Community, an organization that I believe deserves to be supported, because it supports us all.

Jack Pransky
Moretown, Vermont
December 2014

Part I

A History of Three Principles Understanding as a New Paradigm Psychology: One Man's View

An Interview with George Pransky
conducted by Jack Pransky
October & November 2012, September 2013, February & July 2014

In 1973 Sydney Banks, an ordinary laborer, had a spontaneous "enlightenment experience" where he saw how everyone's experience of life is created from the inside-out via Three Principles: Universal Mind, Consciousness and Thought*. He started talking with people on Salt Spring Island, British Columbia about what he saw. As people's lives began to change as a result of gaining understanding from listening to Syd, a community began to gravitate around him. The word got out and people started coming over to the Island to hear him...

THE MEETING

JP: Explain how you met Syd Banks.

GP: I worked as a partner with John Enright in a program called ARC [Awareness, Responsibility and Communication]. John was a well-known Gestalt Therapist. Someone had told him about Syd, and he went up and heard him. I wouldn't have been up there had it not been for John being intrigued by the results he saw. He was intrigued by how low-key Syd was, yet he seemed to have an impact on people. He was intrigued by the fact that Syd didn't have any technology, that he just

---

* Note: I have chosen to capitalize the word, "Principles," when referring to "The Three Principles" (which I also capitalize), and when referencing each of them, to distinguish them from the common use of these words. Some will disagree with this because of the perception that it makes it into "a thing," but, to me, this helps others understand we are talking about something vastly different from the norm.

sat there and talked to people, and it was obvious he was affecting them. So he told me about it. I got intrigued and went up to a talk he was giving.

JP: Describe the feeling you had when you met Syd for the first time.

GP: Well, when I first walked into the room with the people on Salt Spring who had been learning from Syd I was immediately hit by a number of really strong feelings. One of them was I was frightened by how anxious I felt. Now, in retrospect, I was frightened by the contrast between the anxiety I lived with and their ease. I was frightened by how anxious I was and how calm they were, and how serious I was and how lighthearted they were. I hadn't even seen Syd yet, but the contrast frightened me big time, and I was wondering whether I should leave or come back later or something. It was just straight fear and anxiety.

Now, when Syd came in and sat down and started to talk, without any basis whatsoever I felt really hopeful. I didn't know why. I didn't understand it, but I felt like a load was lifted off of me. And when I looked at the other people in the room in some ways it made sense to me; there was something congruent about the way they looked and what he talked about. I didn't understand the particulars. So then I felt a combination of ease and hopeful. I wasn't self-conscious as I was earlier, and I just listened. It was kind of like being in a tub of warm water. It was just very reassuring and very liberating. It was a really nice feeling.

JP: And then you met with him?

GP: Then he sent someone over to invite us to his house, which, frankly, I thought was odd. There were only about 30 people there, so why didn't he just come over and invite us? I thought it was odd that he would send an emissary over, but that's in fact what he did: "Syd and Barb would like you to come over to their house, if you would like." I didn't know that he had never spoken with a mental health professional one-on-one, so at the time it didn't make sense to me that he would want me to come to his place.

JP: How long had Syd been talking with people about what he had realized, before you showed up?

GP: Maybe three years—something like that—maybe a little more, maybe a little less. But prior to us showing up he was doing everything he could to talk to people. He was picking up hitchhikers. He was talking to people in line at the supermarket. He was doing everything he could, and originally he would have gatherings at people's houses. It had only been maybe about a year that he actually had public talks. So I didn't know that he hadn't really had people up from the States very much, and he hadn't yet had any mental health professionals that he knew about, or at least had a chance to talk with. So that was the back story to it.

So Linda and I went over to his house. And he had this absolutely gorgeous property. It was on the water, and one thing that stood out to me was how he understood what we were interested in, and he really showed us around. He would point out things to Linda that she was interested in, and he would point out things to me that I was interested in. So he was really a gracious host, and the thing that stood out to me was how much time he seemed to have. You got this feeling, "We have all the time in the world, George." We're walking around the house, and people from the Island start to show up. So by the time we sat down there were about 15 people there.

So Syd said to me, "Is it true that you're a mental health professional who helps people?" I said, "Yes, absolutely." He said, "If you wouldn't mind, I've never met a mental health professional. I consider myself, in a way, in the mental health business because of the experience I had. I try to help the well-being of humanity as best I can and ease the suffering that people have, even though I don't have any degrees or anything, I just feel like it's what I've been thrust into; I didn't have a choice. And I have no idea what a mental health professional does to help people. So if you wouldn't mind and if it's not putting you out I would love to hear what you do in your work." So I did my best to explain to him what I did. I described it in great detail. And he would ask me questions. Like, I'd say, "Well, I take the person back into their memories to heal their memories." So Syd said, "How would you do that?" I said, "Well, it's a little bit like what Freud did." And he said, "What did Freud do?" He didn't know anything! And I said, "Well, he had people lie on the couch and free associate, just talk off the top of their heads about the memories they had in childhood and he would listen and take notes. Well, I don't have people lie on the couch or take notes, but we do have these exercises, like asking people to remember a time that they were resentful..." And everybody who was there laughed. They thought that was hilarious.

JP: [laughs]

GP: I didn't know what they were laughing about. In retrospect, they were laughing at how different my understanding of life was. I was like a foreign culture to them, so they were getting a kick out of all the answers we gave to Syd. And, finally, Syd didn't say anything, but he kind of gave a signal that they should stop that, like, "Hey, what are you doing?" And they got the message that they shouldn't be laughing at us [laughs]. I never had anybody laugh at me in my entire life.

JP: [laughs]

GP: So I gave him examples of specific exercises that we did, and he kept asking, "What else do you do?" He kept asking. And I basically described the ARC program that John Enright and I did in great detail, which was based on Gestalt Therapy and two-person exercises. While I was doing that he was as involved as a person was if they were watching a movie they loved. He was totally into it. He showed no emotion. He was respectful and he couldn't get enough of it.

And then at some point he said to me, "George, can I ask you some questions about this, just so I can understand this better?" And I said, "Sure." He said, "Well, George, it sounds to me like that would be very uncomfortable and unpleasant for people." And I hadn't really thought about that, believe it or not. That had not even occurred to me, which made me look like a very non-compassionate person. I was putting people through discomfort. I kind of thought about it as an occupational hazard or something. So I said to him, "Well, yeah, I would say that was the case, Syd. It is hard for them." And then I felt really on the

4

spot. It wasn't just him and me—all these people were looking at me and I felt on the spot, attacked in a way. And I defended myself. I said, "Syd, it's part of a process, see? People go into this process and they go through this admitted pain and suffering, but it's for a purpose, and when they come out the other end then they are feeling good. They're healthy."

So he said to me, "Do they come out the other end healthy?" And I didn't hear the question. "What was that, Syd? Would you say that again?" He said, "You said that they go in and they are unhealthy, and they go through this painful process and then they're healthy. And I want to know if they do, in fact, come out at the other end healthy." And I said, "Well, not very often." Okay, I was the one who said that, not him, but it really hit me, and I started to feel a little nauseous— physically nauseous and a churning in me. I felt really bad, like the way people do when they suddenly get a bad cold or something. Well, I interpreted that he did something to put me down to account for the feeling I had. I figured he did something! I didn't know what it was but I knew I wouldn't feel that way on my own. I wasn't feeling this way before I talked to him, so it must be something he did. So I got very upset and angry, and I challenged him. I basically said to him, "Well, what are you saying? What would you do? What's your point here?" And he talked to me about teaching people happiness, teaching people what I knew about happiness and well-being. Well, that really made me worse. If I started at 100, and I dropped down to 60 when I made the comment about helping people, when he made the comment about teaching people what you know about happiness I went down about to a 20. I just dropped like a rock. And then I realized I didn't even see myself in the happiness business. I saw myself in the treatment business, and I didn't really know anything about happiness and well-being. *I* wasn't happy! My relationship with Linda was really bad. My life was hectic, frantic, I couldn't sit down for five minutes, I was such a Type-A person, and he's talking about happiness and peace of mind! And this time I felt like he really did do something because he was the one who said it, not me. Last time you could have accused me of bumming myself out, but this time it was him doing it!

JP: [laughs]

GP: I was embarrassed, to be honest with you, Jack. So I said to him,"Syd, you know, there are tens of thousands of mental health professionals, and some of them are unhappy themselves. They have broken marriages. They're using alcohol and drugs. This is an unbelievably stressful profession; they take their stress home with them. I don't see how it's realistic for them to be helping people by talking about happiness, because some of them don't know anything about happiness. All they know about is mental illness and treating mental illness, and that's kind of how the profession is defined. It's not defined as a happiness vendor or provider; it's defined as treating real illnesses." So he says to me, "Well, if they're not happy themselves, then it would seem to me that they're in the wrong profession. It would be like a mechanic who couldn't even fix his own car helping other people fix theirs."

Now that, to me, was a blatant attack. It wasn't subtle; it was blatant! And I absolutely didn't appreciate it. So I got up, I grabbed Linda by the hand and I said, "We've got to catch a ferry." Linda wanted to stay. So she pulled me aside and said," George, I am fascinated by this conversation." And I said, "Well, I'm not. You can stay, but I'm leaving. I've had it!" So I left and she went with me. We got in the car, made good-bye noises to Syd. I think everybody could tell that we weren't happy campers.

We drove back to California, and on the way back I was fit to be tied. I was churning. I was so upset I had trouble sitting in my seat. I just thought it was a terrible thing what had happened, and I was complaining to Linda about it: "He says he's only got a ninth grade education, Linda, and he's criticizing a profession that's been around for 150 years! I mean, give me a break! It would be like me saying that architects don't know what they're doing, or physicians, or anybody, right? These people are professionals! They went to school. They got licensed. They're experienced. I mean, how does he have anything to say to us? Anything! I mean, where are his qualifications?"

6

And Linda said to me, "Then why don't you just forget it? Just write him off, say we wasted our money." And I said, "We did waste our money. This was a terrible idea coming up here. I can't imagine what we were thinking." So she says, "So let's just forget about it and drive back as if it never happened." I said, "Sounds good to me."

Well, I couldn't forget about it. It just was galling me. Finally I said to her, "I can't forget about it. It's driving me crazy. It's ridiculous." I used all these adjectives. And she said, "Well, George, if you can't forget about it, there must be something to it for it to be getting to you like this." So I said, "I don't know, maybe you're right."

Then I felt this powerful feeling of calm. It was just amazing! I felt so peaceful that I couldn't remember feeling that peaceful in my lifetime. I couldn't remember a single moment when I felt that peaceful. That really affected me. I thought to myself, "I go up to this island, I was there one day, I listen to a guy talk, I go over to his house, and now I have a feeling of peace that I didn't have my entire life. What's going on?" So I was kind of in puzzlement and curiosity. And I was also just really enjoying the trip back and enjoying Linda, and it was like a new world, Jack. It was as if I stepped into a new reality, and it was a wonderful thing.

I came back to San Francisco and my eyeballs had changed. I was suddenly seeing the pace of life there. I was seeing how people's thinking was affecting them. I was seeing the insecurity of everybody, including myself. I went to do a seminar with John, and I saw that we were causing suffering to no avail. People were getting relief but I could see how it was temporary, how it was just getting things off their chest, and how they were getting ideas that could help them but there wasn't anything fundamental happening. So the next few months were very difficult; they were upsetting, but they were also enlightening in the sense that it was a brave new world, like I was living in a world as a stranger in a strange land. Every day, life was refueling and fresh, and I was experiencing life in such a different way that I couldn't quite get it together. In a way it was like I had reverted to a young child. I was interested in everything; I was curious about everything. I was wondering about stuff. I was seeing possibilities. I also felt insecurity and fear about the future and what the implications were, so I was in and out of those two things.

JP: Did you wonder at the time what had come over you?

GP: Yeah. I couldn't understand it, and I kept going back into my head about what happened. So I would actually say to myself, "I went to the seminar at seven o'clock and I sat down in my chair, and Syd came in and he talked, and I couldn't remember much of what he talked about…" So I went over it in great detail trying to find some explanation for how I was so profoundly affected.

JP: Did it seem weird to you that you were in a state of anger and frustration right before that, and then suddenly you were calm?

GP: At that time—now this is in retrospect—the new reality I had was so compelling that I didn't have much memory of all the other things that had happened. Even the consternation I felt in Salt Spring wasn't a part of my memory. It's only in retrospect that I see what was happening. At the time it was not very visible to me.

ENTER ROGER MILLS [*Note: Roger Mills was later proclaimed by Syd to be the other "founder," with George, of what first became known as Psychology of Mind.*]

JP: So when did you talk to Roger about what happened to you?

GP: Well, I came back to San Francisco, and at that time I was a hired-contract faculty member of the program that Roger was doing. In his program he brought in something like seven different teachers and in the course of seven weekends each teacher had a separate weekend in this class of 35 people, and I was one of the seven. So it happened to be my turn to go up there and teach my class. So I got up there with Roger, and Linda told him about the experience I had with Syd. He got curious. And Roger said, "You know, I do see a difference, George, in where you're coming from, but I don't really understand how that could be attributable to listening to some guy talk for an hour." And I said, "Well, me neither, Roger. It doesn't make any sense to me." So he asked me what Syd talked about, and I didn't really know. We told him about the people up on Salt Spring. And Linda said to him, "You know, Roger, you should go up there, and if nothing else we'll understand this a lot better and we can talk about it." So he went up to Salt Spring. And then we didn't hear from him. We knew he was planning to go up there, but he didn't call us or say, "I'm up here." We didn't see him for some time, maybe a few months.

Then we came up to Eugene in a few months, and there was big change in Roger. The major personality traits that I would characterize him with were much different; he was much less of all those things. He tended to be aggressive and talk a lot, and he became much quieter. And even though he was aggressive he tended to defer to others and took a low profile, and now he was coming out and speaking his mind about things when talking with his colleagues. And there was some sense of security that we had not seen in Roger. At the same time there was a humility that we absolutely hadn't seen in him. He was at the same time much more humble and yet much more confident, and it was really impressive to us. So we talked to him about it, and he didn't have much to say about it. He said, "Yeah, I talked to Syd." He couldn't understand why everybody wasn't listening to Syd. So we went back to the Island to spend a little more time with Syd. Then Roger told us that he was leaving his job and moving to Salt Spring. He was taking his daughter and the two of them were going to pack their stuff and move to Salt Spring.

A CLASH OF PARADIGMS

At that time John and I were having problems professionally—not personally—because I couldn't get behind [no longer believed in] what we were doing, and people were leaving my seminars in droves. John would do a seminar for 35 people, and I would do one and have 15 refunds. There was no energy, no intention, no integrity to what I was doing. I was mixing what we were doing, trying to do what we were doing in a different way, and I wasn't behind it. And pretty soon my attendance for the seminars went down. And this is while Roger is up on Salt Spring.

So John Enright said to me, "Look, George, this is absolutely not working out. I mean, you're killing us here! Our reputation is being affected, and I don't know what to do. If I was your boss I'd fire you. But you're my partner; I can't fire you." That really shook me up—that he would actually fire me if he could! I said, "Well, geez, John, I don't know what to say. I don't want to ruin things for you, but I can't get behind what we're doing after what I learned from Syd on Salt Spring. I'm haunted by it. I'm just doubting myself. I just don't really want to take people through their past and their negative feelings and their problems. I mean, is it serving them? Are we doing the right thing here? Shouldn't we be teaching mental health to people?" John said, "How would you do that?" I said, "I have no idea. That's my problem, John. It's not like I have a solution to this. I know what the problem is, but it's not like I have a solution." He says, "Well, we've got to do something, and we've got to do it quick." So we left that conversation. When we got together again John said, "Look, why don't you go up to Salt Spring"—I had told him Roger was up there—"and spend some time, listen to Syd, get his message or his technique or his process, whatever it is, bring it back, and either it will be a terrific thing and will be our new method, or it will fall apart and won't be anything and you can go back to teaching what we were teaching before."

JP: So John, himself, wasn't touched after hearing Syd?

GP: No. On a scale from 1 to 10 [10 highest] he was 9 on intrigued but he was a 1 on touched. But he respected it.

JP: But when he was telling you to go up there, he at least kind of had an idea of the direction Syd was pointing to.

GP: I'm not sure he had an idea of the direction, but he was absolutely recognizing that there might be something legitimate there—something we weren't a party to. It wasn't like, "Go get it out of your system." So I said to him, "Well, John, can we afford to do this?" And he said, "George, we can't afford *not* to do this. With you here, our organization is dead. So you being gone is adding to the bottom line."

JP: [laughs]

GP: So I said to him, "Well, John, I can't afford to take a summer off." He says, "Our organization will pay for it. We'll pay your expenses. We'll give you a salary." So I said, "Let me get this straight. I go up to Salt Spring Island for the summer with my family, you don't care what I do up there, and you're going to pick up the tab. Right?" John says, "Right. But the other part of the deal is, we're still partners and we want you to bring back something we can use or get over your attachment to this. George, that's part of the deal. You can't come back and do your own thing. You can't go up there for a vacation. You're up there to learn. You're up there as a student and you're obligated to come back and share what you learn." So he says to Frank Doherty, our other partner, "Is that okay with you, Frank?" Frank said, "Yeah. It's great." So we did. We packed up the Volvo, we got a place on Salt Spring Island, and Linda and I and the two children went up to Salt Spring to spend the summer.

IMMERSION

JP: When you were there, what did you think about being around the people who were around Syd?

GP: Well, being around those people was 80% of our education, and 20% was Syd. I was very puzzled by the way they lived up there. It was very surprising and puzzling. For example, Linda and I typically spent a lot of our time talking about problems, goals or logistics—those three things. It consumed about 90% of our time and energy. They did hardly any of that. They didn't talk about their problems, they didn't talk about their goals, and they talked very little about logistics. So we didn't understand how they could survive doing that, and we would ask them about it. And they would say, "We don't talk about our problems because it's a bad idea—it doesn't help us to solve problems by thinking about them and talking about them. We don't concern ourselves with goals because we kind of live in a world of opportunity—we just take things as they come, so we don't have any aspirations, really, other than what life presents to us. And we minimize the logistics because we think it's a better strategy to live in real time than to have plans—it's not like we don't have plans, but we don't have very many of them." Linda and I were, "What's with that?!" Then we were interested in what they *do* talk about and how they live. That was an education. They just enjoyed the moment. They got a kick out of things. They kind of fantasized about what life could be like; they kind of pipe-dreamed. They laughed a lot. And that wasn't just one couple. That was all of them. Everybody we were with seemed like they were marching to the same drummer.

JP: Well, that raises an interesting question. If I picture myself being in that position, I would have wondered whether I had walked into a cult. Did that cross your mind at all?

GP: It didn't cross my mind because of how little direct influence Syd Banks had on the people. In other words, there were no things you had to do, nothing you had to pay tribute to. People were living their individual lives, and then there was Syd Banks doing the occasional seminar—like we went up to Shawnigan Lake and spent the weekend together. So that was it. There was almost no organization. It was all just people living their lives, and then they would come together and listen to Syd. So I wasn't concerned about any undue influence or any requirements; there were no requirements. It never occurred to me because there was nothing required of me. So I didn't question it because I was familiar with like-minded people. I had that in Newton when I was a kid; I lived in a 90% Jewish town and every father said the same exact thing. And there were like-minded people in San Francisco—everybody was into self-improvement. So it didn't alarm me in any way. I was used to a bunch of people coming from the same place, having the same beliefs or outlook on life. That was nothing new. It wasn't even as strong a thought system as what I had in San Francisco. So I didn't have any thoughts of that.

JP: What were your conversations like with Syd when you were up there?

GP: Well, one thing is, Syd would talk to us about Truth. And he would also talk to us about the community. It was very interesting. So we got to see how he related to what was happening. That was very interesting to us. And we became, in a way, confidants to Syd because we were outsiders. I remember one time we were sitting in the Crest Restaurant, which was owned by one of the people who was listening to Syd. At that time Syd was living off the donations of the Foundation for Higher Consciousness or something like that, and everybody was paying dues and those became Syd's living expenses. So we're sitting in the Crest Restaurant and he's not paying attention to our conversation. You could tell, he had his head back and was listening to other people's conversations. And he says to me, "Oh, this has turned into a trip." I said, "What do you mean?" He said, "Everybody is talking about what they should be doing, what they should be thinking, what they shouldn't be thinking, about other people's level of consciousness. All they're talking about is my evening talks. This is not good." He said, "Would you mind if I excused myself? Just tell them to cancel my order. I'm not really hungry. But I want to have dinner later with you. You've got to promise me we'll have dinner later." So we said, "Sure." And he apologized five or six times and he made sure we were going to have dinner that night. Well, the next day a letter comes to everybody: The Foundation is disbanded. No more dues. I'm not accepting any money. No more regular meetings. He said, "I just want people to live their lives and enjoy what they've learned and what it's done for them."

JP: How did that affect you? Did you find that behavior at least striking, if not puzzling?

GP: Well, Jack, I was unbelievably impressed that he did that. I can't tell you how impressed I was! I thought, "Wow, this guy is for real!" Of all the things I saw that summer, that gave Syd Banks the most credibility. Because a lot of people in his position would think it was a plus, not a minus, to have followers; they would want supporters. I also thought to myself, his income is going from several thousand a month to zero overnight—at his own doing! He's the one who did that. So I understood it, at least I thought I did, and I thought it was noble. It made me feel like this is more legitimate than I ever imagined. If there were any remaining doubts I had about it being a trip or a cult, or does the man walk what he talks, they were all gone. So I was all in when I saw that.

Then he talked about people's level of consciousness in the community; that people sought out others who were at the same level

13

of consciousness. And he basically said to me, "George, you want to seek out people with a higher level of consciousness in terms of who you hang out with, your friends." And I said to him, "How would I know that?" Syd says, "If you don't know, then you have to listen better. There's a whole different feeling. There's a nicer feeling. There's a humility that comes. When you're with people who have a higher level you'll feel it. You'll be uplifted." And that affected us. And we started to notice that. It was kind of an eye-opener. Listening to him talk about lessons about life was very, very interesting.

They had parties there, and they were so great. They played music. They were already high-spirited people. And I noticed that Syd would leave just when things would get going. So I would say to Syd, "Why are you leaving the parties early?" And he'd say, "Well I like to leave on a high. Parties come to a climax, a summit, and then you'll notice the energy going down and people getting tired and people ride that wave, and Barb and I like to leave right about then." I said," So it's like quitting when you're ahead?" He says, "Yeah, I guess that would be right."

There was a movement in the direction of less thinking rather than more. So there was a lot of quiet that I wasn't used to. So we'd be with Syd and some of the people at the table and nobody was saying anything, and everybody was comfortable with it. That was really interesting to me. So there was the learning at Syd's talks, and then there was kind of a lifestyle, if you will, that was how they went about their lives, which was different from what I was accustomed to.

JP: Do you remember any of the insights you had that summer?

GP: Well, all these things I've been telling you were the insights, and then I also had insights about the nature of life. For example, I saw that you didn't have to plan your life, which I thought previously, because, to use a metaphor, there was a trail of breadcrumbs that I would call opportunity and if you stayed awake, kept your eyes open, you would see those breadcrumbs and take the opportunities as they occurred. So that was a really powerful insight, because being in a good place was both a means as well as an end. There was a logic to a higher consciousness, and people who saw the logic lived nice lives.

QUESTIONING PSYCHOLOGY

GP: The other thing is I saw what I was doing with John and what other people were doing in their approaches in a very different light.

JP: How so?

GP: Now, Jack, I have to use what I see now. I didn't think this at the time, but it's what I would have said if I had known what I know now. I saw that *awareness* was kind of the currency of all these other approaches: for human beings to become more aware of themselves, of their thoughts, their feelings, their behaviors, and that was kind of like a horizontal dimension. And Syd Banks was talking about a vertical dimension called *levels of consciousness*. And improvement in levels of consciousness solved all the objectives of awareness; it accomplished all that greater awareness was trying to accomplish. And I also saw that awareness sowed the seeds of its own destruction, so to speak— undermined its own objectives, because when people became more aware they became more self-absorbed, more self-conscious, and that took them away from the well-being they were seeking. They put things on their mind, rather than taking things off their mind.

JP: So they were becoming more aware of the level of consciousness they were on.

GP: Exactly, Jack, and they were finding ways to leverage the level of consciousness they were on, and not only couldn't it be leveraged, but it tended to lower their level because they went into thinking more and they became more in touch with their problems and their weaknesses. So the thing they became aware of was actually weighing on them, which made them likely to go to a lower level than to stay at the level that they were on at the time.

JP: So at what point did you start to talk with Roger and Syd about a new direction for psychology? Was that when you were up there, or did that happen later?

GP: Well, I actually saw clients up there that came from out of the blue. I ended up making more money that summer than John and Frank. These clients called up, organizations called up—I don't know why they called up—and they said, "We heard you're learning something new, and we're interested." And I said," Well, I'm not really working up here." They said, "Can we come up?" And I said, "Sure." They didn't ask about seeing Syd or anything. They flew up and we talked. I didn't know what to say to them so I just told them what had happened to me. So even though I was actually seeing clients I had a deal with John to bring back what I learned, it's getting late in the summer and I didn't think I learned anything.

JP: That's funny.

GP: So I said to Linda, "I don't have anything to bring back. Nothing! I haven't learned anything. I don't see any application in this. What am I going to tell John?" So Linda says, "You should tell Syd that." I said, "Great idea!" So I went to Syd and I said, "Syd, look, I made a deal with John. I told him I'd come up for the summer, I'd learn what this is about, I'd bring it back and that would be our new program." And he said, "Oh, that would be tremendous!" I said, "But Syd, I'll be honest with you, I have not learned anything that I can bring back. I've had a wonderful summer. I feel like a million bucks. I love what you're teaching on Salt Spring. But I really don't see how it has anything to do with what I do, or psychology."

So he laughed and he said, "George, believe me, you can help people with what you've learned. Now, you saw clients up here?" I said, "Yeah." He said, "Well, what did you teach them?" I said, "Well, nothing really, Syd. I talked a little bit about my story and what little I understood about what you said." And he said, "What did they think of that?" I said, "Well, they thought it was tremendous, but I can't see that being what I teach." Syd said, "Why not?" I said, "I don't know. There was nothing to it." He said, "That's how I feel about what I teach." I said, "No, really, Syd." He said, "No! Really! You don't know what you're saying, you don't know how to say it, you know what you're trying to say, and that's about it." I said, "You're kidding." He says, "No." I said, "You're saying that's how it looks to you?" He said, "Yes." I said, "So you don't know what you're teaching?" Syd said, "That's right. I know what I'm trying to teach." I said, "Well, how can you teach something that you don't know how to teach?" He says, "It's what you're trying to teach. It's your message. It's understanding. It doesn't matter how you get it across." I said, "Well, how am I going to—?" Syd said, "George, stop! You will get it across, because it's in you. Now, what's in you is not what's in me—I understand I'm not the one doing the teaching—but you can teach what's in you, what you see."

Then he said, "You know what you could do, you and Roger? You could play my tapes to people"—there were maybe 15 or so tapes at the time—"bring one of my tapes, play it for whatever group you going to, and then just answer their questions and give them your understanding of what was on the tape." I said, "That's a fantastic idea!" And Roger liked it too. So Roger and I thought that was going to be our approach. Well, I talked to John, and I told him that plan, and he said, "Well, first of all, George, I really don't think people are going to stand for that. I don't think people are going to pay money to hear a tape. Secondly, I don't see how I can do that; I didn't spend a summer up there. So, I don't see how that's going to work." I don't know if I have my timing right; this may be way later, but we did try it and people didn't stand for it.

JP: [laughs]

GP: I think that was later. But when I went back to California, John and I had an annual professional deal that was kind of our signature program. It was an eight-day event where professionals from all over the world and the country flew to California for eight days to spend time with John, Frank and me. And it was at this retreat site in the mountains near Sacramento—it's probably ten or eleven days for them because they have to fly in, drive out 4½ hours, get there, there was a raft trip in the middle of it, so it was a big deal. When I got back from

17

Salt Spring for the summer I had about a week before this event. So I'm thinking, "What am I going to say? This is so different from what John is doing, what are we going to do? What are participants going to do? It's going to look like a bait and switch or something." So I went back and I talked to John and Frank and I said to them, "I can't do it. I can't do what you guys do. I don't believe in it. I don't think it's a good idea. I don't think it's helpful. There's something better." And they said, "What's better?" I said, "Well, I'll teach them this whole new thing about thought and levels of consciousness." So Frank and John say, "Well, teach it to us." Well, I didn't know what to say. I didn't have a way to teach it. I just told my story. I didn't have anything much more than that. So they said, "George, here's what we're going to have to do. We're going to have to divide the group up and have some people go through your program and some people go through ours, and if people want a refund they can have a refund." So I said, "Great!" I thought that was very gracious of them. So we come to the eight-day and we get the group together and we say, "Frank and John are going in one direction, and George is going in the other direction." Roger was there but he didn't want to have any part of this because it was our thing and he felt as humble as I did about what to teach, so he didn't say, "I'll help you," and Linda was no help either; she didn't know any more than I did, in her mind. So we get down there and we say to the group, "You're going to have to choose where you want to go, and if you want a refund we'll give you a full refund, and we'll give you $100 toward expenses." So John doesn't do a presentation. He said, "You all know what we do: two-person activities, etc." So I gave my presentation and I didn't have a clue what to say. "Well, it's got to do with thought and levels of consciousness," and this and that, and of course they heard it as something they already knew, or they didn't have a clue what I was talking about. There are 80 people there, and I think 75 go with John and five go with me. And the five were Roger, Clytee—she and Roger weren't together yet—Linda, Keith Blevens and Rick Suarez.

JP: Rick Suarez was there? [*Note: Along with George, Roger and Keith, Enrique Suarez was one of the early formulators of this psychology.*]

GP: Yes, he was a client.

JP: I thought Keith had called him and told him about it.

GP: Rick was Keith's supervisor for Keith's Veterans Administration clinical internship, and Keith had brought John and me to Dallas where he was living, and Rick came to our seminar with his wife, Ginger, and they really liked it. So they came up to the eight-day. By the time of the eight-day Keith may also have called Rick and told him about Syd. Anyway, Rick resonated with a different direction, so he became one of the five people.

So anyway, I didn't know what I was doing. So at the end of the first morning—and this will show you what a gracious, wonderful person John was—he asked, "Well, how did it go, George?" I said, "You know, I absolutely, positively did not do justice to it. People have no idea what I'm talking about. They are not relating to it. I don't think I can pull this off, John. I just have no idea what to talk about. And I don't feel right about giving even a few people a half-baked experience because they put aside all this time in their lives. But John, I'm telling you, this is a whole new deal. This is the future of psychology; I'm just not up to the task." So John says, "Let's bring Syd down here." I said, "Oh, John, I would love that, but it's going to be massively expensive. I mean, he's got to get down here right away." He says, "We'll hire a private plane." I said," John, we will absolutely eat up every penny of profit and possibly go in the hole if we do that." He says, "George, I've never seen you so taken by something. I can see your frustration that you can't offer it. We'll bring him down, and we'll give them all a choice again of whether they want to listen to Syd or listen to us. I said, "Well I'm going to make up every dollar we pay of Syd's expenses—" John said, "I won't hear of it. We are bringing him down and that's it. I'm doing this for professional reasons, not for personal reasons."

So I call up Syd and I said, "Look Syd, we're doing this seminar, I'm trying to get across what I learned on Salt Spring a week ago, and I can't tell you how badly it's going from my perspective—" He said," George, I won't hear that. I know it's going better than you think." I said, "Well, perhaps, but would you consider coming down here and teaching? We will pay you for your time." Syd said, "Sure. You don't have to pay me, though." I said, "No, we want to pay you, but you're going to have to take a private plane." He said, "From Salt Spring?" I said, "Yeah." He said, "So I get on a plane at Salt Spring and then, what, fly to Vancouver?" I said, "No, you come directly to Sacramento." He said, "Okay."

So he comes down and he talks to the whole group for an hour, and they were into it. So people did it. They sat in a room and Syd talked. And he talked like that for four days. It did a lot for me, Jack, to see these people, particularly the therapists from Germany, listen to him for that amount of time and seem to resonate with what he said—even though it didn't really go anywhere. They didn't come back and say, "We want more." But it did something for me that he could talk like that and my peers could respond to it. So I was thrilled. And it made me think that there was a future to this. If my peers could listen to him like that and not object and not have a problem with it and calm down and their level of consciousness went up—and you could see that they were more relaxed, you could see the couples were closer—I thought, I absolutely could do that! Not as well as him, but if they could respond to him, they could respond to me. And then I realized my lack of confidence was no small factor in my inability to talk to the group. So that was the first glimpse I had that this could be brought into the field of psychology. I got that glimpse, and I thought, "It's just a matter of time before Roger and I are able to get this across to people."

JP: So how did it happen that you and John parted ways?

GP: Well, we saw from the eight-day that John was not going to go my way because he said he had too much at stake, even though he brought Syd down there. He said to me, "Look George, you don't have a reputation. Your reputation is you work with John Enright." He was very humble; it was just realistic. "You're not giving up anything. You have no reputation, even as talented as you are doing the work. I'm nationally known as the second or third best Gestalt therapist in the world. I have a Yale degree. I can go anywhere and people flock to me, and 90% of the people who were here would go with me if we split up. I don't want to leave all that behind." I said, "John, number one, it's the future of psychology! Number two, you would be ten times as happy as you are now if you went in this direction. Look at how lighthearted I am compared with you. I mean, you're serious, you know? He said, "I know. I wish I was like you, George. You're so lighthearted and you're so excited about what you've learned." I said, "John, you could do that. You have that in you. And your reputation would bring people in. You just have to tell them you're doing the opposite of what you were doing." He said," I can't do that. I love what I do. I love the intellectual part of it. I wish I could, but I can't."

[Side note: Now, on his deathbed, he told me that he thought it would blow over. I said, "John, I'll buy that, but at some point you knew it wasn't going to blow over. Why didn't you come back? God knows I've been on your case enough about it." He said, "I thought it was too late." I said, "Then why didn't you tell me?" He said, "I was too proud. I didn't want to come to you and say, 'Look, I should've gotten into this ten years ago,' and I blew it." I said, "John, that's inexcusable." He said, "I know. I know that now, George, you don't have to tell me."]

So, we sent out a letter, same as we did at the conference, stating, here's what John is doing, here's what George is doing. And we had 5000 people on our mailing list, and 4990 said that they were going to go with John, and 10 or 20 said that they were going with me. And that was the parting of the ways for us.

CREATING A NEW PSYCHOLOGY

JP: So at that point you were out of a job?

GP: Yeah. But Syd was behind us 100%. We brought him down to talk at U.C. Berkeley. He did a talk for anybody that was interested. And he came down—Roger was living there then—and Syd met with us and he talked with us and he raised our level. We had a course at John F. Kennedy University—I don't know how long a time that was, Jack, but it was a time when Syd was grooming Roger and me, and we were doing a lot of stuff. And I was filling up these seminars for Syd when he would come down.

JP: Was Roger's grant still going on then? When I interviewed Roger for my *Modello* book, I thought he said that the grant showed the results.

GP: The grant showed the results of John Enright's and my work, but it didn't show results of what we'd learned from Syd.

JP: He did say the grant showed ARC's results, but I also thought he said that, after Syd, results improved even more.

GP: First of all, it wasn't long after Roger went to Salt Spring that he left Eugene. So he wasn't there very long afterwards. And when he was in Eugene, his boss would not let him do anything, because he was completely freaked out about the Syd Banks stuff. Roger said to me, "Let's you and I go around, get it funded by 'Mental Health' and teach this understanding around the state or in the schools." His boss said, "You're not teaching this stuff anywhere. It was a stretch for me to have Enright and Pransky come in here"—because it was nontraditional—"but this Syd Banks stuff is absolutely unprofessional, and you are not doing it!" So Roger had no leverage whatsoever after he met Syd Banks, and as a result his work at Oregon did not show anything about Syd's approach.

P: Okay, back to Syd meeting with you and Roger. Why was he grooming you, and what for?

GP: Well, Syd absolutely did not want to be the face of this understanding because he knew he could not stay out of the guru role if he did that. If he went out into the world and did talks, he looked so much like a guru he couldn't get out of it. So he wanted it to go out professionally. And he picked Roger and me, not because of our talents but because we were really the only two professionals at first who were even interested in what he had to say.

JP: That was all before Rick Suarez became involved?

GP: Yes, that was 1976, and I think Rick was around 1979—I'm not sure exactly, but it was definitely before Rick. We were a long way from understanding what Syd was talking about and from having even the personal traits or character to be in a leadership position. Syd really had no choice. So he just put huge amounts of energy into Roger and me. He changed our personalities and taught us a crash course in his understanding and watched our every move and came down on us when we were in the wrong direction. It was like taking a minor league baseball player and having a few months to get him to be at least above average, if not a star, in the major leagues.

JP: [laughs]

GP: He didn't see anything else to do. He did his best with us. He came down to San Francisco. We went up there. He was on the phone. He was asking us about everything we did. He was on us about the mistakes we made. He was reading the riot act to us. And he just pushed us.

JP: When he read the riot act to you, can you think of any instances where he thought you were off base?

GP: Well, for example, I had a person who was an excellent speaker, a professional self-help person, and I had the idea that he would be a good person to bring into this. Syd came down to San Francisco and met him, and he was appalled. The guy was all speeded up and full of himself, he had no idea about the understanding, and Syd was not so much upset about this guy but with the fact that I was so stupid for picking this guy out. He was thinking, "Where is George Pransky's understanding that he would pick this guy out?" And he just wailed on me about grounding [*Note: Meaning, being well-grounded in the understanding.*] "It doesn't matter how much speaking ability he has. It doesn't matter how much experience he has. It doesn't matter how good he is with people. It's the specific grounding!" And he just hammered that point. And to his credit he just saw this problem and he zeroed in on it. And after he was done I had different eyes. I could see *grounding*, which I never could see before. It had been invisible to me.

JP: So whose decision, ultimately, was it that this stuff be turned into a psychology?

GP: Syd's.

JP: Did he say to you, "I want you and Roger to turn this into a psychology"?

GP: No, he didn't see it that way. What he said was, and this wasn't to us—I overheard this conversation—someone said to him, "Why is this coming out through the field of psychology? Why isn't it coming out, for example, through religion? Or, you said this was physics; why is this not coming out through physics?" And Syd said, "Because psychology turned up on my doorstep. It wasn't my decision. If two religious people had turned up on my doorstep and they really caught on like Roger and George did, and they dropped what they were doing and dedicated their lives to it, I would have it go out through religion. If two physicists had come to me, I would have had to go out through physics. I don't care. But it so happened that two people in the mental health field showed up on my doorstep."

JP: Roger told me that Syd thought it would best go out through psychology.

GP: Well, I'm guessing at this, Jack, but knowing Syd as I do, I think he said that because that's how it was. In other words, given that he was stuck with psychology I think his thoughts went to: "Oh, it's a good thing, because psychology has professionals who are helping other people, and that's a way to do it." That's my opinion. He never said that to me.

JP: But when he found out you were a mental health professional, he asked you all those questions?

GP: Oh, he absolutely wanted to go out professionally. So if he had had two ministers in training or a graduate student in physics he might not have been interested. But the fact that we had degrees—it didn't matter what the degrees were in—made a big difference to Syd. Syd thought that degrees carry a lot more weight in the world than they really do. He thought that if you're a "psychologist," as he called us, and have a Ph.D. nobody's going to question what you're saying. But this may be

24

because of his ninth grade education and background. So he was thrilled that we were professionals. It was much better that we were mental health professionals than, say, nutrition professionals or engineers. There are a lot of professions that he wouldn't have found very desirable, but there were four or five options—psychology, psychiatry, philosophy, physics—that he would have taken if he could have. But he did like the fact that mental health professionals are in the well-being field, and that they had degrees and reputations in that field. I'm making the point that Syd said, "Psychology chose me. I didn't choose it." There's no way that Syd would say, "I wanted it to go through the field of psychology." When asked he said, "That's what showed up."

JP: Did he say anything specific to you and Roger that you remember about taking it out into the field?

GP: Sure. He said, "This is going to be the new psychology! The old psychology is going to collapse. Any clinic or hospital that takes this on will be like the Mayo Clinic. You should go out to the A.P.A. [American Psychological Association] and make this announcement of the new psychology. So he absolutely wanted us to take this out and get it into the mainstream of psychology.

JP: Before you and Roger had started teaching this, were Elsie and Chip involved in teaching it at all? *[Note: Elsie Spittle and Chip Chipman, who were with Syd on Salt Spring Island, have been the two non-mental health professionals who have probably done most to share this understanding.]*

GP: Elsie was really the first person, to my knowledge, to teach this understanding besides Syd Banks. To my mind she showed a lot of courage and had a lot to say. She was a housewife, and Syd brought her up to teach with him. So she would sit next to him, or she would be the opening act, if you will. She would go in and talk, and then Syd would come in and she would introduce Syd. Then every once in a while she taught on her own. Around that time Chip had gotten a job as a draftsman on Salt Spring. So neither Chip nor Elsie had any kind of private practice.

JP: Okay, back to this understanding being put out as a psychology.

GP: Well, Syd was thinking that we would go out with our message and go to the powers-that-be in psychology—there really aren't any but he thought there were—and present this to them, and they would buy it. And then this would be the new psychology and the new psychiatry. So he did give us that: Go to the world and bring this to the field.

JP: Did you and Roger sit down with Syd and try to figure it how to do that together, or did you try to come up with it on your own at that point?

GP: Well, Syd suggested we should put our heads together. Keith had moved up to California to work with John Enright and me, and he started going to Salt Spring, and he was really into this understanding. This was around 1977. So we decided the way we would put our heads together was to form an organization, and all three of us would be partners of that organization. So we started New Psychology Consultants, or something like that. We had no idea how to build a practice. We didn't have any business. Nobody came our way. We didn't have any clients, because I had lost everybody that worked with me when I was with John. Most people were pissed off that I was a turncoat.

JP: You, Keith and Roger wrote the first papers together. How did you come to write them?

GP: We knew that we needed something to introduce ourselves to the world. So we just sat down and said, "Well, we'll write a paper and we'll get the paper around, and people will be interested in it. We'll do seminars…" and stuff like that. And we sat down and we wrote it.

[*Note: "The New Psychology: Seeing Beyond Techniques, Methods and Approaches" and "A New Framework for Psychology." These papers were subsequently reprinted in the Appendix of George's 1998 book,* The Renaissance of Psychology].

JP: How did you put it out?

GP: Well, we just sent it out to everybody we knew. John sent it out to his mailing list. I think we put ads in a psychology magazine. We just sent it out grassroots to anybody we could get our hands on. We thought these papers would attract hundreds of mental health professionals and psychologists. I don't think we got any response from anybody whatsoever—except from the A.P.A. [*American Psychological Association.*] The A.P.A. sent us a letter and said that we had no right to talk about a breakthrough; only the field, the A.P.A., could do that. We sent them back a letter saying that we think this *is* a real breakthrough, and we feel like we owe it to the world to announce this. And then we didn't hear from them.

JP: Were you all living around the same area?

GP: We lived near each other, but believe it or not, Jack, we had no plan whatsoever. We didn't have an office. I don't think we even set up seminars. We had the idea that if you get a better mousetrap people will beat a path to your doorstep. We had that philosophy. And we also thought that philosophy was implicit in this understanding—that you don't have to do anything; "if you build it, they will come."

JP: How long did this organization last?

GP: Well Roger went to work—he got a job with, I think, the University and he supported us for about a year or year and a half?

THE ADVANCED HUMAN STUDIES INSTITUTE

JP: In the meantime, Rick Suarez had been one of the five people in your seminar. Was he starting to do work on his own with this new understanding?

GP: Rick was very taken. He left the seminar, called Syd and went up to Salt Spring. So he may have been talking with Syd and visiting with Syd, trying to figure out what to do, how to get this out. I think he came up with the idea of the Advanced Human Studies Institute in Florida, and I think Syd might have suggested that Roger do it with him. So when Syd said that, Roger said, "Great!" So Roger moved to Florida.

27

Then Keith moved to Florida to go to the Institute down there and stayed down there for a couple of years. Now it was just Linda and me. We moved out of our Point Richmond house and bought a house in Oakland, and then we started a practice in Oakland.

Then Amy Crystal was a client of ours—she was teaching Jenny Craig or something like that, and she had a counselor's license—so we tapped her because our referral rate was so high that we needed more people. Then Kimberly Kadoo got involved and we took her in—Amy knew her in some way. So she came in as an interested professional and was just blown away. She just couldn't believe it. She couldn't get enough of it. She wanted to sit in on it with all the clients. She wanted to go to everything we did down there. So she just got immersed in it. Syd became very impressed with her and suggested that she go down to the Institute and work with Rick. And when these people went down to the Institute the people there saw, "Wow, these people are good!" So they hired Kimberly and she never came back. She was originally going to work with us and be in our practice, but she went to the Institute for training and she never came back to us. Same thing with Amy. I brought Bill Pettit in, and he got involved, and then he went down to the Institute, and they said, "Oh, stay here. We want you here." So, for a while there, I was kind of the minor leagues for the Advanced Human Studies Institute.

JP: [laughs]

GP: And Christine Heath and Joe Bailey and others went to that, and that Institute brought in a lot of people, like Rita Shuford, Sandy Krot, Darlene Stewart, Jeff Timm…

JP: How did it shift, in Syd's eyes, to the Florida Institute and away from you? What happened?

GP: Syd was understandably impressed that Rick and Roger put that Institute together. He saw that Institute as the vehicle for getting the understanding out. The Florida Institute provided a clinic and professional training. He also liked the fact that they wrote that book, *Sanity, Insanity and Common Sense.* He thought that was needed, and he liked that it was written by and for professionals. I don't think Syd realized the size of our practice, our results and the number of professionals we were training. I'm guessing he thought that the Institute in Florida was a more professional operation, not just a couple of people with a private practice. And maybe Syd kind of felt like I didn't know what I was doing, but I'm just guessing what was going on in his mind.

JP: So after all that had happened before, how did that affect you?

GP: I didn't really care.

JP: You didn't?

GP: No, I still went to Syd's seminars. I would go up to see him. So it wasn't like I was an outcast. It wasn't that I was so bad; it was that they were so good, you see? Later there were times when Syd thought I set truth back a hundred years and he was really pissed at me, and that was really hard for me, but this was not one of those times. It was more that he was getting behind Rick and Roger and the Institute, and he wasn't so behind me. He would come down occasionally, but all he would talk about was the Institute.

JP: Why didn't you become part of that operation?

GP: That isn't known to this day. When I went to the Institute Rick pulled me aside and said that he didn't think he'd be there forever and I might be someone who could take his place. A few years later Rick said to me, "Why don't you move down there with Bill Pettit?" So I told all my clients I'm moving to Florida. Then I got a letter from Rick saying that my application was incomplete, and because my application was incomplete I couldn't come to their Institute. I couldn't move down there. I really don't know what changed.

JP: That is really odd. What happened?

GP: Yeah, that was bad, but anything I'd have to say about why that happened would be pure speculation. But here's the good part of the story. Even though Syd wouldn't give Linda or me the time of day, basically—every once in a while he'd call us, but he was totally into Rick and Roger and the Institute—I sent a lot of the people down there who went to the Institute programs, and they had all been trained really well. A lot of those people got hired and became leaders down there. So he saw that we were doing something right in terms of training people.

The other thing I didn't know, like when Amy went down there originally, they asked her about her client load with me. She said, "Oh yeah, I had a full client load." And they said, "What about George? He probably didn't do much." And Amy said, "Oh yes, he had a full client load, too." And they would say, "Wait a minute, how many clients did you have?" And Amy said, "We were deluged with clients." "How long did you have them for?" "Oh, we had them for an average of eight or ten sessions." "How many new clients did you have a month?" "Oh, I don't know, 10 or 15." So the word of our success in Oakland kind of filtered down there. But for a long time Rick was kind of Syd's golden boy.

THE FALL OF THE INSTITUTE

JP: So how did Rick go from being Syd's golden boy to him not being around or involved anymore?

GP: You might say that Rick and Syd developed some irreconcilable philosophical differences.

JP: What do you mean?

GP: That's an interesting story. Rick was very intent on getting Syd's message established within the psychological establishment, so it would become mainstream. He wanted to infiltrate the field from within. And in order to do that you had to look like the field. He would say: "You have to be professional. You have to dress professionally. You have to talk professionally. You have to conduct yourself in a professional way." You couldn't talk about Mind right away because it was too ethereal; you had to talk about Thought and Levels of Consciousness first, then you could maybe stick Mind in, but you had to be careful talking about it. The results you talked about had to be measurable, not anecdotal. It had to be something like: a person had an eating disorder and now he doesn't have an eating disorder; it couldn't just be he felt a lot better when he left. So there were a lot of professional standards that Rick superimposed on it, and he trained his people about that. He said, "Look, this is how we're doing it, folks." They did a conference in Hawaii, and Elsie and Chip had become part of the Institute by that time.

JP: Chip and Elsie were part of the Institute? How did they get down there from Salt Spring?

GP: When the Advanced Human Studies Institute moved to Tampa—it might have been the early to mid '80s—I'm guessing that Syd said to them, "Why don't you go down there. They've got a good thing going." So they moved down to Tampa and Chip started working with businesses, and he supported the Institute very generously. He took all the money he made and gave it to them and took a salary for himself. I think Elsie became head of the Institute at some point.

JP: Sorry, I digressed.

GP: So anyway, they decided to put on a big conference, and Rick said, "There are going to be professionals at this conference, so remember, don't talk Mind," and you had to tell your story in a professional way, not the kind of personal sharing that you often hear in this community—which I think is wonderful, but Rick thought that would not fly with a professional audience. So he laid down this protocol. Well, Elsie felt constrained by the protocol. She wanted to kind of talk from the heart. So Elsie and Chip went to Syd and said, "Rick laid down the law. We can't do [this]. We can't do [that]. He wants it to be very professional." And Syd said, "Oh, that's not good." So he went to Rick. Now, I don't know exactly what Syd said to him or how he did it, but I do know what Syd thought about it.

JP: Which was?

31

GP: Well, to provide some context, at the time, cognitive therapy and cognitive behavioral therapy were very popular and very credible. Rick saw that cognitive therapy and Syd's message both focused on thought—cognitive therapy focused on what we think, while Syd's teachings focused deeper on the fact that we think. Rick's idea was to call Syd's approach, *Neo-cognitive Therapy*, as in, beyond cognitive therapy. He envisioned that Neo-cognitive Therapy would become another branch of therapy that could ride on the credibility-coattails of cognitive therapy. He envisioned that Neo-cognitive Therapy would become increasingly credible and popular as people learned more about it. Rick thought that the powerful results, along with the subsequent research, would make Neo-cognitive Therapy the therapy of the future. In other words, Rick's overall strategy was to conquer the field of psychology from within, to inoculate it with the power of Syd's message.

JP: I do know that Rick's strategy resulted in the first Psychology of Mind research studies, which is a good thing. So what did you think of his approach?

GP: At the time it made perfect sense to me.

JP: But not to Syd?

GP: Syd saw that the teachers were disempowered by these restrictions. They couldn't just get up to speak from the heart and just be. More important, Syd thought these restrictions compromised the message. Mind was at the very heart of the message, and Syd said leaving Mind out of the teachings lacked integrity. Also, speaking from the heart and talking about what people experienced was, to Syd, exactly the way to get the message across. He thought restricting teachers in that way was essentially tying their hands.

JP: What did you think of that?

GP: Once Syd pointed it out I saw that my colleagues weren't teaching with as much impact. The work is in the moment, and when we spoke from the heart it was passionate. I also saw Mind as absolutely essential, and to leave it out was a misrepresentation.

JP: So what happened?

GP: I don't know exactly because I wasn't there. Syd's story to me was that he was very gentle with Rick, but knowing Syd as I do more likely he went to Rick and said something like, "You're taking the heart out of it! The whole thing is about results, and people should talk about their personal results. Mind is more important than Thought and Consciousness. It's a big mistake to try to fit this into the field. That's the problem! If you try to fit into the field, you look like them. The whole idea is to do things different from the field. You don't want to fit into the field at all!" So he just torpedoed Rick's game plan— everything about it, the whole philosophy, everything. And you can imagine how Rick felt. For five years he had trained people, studied what the field could handle, had what he thought was a terrific strategy of how he could integrate this into the field, and then Syd Banks completely torpedoes it.

JP: And then?

GP: What happened was that Rick presented at the conference and, to me, he seemed to be just a shell of his former self, but he made the best of it. Rick went back to the Institute and became reclusive. Now, to give Rick his credit, he had spent years formulating and developing a credible strategy to get this understanding into the field of psychology, which was the charge Syd had given him. He put a lot into it, and he had his ducks in a row. And in one fell swoop it's all gone. And you've got to ask yourself, if you were in his position, would that happen again? So he stayed around the Institute for a little while and then he left. He subsequently went out on his own, opening his own practice.

JP: He left on his own accord?

GP: Yes, on his own accord.

JP: Going back a little, George, aren't you saying you saw both Syd's and Rick's points of view, even though they were opposite?

GP: I did see both of their points. I thought it would be great to get respected in the field. I thought professionalism was good. But it would be wrong to compromise the message in the delivery of the message in the process.

JP: Did you discuss this with Rick?

GP: I did. But he thought we would never get credibility with our colleagues if we didn't make those accommodations.

JP: When I talked to Amy Crystal, all I could picture was this axe coming down and splitting things right down the middle. It was pretty clear that she, Kim Kadoo and Darlene Stewart all went in Rick's direction, and Rita Shuford and Sandy Krot, and I don't know who else was there at the time, all went in the direction of Syd. Why that split?

GP: Well, Amy and Kimberly were higher-ups in the organization, so they worked very closely with Rick, and they felt that Rick was badly treated by Syd. They also bought Rick's philosophy that the only way to get this out in the world was to infiltrate the field, and they saw that Syd was against that. So as far as Amy and Kimberly and Darlene Stewart and Janice Phelps were concerned this was never going to go anywhere. They didn't feel like it was a good strategy; that it was always going to be seen as a spiritual trip. It wasn't going to look like a psychology. So they saw no future in it. They felt it was not right. So they saw no reason to stay there.

JP: After they left, were they still teaching this stuff after that?

GP: I don't really know because we didn't stay in touch. At one point Rick called me up and said, "I'm making a list of Psychology of Mind practitioners that I'm going to recommend, and I'm going to really put a lot of energy into getting this list out there and recognized and, George, I'd like you to be on the list." I said, "Well, I wouldn't want to be on the list, Rick." He said, "Why?" I said, "Because my loyalties are to Sydney Banks. I'll be on a Syd Banks list, but I'm not going to be on a Rick Suarez list." He said, "Well, then can you recommend anybody that I could call and put on the list?" I said, "I won't recommend that anyone be on your list because it doesn't have the endorsement of Sydney Banks and Syd is our teacher. It's nothing against you, Rick. I think that people who continue to listen to Sydney Banks are going to flourish, and people who drop out of that and get on Rick Suarez's list are going to die on the vine." Rick, of course, disagreed. After that, I think Rick considered me in opposition to him, and that was the last I heard from Rick Suarez.

JP: When I talked with Amy, around when I was writing *Parenting from the Heart* and wanted to use a great quote from her that I had heard on an audiotape, she really didn't even want to talk to me or have anything to do with it. I didn't know anything about the history. On those tapes of Amy's I heard, she was very good.

GP: Yes she was. Amy thrived when she was with me. She just became an outstanding teacher and counselor, and was very, very confident in what she was doing. But after she went down to Florida she stopped having much to do with us.

JP: So after all this, Syd wanted to write Rick Suarez right out of the history?

GP: He did, yeah.

JP: How did you feel about that?

GP: Well, I didn't feel right about Rick not getting his due, but I think I was the only one. I thought he should get his due, but I also thought that if we wanted to start again we could. Syd didn't want to acknowledge Rick but he was looking at it very pragmatically, that if he acknowledged Rick I think he thought that would send people in the wrong direction. So giving him the most generous interpretation of what he did, Syd didn't think going in Rick's direction would be helpful to people. Other than that, I think he felt that we needed a fresh start. A way to do that was just start from here and have this be the foundation of it and not concern ourselves with what the Institute or what Rick did down there. Now I, personally, don't think that's right. I think even if a person turns really bad and becomes a monster—which is not the case with Rick—a person's contributions should be acknowledged. I think that Rick put a lot into it, he made a lot of sacrifices, he gave up his own private practice, he contributed a lot to the formulation of it, at the time he was absolutely seen as a person leading us, and I think it should be known that he did move the ball forward at an important time in the development of this understanding. And I said all that in a speech at an annual conference. Now, prior to that, Rick was really attacking what was going on. There was an article written about Syd where Rick was quoted as saying it was a bunch of crap. He said, "You can't put out a fire with a squirt gun." That was his statement. He was really taking issue, challenging people's credentials. At that point I felt like I was right all along, that they should have given him his due. So in my keynote speech I gave him credit. And it really caused problems with my peers. They had kind of an intervention and told me I should have told them ahead of time that I was going to do that. And I said, "Well, I said I was going to talk about the history of the understanding." "Yeah, but we didn't think you were going to mention Rick." But I'm glad that I stepped up and did it.

JP: It sounded to me at the time like there were still a lot of hard feelings.

GP: Oh I didn't say there weren't hard feelings. I'm saying that prior to Rick Suarez getting his due he was actively doing everything he could to undermine what we were doing. That's what my concern was. My concern was we were a party to his doing that by not giving him his due. And as soon as we acknowledged him, he stopped actively undermining it.

JP: Did Roger take over the Institute when Rick left?

GP: He didn't, no.

JP: By that time, had he already gotten the grant to go into the Modello Housing Project?

36

GP: He might have, but I know Roger got comfortable as just a worker-bee at the Institute, and Rick took control of everything, so Roger didn't really get to have that much responsibility. And Syd's idea was that *level of consciousness* was the only thing that mattered, and Elsie had the highest level of consciousness of anybody down there, so he made Elsie president.

NEW LEADERSHIP

JP: So, backing up a bit, with Rick leaving the Institute, how did you get back into the fold, so to speak?

GP: When Rick left the Institute they invited me down to speak at the next conference, and they gave me a breakout session. And my basic message was, "If you're not getting results, the problem is in you and not the client." Their philosophy was, "If the client isn't catching on, they're not ready."

JP: Well, Syd implied that a lot in his early days, like on his early tapes. So are you saying Syd was wrong, or they were misinterpreting what Syd was saying?

GP: Oh, Syd wasn't wrong, but I saw that practitioners could be doing better helping people with this understanding than they were, and that statement served as an excuse that got them off the hook, so to speak. Also, a lot of them weren't doing any intake; they weren't doing any dialogue. They would just go in and start talking to them. Well, it turned out, of 160 people at the conference, all but seven went to my breakout session. So they had to switch it to the main room, where I gave my talk on "It's you, not them." And that was vastly popular. And all of a sudden Linda and I had tremendous respect. They even asked us to come back and do staff development and training of teachers. Then Joe Bailey and Christine Heath asked us to come to Minnesota and train their counselors, and as soon as Rick left Syd was all over me. He said, "You know, George, I want to help you. Why don't we do a seminar down in the Bay area," and "Maybe you can help the Institute in Florida, because it's floundering." Without Chip supporting the Institute it would have fallen apart because they didn't have enough clients. You have to hand it to Chip; he was busting his ass with businesses and he was giving his money to the Institute. But Chip had his own business, his own practice. At the time he didn't really see himself as a leader of all this. Elsie was doing her best to hold everything together.

Anyway, at that time people had a lot of respect for me because of my talk down there, and different centers asked for my help. So I went around the country and did organizational development and worked with them. Well, at some point Syd said to me, "You know, George, if you are teaching this pure, which you seem to be, and you're very successful, you must be doing something right, and I've noticed that these other clinics are bringing you in to help them get things going. I don't know what I was thinking about you. Your way of doing things is so different. You're very out there, very aggressive, and you insist on getting paid well for what you do. That's very foreign to me. But your clinic is doing great and everybody else isn't doing so well. So I have to think that I'm underestimating you in some way." So then Syd kind of looked to me as a leader of the community, and I took on that role.

PSYCHOLOGY OF MIND AND "THE FOUNDERS"

JP: How did the name, "Psychology of Mind" come about?

GP: Syd made up the name, Psychology of Mind. I would say that was around 1978—well before Rick came up with Neo-cognitive Therapy—and nobody liked the name, Psychology of Mind. So we went to Syd and said, "Nobody likes this name. It sounds like 'Science of Mind,'" and this and that. And he said, "What's in a name? It doesn't matter what the name is, and the name accurately describes what this is, because it is a psychology of Mind." So we said okay.

JP: Who came up with the idea of "founders."

GP: Syd. In the late 1970s Syd brought Roger and I together for a conversation. Syd was intent on getting this breakthrough out professionally, and specifically into the field of psychology. He said something like, "Every new breakthrough has to have a story. It has to have a time, a place and a person identified with its origins. So it has to have a founder or founders in its story. The story is that two Ph.D. psychologists met and were inspired by this man from outside the field of psychology, an ex-welder with a ninth grade education who didn't read psychology or spirituality books. They saw the amazing results produced by this man who claimed to have discovered the secret to life. While listening to this man, the two mental health professionals had their own insights into how the mind works. Those insights transformed their lives and inspired them to share what they had discovered as a new way to help clients. Thus was the inception of this breakthrough brought into the field of psychology by these two founders that would provide a new foundation for psychology and psychiatry." He said, "You two are the founders. You will bring this understanding to the world." So Roger asked him, "Why wouldn't you be the founder since you discovered this understanding?" And Syd said, "First of all, I didn't really discover it. I rediscovered it. And when I say 'founders' I don't mean it as in who found it. I mean founders as in who provides the foundation, who established it in the world. I don't want to bring it to the world because I would be seen as a guru, and that wouldn't be good. I want this understanding to be established in professional channels and I don't have the credentials to do that. You guys do."

JP: Why did Syd choose Roger and you as founders?

GP: Well, he really had no other candidates. Syd jumped at the appearance of Roger and I coming onto the scene to build the needed story. He was kind of stuck with us—right time, right place. He didn't know how to get what he discovered into a professional context and then we fell into his lap. In the late '70s Roger Mills and I were the only other two people who were teaching the Principles full-time– Roger in prevention and me in the clinical arena. At the beginning we had no colleagues, no referral base, no training opportunities other than our conversations with Syd. And, in retrospect, we were the people who brought in most of the major players into "the Principles" community. In addition, Linda and I provided considerable financial resources to support Syd's work by bringing in wealthy benefactors. Linda and I also set up and populated seminars for Sydney Banks so that he could reach people with his message. Both Roger and I provided the first professional trainings. So I would say that all these contributions provided a foundation for this new understanding. Ask yourself how many other people contributed to the foundation of this understanding other than the contribution they made with their own practice. In business terms, Roger and I spent considerable non-billable time to help Syd lay a foundation for our colleagues.

JP: Then why would some people like Reese Coppage insist it was a myth that the two of you were the founders? Because there were a lot of people on Salt Spring Island who had gotten involved with Syd and his understanding before you, including Elsie and Chip.

GP: Well, it's certainly not a myth that Syd Banks designated us as founders. It's certainly not a myth that Syd Banks thought that this movement needed designated founders independent of Syd. Were we really founders? There is really no answer to that question. After all, the notion of founders is just made up. It's all in the eye of the beholder. To say that we, as founders, is a myth is to suggest that there is a truth and that isn't it. I don't see it that way. Personally, I would call Roger and I pioneers. We both gave up well-paying jobs and cut our standard of living at least in half to get Syd's message out on a full-time basis. Both of us established successful practices that made Principle-based teaching look both feasible and attractive. Roger pioneered bringing this into prevention work in the community. I would also say that Linda and I pioneered the first business application, mediation application, couples counseling application, and individual therapy applications with a wide range of diagnoses. Our professional training was the first exposure to this understanding for many therapists and counselors.

JP: And Elsie and Chip?

GP: Chip and Elsie and other people on Salt Spring Island were sharing what they learned from Syd amongst themselves and even in public forums before Roger and I came on the scene. They were more grounded in this understanding than we were and better at talking about it. But Syd was adamant that the founders—the people who were to introduce this understanding to the world—had to have degrees and be mental health professionals. Syd had a very high respect for degreed professionals because of his background. He assumed that if degreed professionals presented this understanding to the fields of psychology and psychiatry it would be seen as legitimate breakthrough. Conversely, he thought that if nonprofessionals introduced this breakthrough it might not be as respected; it might be seen as some type of a spiritual trip or some New Age psychology. Given those requirements that's why I said Syd was kind of stuck with Roger and me as founders. The Advanced Human Studies Institute was the next prominent professional presence of the principles. By the time that Institute became established my practice with Linda had instituted professional trainings, applications and a full range of counseling/therapy. It also set up professional seminars for Sydney Banks in the States. So no matter what other people think, the founders' designation came from Sydney Banks and he wanted the founders to be professionally credentialed, going forward.

ANNUAL CONFERENCES

JP: Okay. To change the subject, how did the conferences first get started?

GP: The annual conferences started when the Human Studies Institute started, in 1980 or 1981. The first keynote speaker was a guy named Leonard Shaw, who didn't have a clue about the understanding. But he was a partner with John Enright and me, and he had gone to a Syd seminar and was a psychologist. That was back when I was persona non grata at those things. They had maybe 25 or 30 people, and they had conferences every year in Florida. Then when Rick left it kind of opened the door for a community. It leveled the playing field. So you had George and Linda Pransky, Joe Bailey and Christine Heath, Bill Pettit, Keith Blevens, and Roger Mills, among others, and there was no hierarchy. No one was paying tribute to anybody else; it was all a level playing field. So now everybody was involved in planning the conferences.

At some point we were all together and someone said, "Why are we having the conferences in Tampa? Why don't we have them all over the

EARLY BOOKS

JP: How did your book, *Divorce is Not the Answer* come about?

GP: It was when I was living in California. I know that because I drove up to Seattle and spent the summer up there and wrote. It took me two and a half weeks to write it.

JP: Ha! It takes me about three years to write a book.

GP: I had it all in my head. I had the format down. I knew what my messages were. And I sat down and I wrote, and two and a half weeks later it was done. Then I gave it to a professional editor, but it was mostly just grammar.

JP: What gave you the idea to write it?

GP: I loved relationships as a subject. And I saw all the problems that people were having, and felt that if I wrote a book it would help a lot of couples. And it would help a lot better than me seeing people one at a time.

JP: What did Syd think of the books that were being written, like *Understanding*, by Jane Nelsen and, particularly, Richard Carlson's books?

GP: Syd liked that these books were coming out because it brought new people into the understanding. He wasn't at all judgmental about them and appreciated the fact that people went to the trouble of writing them.

JP: What did you and Syd think about Richard Carlson ultimately making all that money with *Don't Sweat the Small Stuff* and that subsequent series, and never having anything to do with the whole Psychology of Mind effort?

GP: Syd and I both understood that Rich was not a joiner. He didn't want to belong to anything or be a part of a community. We respected that he was that way and appreciated that he was independent and thought for himself. We both thought that Rich was a terrific person and felt grateful that he helped so many people and pointed them in the direction of the Principles.

country? Why should you get the profit from the conference (meaning, the Advanced Human Studies Institute)? I didn't say that, but one of the other people did. And Elsie and Chip said, "Well, we live off that profit. That's a good part of our earnings." And Chris said, "Well, what does that have to do with anything? It's really not your conference anymore. It's the community's conference." So Elsie said, "Are you going to keep the profit?" "No, the profit will go back into next year's conference, and every year we'll make it better and better and we'll be able to lower the cost of tuition." And to her credit Elsie said, "Oh, that sounds good to me." So then we had our annual conferences and we had an annual conference committee.

MODELLO

In 1987 Roger Mills brought this understanding into the Modello housing project, a low-income, primarily African American public housing project replete with problems, and incredible results were shown there among residents. Subsequently, Roger moved into the Homestead Gardens housing project, with similar results.

JP: What did you think when you heard Roger was going into Modello, originally?

GP: Well, I didn't hear about him going into it, Jack, at all. I didn't know anything about it. I knew that Roger was doing prevention work and talking in communities, but I had no idea that he had actually gone into the projects and did what he did. I had no idea. The first time I heard about it was at one of the conferences where they had the Modello people speak. And that was around 1989, two years or so after he went in.

JP: Were you totally surprised?

GP: Oh, I was amazed. This is when I first heard the story of his actually going in there, teaching parenting classes.

JP: Did you think he had it in him?

GP: Well I have a lot of respect for Roger's persistence and willpower, and he was a very competitive person. So it didn't surprise me at all that he would be able to pull that off. He was just incredibly persistent.

JP: It was an amazingly courageous thing to do.

GP: Well that doesn't surprise me about Roger. I mean Roger, at the drop of a hat, packed up his stuff and moved to California without a job. He left a really good paying job in Eugene, and thought nothing of it. He came down to California and didn't have any means of income, and then he went to the Advanced Human Studies Institute. He was a very courageous person. He was an adventurous person. He thought nothing of it. He didn't even deliberate about it. So him doing something like that didn't surprise me in the slightest. What surprised me is that someone could accomplish those results in a community like that, with the crime rate going down the way it did, with people getting off of drugs. And it surprised me that he could get parents to go to parenting classes. I thought that was very cool. That was around the time I moved up to La Conner.

[*Note: For Roger Mills' history in the Modello and Homestead Gardens housing projects, see the book,* Modello: A Story of Hope for the Inner-city and Beyond *by Jack Pransky.*]

LA CONNER

JP: So if you had built a thriving practice in Oakland, what made you move to La Conner, Washington?

GP: I started the practice in Oakland around 1980 and I moved to La Conner in 1990, so I was in Oakland for 10 years. What happened is when I met Syd and did all this with New Psychology Consultants and then started my new practice, I went through all my savings. I had been making 80 grand a year working for John Enright. I borrowed money from my parents and everybody I could. I maxed out my credit cards and we borrowed a down payment on the house from Linda's folks. Linda was working as a nurse to pay the expenses. But the practice developed and after a couple of years we were both working and we were making a very good living, and we had people working for us. And I started working with businesses, and the business thing was really a big money maker, so now our standard of living was high and we were living in an Oakland ghetto. We had drug dealers and people sleeping in our cars if we left them open. They were stealing our kids' bicycles—which didn't bother us—but Linda said, "We don't have to live here, George. I love our house, but…the kids are going to college soon, and I'd like to move somewhere else. Can we do that?" I said, "Linda, honestly, I feel like we can go to almost any location anywhere and start a practice with what we've got going for us. Plus, I'm good at starting a practice now, because I did it already." Well, we got into a quandary about where to go, with all the possibilities, and then a friend said, "I love your house. This is a beautiful house. Did you ever think of selling it?" I said, "Absolutely." So we sold him our house. So now we had no place to live and no place we wanted to go. So Linda said, "Why don't we go up to my folks' place for a while?" And I said, "Yeah, we can live off our savings." So we went up to La Conner—they lived on the property we live on now—it was supposed to be a temporary thing, and we were happy as a lark there. And we started running out of savings.

So I went to the District Attorney's office and said, "I'll take criminal offenders." The next week I had a full practice. We went to the Bay Area every couple of months to make money, and people said, "Can we come up there?" So then we came up with the idea of an intensive, and that created a big referral rate. So it wasn't long before we needed someone else, and we brought in Keith from Texas. And that just generated more business, so we brought in Sandy [Krot], and then we brought in Dicken [Bettinger], and then, later, the kids [Kara Stamback and Erika Bugbee] came into the practice.

THREE PRINCIPLES

JP: Jumping back a bit, if you listen to Syd's early tapes he never talks about "Three Principles." It was all very spiritual. Of course the Principles were always embedded in what he was talking about, but he didn't break them down into Three Principles.

GP: He didn't, no. And I have my own theory about how he came up with them. He had been recommending *Sanity, Insanity, and Common Sense*. He got behind it. He sung its praises. He tried to get everybody involved in it. And he's sitting with someone new to this, and they talked about "the four principles." [*Note: See Part II, 1987.*] And Syd said, "What four principles are those?" And they listed them and said, "They're from the book, *Sanity, Insanity, and Common Sense*." He said, "They are?" They said, "Oh yeah. That's what the book is all about, the four principles." Syd says, "Emotions isn't a Principle." So Syd gets the book and reads the book, and he's absolutely appalled.

JP: Did that play into Rick's falling out with Syd?

GP: No it didn't. When he heard them he thought they were rubbish, and I don't know how Syd handled it then, but that was maybe a year or two before that other stuff happened. That did not sully Rick's reputation, because Syd kind of knew Rick was trying to do his best.

[Side note: Now here is an interesting thing: Three years before the fallout of Rick, Syd went to a garage sale that Rick was having, and at the garage sale was a bunch of psychology books. And Syd said to himself, "This man is not grounded in this understanding if he could sell psychology books, because the old psychology is bad for people. It's not just inefficient or wrong, it's harmful. It makes them self-absorbed. It takes them into their past. It takes them into their negative feelings. It makes them think that their problems are real, that their emotions are information about the world." So he had a laundry list of how the old psychology was actually harmful to the world. So Rick might as well have had a shelf of poisons that he didn't use anymore because he found out they were poisonous and now he's selling them. So Syd told me, "As soon as I saw those books I knew that Rick didn't understand the Principles." So I said to Syd, "Then why did you allow him to be leader if you knew that?" And he said, "Oh, well, I was hoping that maybe he'd go up a level." That's what Syd said. I'm guessing he didn't want to face that the person he had put his trust behind, who was running things, who everybody else was listening to, was not well grounded in the Principles.]

JP: Getting back to Rick coming up with four principles, Syd hadn't read the book before but he was pushing it?

GP: That's right, and he was absolutely appalled. And he says—now this is me—I think he asked himself, "Well, what are the principles, then?" Because it was shortly after that that he started teaching *Mind, Consciousness and Thought* as Principles.

JP: I remember he put out a tape saying it's Three Principles, and they are Mind, Consciousness and Thought. I think that was about 1990 or 1991 or so, just before I came into this.

GP: Yeah. I think it was in reaction to what he saw, that they weren't really Principles. And then he thought, "Wait a minute. Principles is a good thing." And he kind of intuited what a Principle was, and then came up with The Three Principles. But I don't know this for a fact.

THE PSYCHOLOGY OF MIND TRAINING INSTITUTE
AND THE CORE CONCEPTS

JP: How did the Psychology of Mind Training Institute (POMTI) come about?

GP: Well, after the Florida Institute closed La Conner became the gathering place of practitioners of this understanding during those years. They would come up to La Conner. Other than that, and other than the annual conferences, people never got together except around Syd's few seminars. So, at that time we were hiring Syd as a consultant, and Syd said, "You guys should get organized. You should be working together. You should have collaboration. You should be helping each other. You should be figuring out together how to get this message out." Syd said to us, essentially, "At this point in time I think there is strength in numbers. I think you guys are in a position where you could become more credible. This understanding could become more credible, rather than just a bunch of individuals out there teaching the same thing." Now, prior to that, Syd seemed to be very much against affiliations of people, and I think his reasoning, as best I understood it, was that people would become dependent upon each other, copying each other, as in, "They really teach well; I'll teach the way they teach, and do what they do." So there was X-amount of dependency happening, and Syd was really all over us about: Mind your own business. Do your own practice. Never mind what anybody else is doing with the understanding. That's how he was. And, in my mind he was right, because everybody at the time did get independent and start thinking for themselves.

So when we all got stronger and more independent, he came to us and said, "Look, this is a good time for you to form an organization, get credibility in the world, get acknowledged by the field of psychology." He said, "Pick the 10 or so practitioners that you think are the most credible, make sure they have degrees and a lot of experience in the mental health field, so that it will look like you're a professional group, and meet together." So we just took it upon ourselves to set up this Board of Directors for this Institute, and that's when we came up with Core Concepts Courses and all that. We set this up as a Training Institute to get the training out around the country to professionals.

JP: So was it because you decided to do a Training Institute that you came up with the idea of "concepts?" As in, "What are we going to teach at the Training Institute?"

GP: First we came up with the idea of working together. Then we came up with the idea of a Board of Directors, and we thought it should be professional, so everyone on it had to have some type of a degree to be on the Board. That limited it. Anybody who had any kind of degree was on the board. We had Bill Pettit on it, Roger, Keith, Rita Shuford, Carol Ringold, Christine Heath, Joe Bailey, Dicken Bettinger—

JP: Why was that decision made?

GP: Again, this was at Syd's urging. We thought that it should be professional, that it was easy to discredit this, and it's harder to do if you have Ph.D.s on the Board. So I thought that was good; it would be one less thing that people could dismiss us for. So we had a Board of degreed people, and one of our objectives was to provide training for the large community. And we thought, we've got to do a course. But nobody knew what to do in the course because we all taught differently and went about it differently. So I came up with the idea of the Concepts Course. I said, "What is it that we all teach in common?" And I made a list of those, and I brought them to the group, and I said, "I asked myself, what is it that every single person in this room would get across? What ideas would everybody get across in a course, and anything everybody wouldn't try to get across in what they teach shouldn't be in the course, and every idea we all do want to get across should be in the course." They agreed with that philosophically. They said, "That's a great idea! We'll just take the common denominator of what we all teach." And I did these overlapping circles, and in the middle where they all overlapped, I said, "That's what we're trying to do!" And they said, "Well, how are we going to figure that out? Nobody knows what anybody else teaches. That's going to take forever." I said, "As a matter of fact, this sheet of paper I have has that right on it. I'm not saying this is right, but it could be completely right. But you tell me." So they went and they eliminated a couple that some people didn't teach, and they added a couple, but overall, that became the concepts. So I suggested, "Look, we take three days, and we just teach these eight ideas, and this is the order that we teach them in." Everybody agreed with that. So then we had the Core Concepts course.

JP: So then a little later, I think it was you who thought, wait a minute, we have *thought systems* as a concept in there, and it shouldn't be.

GP: That's right.

JP: Why was that?

GP: Well, when I taught the course, when it would come to *thought systems*, it was indistinguishable from what you and I would call the old paradigm. In other words, you couldn't get *thought systems* across without people calling it "schema" or calling it "assumptions," or calling it "beliefs," so it was the only one on there that was indistinguishable from the current thinking. So I went back to the drawing board and I said, "Well, what is it about that?" And I realized that a thought system kind of assumed something that was outside of what people were thinking in the moment, whereas all the other core concepts were in real time in the moment. *Thought systems* assumed that there was a power beyond our control that was influencing us, and that seemed inconsistent with the logic.

JP: Then a few years later I remember the "rigor stage" around the concepts.

GP: There was, yeah.

JP: That kind of backfired, don't you think? I mean, the idea of it was beautiful because I remember you found out people were off teaching very different things when they were supposedly teaching the same concepts. So you thought it would be a good idea to get everyone on the same page.

GP: Well, the thing about the rigor stage is that it got people to pay attention to what they were saying, and that was a really powerful thing.

JP: It was. But there was a lot of intellectual thinking that went along with it.

GP: That's true.

JP: It messed me up a little.

GP: Yeah, there were a lot of people getting in their heads about saying it right.

JP: Yeah, it drove people right into their heads.

GP: That's true.

JP: It seemed like a good idea at the time.

GP: Well, the spirit of it was a good idea, but we didn't really know what the implications of it were going to be. And that's true of every stage. We couldn't see what would happen.

JP: I remember you and Roger kind of had a falling out around the rigor stage. Roger thought his people were losing the feeling by trying to say it right.

GP: I don't think Roger and I ever had a falling out.

JP: I remember there was some conference when the two of you got up on stage together and hugged each other and it was a big deal because things were not so good between you before that, and I remember Elsie getting up and saying at the time, "I feel that the lid has been taken off."

GP: Well that wasn't Roger and me. That was the people under us. In other words, our constituents saw a friction between Roger and me, but I never saw a friction between us and, as far as I know, neither did Roger. But his people thought that we were in it just for the money, and we weren't really into helping society. His people didn't like that we worked with a really high demographic. And my people thought that Roger exaggerated his results. Roger and I never felt like there was conflict between us. Now later, when there was an incident between Syd and me around my tapes, Roger backed Syd 100%. But I expected that of Roger.

JP: What happened to the concepts, ultimately?

GP: Well, what happened is Syd. Syd busted "the concepts," just like he busted the "four principles." What happened is, I think it was Elsie who was talking with Syd, saying she was confused about which concept was which, and he said, "What concepts?" He didn't even know we were teaching concepts. He had no idea. So he said, "What are they?" And she went through all the concepts [*Note: See Part II, 1996*], and Syd said, "You don't have to break *thought* down. You don't want to do that. You just want to teach the Principles, the essence of it. The other things at best are just metaphors that come to mind. But it's a mistake to break it down like that." Syd said, "It's not that complicated. It's just the Principles of Mind, Consciousness and Thought, and that's all you have to teach.

JP: So given that you are the one who pretty much had the original idea to have concepts, what did you think of all that?

GP: I thought he was right. I thought, "Well, there's something to be said for that." Now, I still thought they were useful to me in what I was teaching, but I didn't think everybody had to teach that. I thought, "Well, this is just my way." So I thought it went from being a good idea of what to teach to something that was just my way of teaching, and I didn't see a downside to it. I just thought it was better that people teach their own way, and the simpler you taught it the better.

TEACHING THE THREE PRINCIPLES

JP: I remember, somewhere along the way, Syd said to you that he wanted you to teach the Three Principles, and you said something like, "That's your department, not mine." So how did that all come about, and what was the story there?

GP: Right. That is a hell of a story, Jack. I forgot about that. Syd and I were down in Orinda with Don and Barb Carlson, and we were staying at their house. I think we were doing a seminar, and Syd was talking about the Principles this and the Principles that, and he said, "You know, George, the Principles are psychological as well as spiritual. They are Principles of psychology." I said, "I know that, Syd." He said, "Then why don't you teach the Principles? Why aren't you teaching the Principles instead of me teaching the Principles?" So I said, "Well, I don't think that's in my expertise. That's not really my thing." Syd says, "Well, that's what the field needs to hear. They need to hear these Principles." I said, "I know Syd, that's why you're here." He said, "No, you should be teaching them." I said, "Well, I don't even understand them myself, to be honest with you. They are over my head." He said, "George, you have to teach them. This is ridiculous! And all your peers have to teach them, too. You are a leader. People look to you. If you're not teaching them, they are not going to teach them." I said, "I know, but I don't think anybody can teach them but you." Syd says, "That's not true! They wouldn't be Principles if that was the case."

52

Then he said, "Would you like to teach the Principles?" I said, "Well, yeah, if I don't have to talk beyond what I know, I would." Syd said, "Okay, you just have to know more then." So he says to Don and Barb, "You have a beautiful place up in Sonoma County, right?" They said, "Yes." He says, "Let's all of us go up there, and I'll tutor George about teaching the Principles." So Don and Barb and I went up to their Sonoma ranch, and it's beautiful weather, and Syd and I are out on the porch. And it's funny, Jack, because I never took the Principles seriously until that moment. I was just kind of, well, you know, what are you going to do? So I started listening and asking questions and challenging, and he gave me a crash course on the Principles.

So we are at the ranch and he says, "You have to teach this to your colleagues." So we had a meeting at the faculty club and we invited everybody, and I told Syd, "I want to teach it with you." And he said, "No, if you teach it with me people will think that I'm essential to teaching the Principles. You teach them." I said, "Syd, I just learned this a month ago. How am I supposed to teach it?" He said, "You'll teach what you know, George." So I did. And when I taught it, nobody had a clue what I was talking about. It went way over their heads. And I said to the group, "My God, you don't have a clue what I'm talking about, do you?" And they said, "No." And I said, in front of the room, "Syd, this is messed up."

We took a break, and Syd said, "What, are you crazy? What do you think I've been up against all these years? People don't see it until they see it. It's like the will-of-the-wisp. It's invisible until it's visible. You are that way. You couldn't see it." I said, "I know, but it seems obvious now." He said, "Well it's obvious to you because you see it now, but it's not obvious to them. What I see isn't obvious to you, George," I said, "I know but I thought I put it out so clearly. They are not getting what I say!" Syd said, "George, what you're teaching now is more profound and farther from the intellect than what you used to teach, so people are having a hard time. But that's good! And you have to be more humble and more compassionate because it's hard to see something you don't see." And little by little people began to catch on.

JP: I remember it took a long time for people to go from only teaching concepts to only teaching Principles. That wasn't easy for people. Now I can see that the concepts were distracting people from seeing the deeper meaning of the Three Principles. It seems so obvious to me now, but it didn't seem at all obvious then. I kept thinking, regarding prevention, wait a minute, *moods* as a concept is what first affected the Modello folks. They were able to hear moods at the level they were at. How can we give up teaching things like that in a community? How can we just start teaching Mind, Consciousness and Thought in a community?

GP: I know. It wasn't easy for people. But it was a turning point for our teaching.

JP: People started teaching with so much more depth and simplicity.

GP: True.

TAPES

JP: Jumping back a ways—it's hard to keep this in chronological order because so much was happening simultaneously—how did your tapes come about? I know, early on, someone had made a number of tapes of some of Syd's early talks, but how did you get into making tapes?

GP: Well, it was when I was in La Conner, so around 1988 or 1989 must have been my first tapes. I would be working with a client, and they would have a particular problem and I would come up with an insight about how to help them, and the insight would be very useful to the client. And then I would be doing a seminar or seeing another client or something else, and I would have that same idea, and it would do great. So after I saw an idea did great over time I thought, "I can see this helps the general public. I could make a tape on that subject, and I'll distribute it to every client I get." Well, after a while I began to see what ideas would be helpful to the public, without having to wait to see what they were. I would be able to tell a great idea from a good one, and every time I came up with a great idea I would make a tape. And then I discovered the ability to come up with great ideas about any subject at will. So, if you gave me "anxiety," I found my ability to come up with a great metaphor, like the trees in the forest [*gravitating to the light*]. I would come up with great metaphors. Then once I discovered I could make tapes on any subject, then I started thinking, what subjects do people struggle with the most? Then one of my business clients said, "You know, George, you should do a tape of the month club. People love your tapes." So I did a tape of the month club. Every month I would make a tape on a subject that I thought was a good subject, so now I have over 100 tapes.

JP: We can talk about what happened to your tapes later, but first...

IMPROVING TEACHING AND
GETTING THE PRINCIPLES OUT TO THE WORLD

JP: ...do you remember anything about the POM Teaching Fellow program in La Conner in 1996?

GP: Maybe that was this: I had this client who was a very successful businessman and owned several companies. He came up to meet with me in La Conner, and he liked what he learned himself and what his company learned. He said to me, "Don't you think it would be great if we had 10 or 20 people who are teaching what you're teaching?" I said, "Well, there are a lot of people out there teaching." He said, "Yes, but they are not successful at building their practices, and I'm assuming that they just don't understand enough or are not offering enough, or the world would be beating a path to their door." So I said, "Well, I'm not in a position to say that, but the logic is sound." He said, "I'll tell you what I'll do. I will fund a project to train your colleagues, and the way it will work is you pick out people that you think are very promising—I don't want you to pick people who need a lot of help—your top-level most promising people—bring them to La Conner for as long as you feel is appropriate, and I will pay you to train them. I will pay them for their time, for what they would have made had they stayed home and done their practice, and if you don't have enough clients to have them work with you, I will fund you seeing pro bono clients, people who need help. So they come up there, you're able to talk with them and have them sit in with your clients, debrief them, and nobody is the worse for it financially." He said, "That's what I want to do. I want to get this out into the world, and I want to quadruple the number of practitioners." So I thought that was great! So I don't remember all the people I had up there, but for sure I had Keith and Christine Heath and there were maybe seven or eight people that I had up there. They came up one at a time, they were there for a week or two, some longer. They sat in with clients. I would debrief them; Linda would meet with them. They asked a bunch of questions. There were a lot of things we did that they never even thought existed, like the kind of intake we did. They didn't really do any intake. It was all teaching—just sit down and here's the understanding. So the whole idea of intake, the whole idea of checking in with people, seeing what they heard, they did some of that but it wasn't intake-heavy like it was with us. They saw how people came for an intensive with us for a period of time. So I'm thinking that was the Fellowship.

JP: What about the trainings you did for us teachers?

GP: Well, we needed more teachers ourselves, and we thought there needed to be more teachers in the world. So we had, by invitation only, 25 people, like Joe Boyle—just a whole bunch of people, up to La Conner for three or four days.

JP: I was part of that. It was great! I really got a lot out of that.

GP: I don't remember who was there. We did two of those.

THE PSYCHOLOGY OF MIND/AEQUANIMITAS FOUNDATION

JP: Do you know how the idea for the Psychology of Mind Foundation came about?

GP: I do, as a matter of fact. After we met and we set up the Core Concepts courses and stuff like that, then we had the idea that we could set up a nonprofit and get funding. We had all these grateful clients and businesses, and if we set up a nonprofit and said we're looking to do good things in the world we could get funding. At that time we had the connections to do good things in the world—well-established, high-powered business people with good reputations, and they all had connections, so we started putting people on the Board who were well known, who could support us financially somewhat, good connections, credible, a bunch of like-minded people. So that was our new plan. We had John Wood on the Board, Kevin Gleason, Reese Coppage—clients who were successful businessmen.

JP: When did it become the Aequanimitas Foundation? What made it change to that?

GP: Well, Judy [Sedgeman] became very active in the leadership of it, and she basically felt like the Psychology of Mind Foundation was not a good name for it. They thought of all kinds of names, and she came up with Aequanimitas—it was used in medical practice, and it describes the exact kind of thing that we're doing. So she simply came out with that.

THE SYDNEY BANKS INSTITUTE OF INNATE HEALTH
AT WEST VIRGINIA UNIVERSITY

JP: Which brings me to West Virginia University. How did that get started in the first place? I remember you had gone down there and had done some training, and you were very excited about it.

GP: Here's how that happened: The Dean of West Virginia University School of Medicine was a man named Bob D'Alessandri. He was in a group that was a network of head administrators of medical schools, Deans, heads of HMOs—so they were very, very high level medical professionals. They had a forum that would meet, like, once a year in a really nice location, and they would bring in a guest speaker. Someone in his forum had heard me speak to a group of physicians in San Francisco, so that person asked me if I would talk to their forum because it was going to be on an island that was about an hour and a quarter drive from us. So I said, "Sure." They had a dinner, they invited me to it, and then I gave a presentation. And at the presentation was Bob D'Alessandri, Dean of the West Virginia University School of Medicine. He was really inspired by it. And he came up to me afterwards and said, "Why couldn't you teach this to students to significantly improve their learning?" I said, "Well, you could, Bob." He said, "Because the insecurity that they have, the pressure and all that stuff is the reason why they don't do better. This would be a great thing for students." I said, "Absolutely." So then he called me back that week and he said, "George, I and one of the other Deans would like to come up there and go through your program and see what you have to offer." So he did. And then he said, "While I think this would be very important for the students, right now we need this for the faculty because, as an example, we are in budget negotiations and everybody is feathering their own nests. There's no big-picture thinking. Everybody's trying to get as much money for their budget as they can, and I realized after I went to your talk that we were never going to get anywhere this way. And all it is is insecurity and everybody is just frightened and acting for themselves. I got from your talk that this doesn't have to be the case, so I'm thinking that if you talk with them at a seminar that would make a big difference." So the other faculty member, the Chair of the department, said, "Well, why don't we have George work with the budgeting team." And Bob said, "I think every single chair of this University medical school should go through this program." And the Chair said, "You can't do that, Bob, because where are you going to get the money?" And Bob said, "Where there's a will, there's a way. I've never felt constrained by budgets, and I don't want to start here." I think he brought seven or eight more people up just to get enough buy-in. They didn't go through the program; they just came up and asked me a million questions. What was in it for them? And this and that. And they agreed that this would be a good thing. Then Bob said, "Let's do it!" And he brought every Chair of the University medical school departments to La Conner, and we did four day programs with them as a group.

JP: So, out of that?

GP: So he asked me if I would move to West Virginia and be on their faculty.

JP: I remember that, and you were very touched and thrilled with the idea that a major university accepted you.

GP: I was thrilled with the idea, but ultimately I didn't want to do it. And the reason was because I've always been adverse to specialization. I love doing new things, being in over my head, and I've always seen myself as part of the R & D—Research and Development—branch of the Principles, self-appointed—

JP: [laughs]

GP: —that I would bring the Principles into areas, and then other people would say, "Oh yeah, that could be done," and so forth. It was kind of, like, finding out what it takes to do it. So I didn't want to go to West Virginia. But Judy was working for us at the time, and Judy wanted to go. So I talked to Bob, and he had gotten to know Judy, so he brought her down there and she became a faculty member. And then she convinced them to bring in Bill Pettit.

JP: Before that, I was under the impression, probably wrong, that you had started to work with them, and something happened and you left there.

GP: No, I never agreed to be a part of the University. I agreed to go down there. I agreed to do this and that for them, but always as a contracted employee. They made me a faculty member, but I was adjunct.

JP: I remember at first Syd was thrilled that the Sydney Banks Institute of Innate Health got created. So, what ended up happening to it?

GP: You'd have to ask Judy Sedgemen or Bill Pettit. [*Note: See Part III B*] But see, from the time it was discovered that limes prevented scurvy it took 200 years for limes to be standard issue on British Naval vessels. From the time germs were discovered it took 50 years for sanitation practices, sterilization in surgery and communicable disease control to become mainstream. It's very difficult for fundamentally new thinking—new paradigms—to infiltrate an existing institution like academia. The foundation of academia is credentials, research and new ideas being built from old ideas. Along comes Sydney Banks, saying that his advanced understanding of psychology, which flies directly in the face of the psychology currently taught at that university, originated from his epiphany in a moment of enlightenment. Syd did not have education and training in the field of psychology; he had only a ninth grade education. The fundamental understandings that he contributed did not come from research studies or an advancement of already existing ideas. They derived from his own understanding via the profound insights that came to him out of the blue. Bill Pettit was loaded with credentials but he overtly turned his back on his education and experience and proclaimed that the Principles Syd discovered represented a more true, more essential understanding of human psychology. Right from the start Sydney Banks and the West Virginia School of Medicine were like oil and water. Judy couldn't bring in credentialed mental health professionals because her colleagues would challenge those credentials. She was smart—she brought in non-credentialed people like Chip and community people because they wouldn't be saying that their professional education in mental health flew in the face of what they currently understood. The medical school faculty liked the results that Bill Pettit and Judy produced but attributed those results to Bill and Judy's personalities. They were impressed by the guest speakers that Judy brought in. They even listed improvements in their own personal lives from exposure to the Principles. But the department head held the line, stating that the traditional psychologies were the "real psychology," independent of the results produced by the Principles. For example, all the medical school students were required to take a course in mental health and mental illness. You would think that would be a perfect opportunity for Judy to teach people the generic nature of mental health and mental illness via the Principles, but the department insisted that course be based on the traditional psychology paradigm.

From the minute Sydney Banks was introduced to the University the conflict between paradigms began and just played out over time. His visits down there added fuel to the fire. Naturally, his visits and even his conference calls were discouraged. The department head was between a rock and a hard place. Even as he liked and respected the work of Bill Pettit he wasn't about to say there was a new psychology paradigm at his institution. The department head didn't understand what he had with this new paradigm. If he had truly adopted this paradigm at the medical school at University of West Virginia it would have been the psychology and psychiatry equivalent of the Mayo Clinic. But because of this lack of understanding he was frightened, thinking that he was introducing an approach that would embarrass him with his peers.

JP: Did you see this kind of thing play out a lot?

GP: Yes. For example, one-time Syd and I did a retreat for the vice presidents and directors of a large corporation. After our morning presentation it was clear to us that people were really full. We thought they needed to decompress and reflect on what they had heard; we thought that was absolutely the best use of time. We wanted people to take the rest of the day off and let their learning soak in. But it was a problem for the business leaders. Taking 70% of the work day off enjoying yourself made no sense for them, even though it was suggested by someone they trusted. They had trouble getting past their well-entrenched thought system about "keep your nose to the grindstone." They did go along with it, and ultimately saw how that day moved the ball forward, which was a lesson that fed into their leadership on a go-forward basis. But it was an awkward conversation prior to their deciding to trust us.

JP: Okay, so back to what happened to the Sydney Banks Institute, do you know where Syd was coming from about it?

GP: Well, I don't have very much direct knowledge of it, but I did hear it from both sides and I tend to think that both sides were accurate in what they saw. So from Syd's side of it he felt like they weren't bringing him in. Judy was bringing in occasional people like Chip, but she didn't bring in any Ph.D.s, like myself or Keith, and Syd thought that was not a good thing. He also felt that he was getting paid and was supposed to be the inspiration behind it, and he didn't have the opportunity much to go in there. He offered, but they wouldn't bring him down. So that's Syd's version, and I think that was accurate. What I understand of Judy's version of it was that when Syd came down he didn't treat the department head very well. So the head of the psychology department introduced Syd, and Syd basically badmouthed psychology, saying the answer is not in the past, it's not in dealing with the details, it's not this and it's not that, and Judy and Bill know what they're doing. You can understand how the head of the department felt a little disrespected because of that. Syd sounded like he did not respect the head of the department and kind of talked as if the guy wasn't there. So that kind of soured Syd's relationship with the University. They were afraid to bring him in. Now, in terms of the other people, like myself and Keith and Roger, she said she didn't want to bring us in because our credentials would not stand up to what they would require down there in the medical school—the kinds of degrees we had weren't really respected by them.

JP: Did Syd ultimately have a falling out with Bob D'Alessandri?

GP: Not really. Syd was very disappointed because he thought he would get, like, a faculty position or some type of honorary degree. Bob initially had said to Syd, "I think I can do that," But later he said, "I just don't think I can do it." I don't know how much of that had to do with Syd's relationship with the University. I don't know whether Bob had just thought he could and couldn't, but that was a real sticking point for Syd. He felt like he was supposed to be a much bigger part of it, and he wasn't. So he was disappointed. But I don't think he had bad will towards Bob. And in a university it's really crucial that a strong relationship be built with a department head, and I'm not sure that happened.

JP: At one point Judy and Bill called me up and asked me if I wanted to move down there and become part of that program—join their team— but it never materialized.

GP: Really? I didn't know that.

JP: Yeah. So was it Syd who said, "I don't want it to be called the Sydney Banks Institute anymore?" Or was it the University?

GP: I don't know. That's a good question. I know Syd was glad that they didn't keep calling it that, but I don't know whether he initiated it or not. But you know, it's easy to see how hard it would be for a university to wrap their heads around a theosopher, a person who doesn't have degrees, a person who learned on their own, whose ideas were original. When I talked with the head of the department and asked him, "How do you figure he knows this?" He said, "Well, he learned it, that's for sure. He just doesn't want to admit it." So I said, "Do you think he studied?" He said, "Oh yes. There is no way he could have known it if he didn't." So I said, "What if he just intuited it?" He said, "No. Not possible."

HEALTH REALIZATION AND SANTA CLARA COUNTY

JP: What is your understanding of how it went into Santa Clara County in the Alcohol and Drug Program there? What did you think of all that and what ultimately happened?

GP: I really know nothing about how it got into Santa Clara County. [*See Part III C*] I know that Roger was involved, but I don't know any specifics. Bob Garner was a leader who bought into the understanding. Without him it never would have happened. I thought it was wonderful that it got into the County because it helped so many people. It also added to the credibility of the Principles. What ultimately happened was when Bob Garner retired, his replacement stopped the program, which was not a surprise. I saw the same thing happen at BAE Systems and West Virginia University School of Medicine. When leaders take over they often go with programs they are familiar with rather than something unfamiliar or don't understand, as in the case of Santa Clara County.

JP: I remember one day Roger called me up and essentially said, "No more Health Realization!" Given that "Health Realization" was a name Roger created, and given that Santa Clara County Alcohol and Drug Services now had a "Health Realization Division," and given that my business was called the "NorthEast Health Realization Institute" and it was a name I really liked and it resonated with the prevention world, and especially because some of us had spent years trying to get that name recognized in the prevention and human services fields and we were just beginning to make some headway, I was not happy with this.

63

When I asked Roger why, he was very vague about it but he attributed the decision to Syd. I heard later, second or third hand, so I don't know if it's accurate, that Syd heard about someone teaching what they were calling "Health Realization" who was apparently misrepresenting the understanding, and he jumped to the conclusion that it was about "Health Realization" in general. Do you know how and why this all came about, and what did you think of that?

GP: I don't know how it came about, but I do know the logic behind it. Syd observed that there were a lot of people teaching the Principles under different names. For example, Roger and others talked about the Principles as "Health Realization," while Pransky and Associates taught the Principles at BAE Systems under the name, "State of Mind" program, and West Virginia University was calling it "Innate Health," and others were calling it some other things. Syd felt that these different program names diluted the visibility of the Principles in the world. In business terminology he was suggesting that we had a branding issue. He thought it would be better if the world saw all these teachings as one thing, and calling it "The Three Principles" seemed to him to be the best name because it was the most truthful and to the point. I understood that people name their programs with marketing in mind for their particular audience. I did feel, however, that creating a single brand called "Principles" would ultimately get more visibility in the world. It did mean that each practitioner would have to give up some promotional potential and encounter some organizational complications by sticking to this single brand, but the greater good would be served by that sacrifice. I thought it was great that Syd would suggest we do the right thing and not be concerned with the implications. He was truly a man of integrity.

HUMANNESS

JP: Let's get back to your tapes. I loved your tapes. I used to listen to them over and over again until they sounded like old news, and then I knew I "got it" and it was part of me. They really helped with my grounding. But you took them off the market for a while. Why? And are they back on?

GP: Yeah. Well what happened was my tapes were apparently interfering with Syd's tapes; he thought that people were buying my tapes instead of his tapes, which were the closest to the truth as he saw it. I argued that my tapes sold his tapes. I would get my tapes out and then people would buy his tapes to get more. But he got really indignant that my tapes were undermining his message. Now, here's the thing, Jack, this is one exception—I never did anything Syd wanted me to do unless I thought it was a good idea—so with this exception I never did what Syd asked me to do unless I would've done it on my own, and there was a period of time when I could not see taking my tapes off the market. They were helping people. I felt if people were taking my tapes over Syd's there was a logic behind it. It just didn't feel right to me. So I didn't do it and it became a tremendous source of conflict between Syd Banks and me. And then it spread. The whole community came down on me. But I said to each of them, "Look, I'm not taking my tapes off the market until I think it's a good idea, and talking to you not only hasn't made it a good idea, but it's made it a worse idea because I think it's a bad role model. X-number of people look up to me, and if I sell out it's not going to sit well with others. The reason I have any respect in the community is because people see me as a straight shooter and as honest." So it was a difficult time.

JP: When was that?

GP: It was around my 60th birthday party—I now just turned 72, so that was around 2000. So there was a period of maybe a year or more, maybe even two years, when I was completely on the outs with Syd Banks and others over this issue.

JP: So when things like that happened, what did you think about the way that people treated each other in this community, and the way Syd sometimes treated people? What did you make of that whole thing?

GP: Well I didn't like it when Syd got harsh with me. There were also times when he was somewhat estranged when we weren't on the same page; that was difficult for me as well. But, I also saw it as taking the bitter with the sweet. In other words, I had gotten so much from Syd, and my life was so improved by Syd, that it was a small price to pay.

That's one thought I had. So in the grand scheme of things, me having some unpleasant moments with regard to Syd didn't really matter, because if I hadn't met him I would've had many difficult moments, even years, anyway.

JP: [laughs]

GP: The other thing is, I never knew what Syd knew that I didn't, you see? So even though this thing about the tapes didn't make sense to me, I didn't rule out the possibility that Syd knew something I didn't here. There were a number of times when we didn't understand why Syd would do some of the things he did, and he turned out to be right. So after a certain amount of time I did say, "Well, look, if Syd thinks it's getting in his way, that's good enough for me." So, with that leap of faith and openness I later saw the truth of it for myself.

JP: In this community there were times that a lot of different people were on the outs at various times. You said it troubled you. Did you try to do anything about it?

GP: I felt like I couldn't do anything about it.

JP: That's the thing that always troubled me most, the way people sometimes treated each other, Syd included.

GP: Well, me too. But I had no solution, Jack. But see, now I see it very differently than I did then. I have new perspective on it now.

JP: How so?

GP: People need to understand that Syd wanted to get this message out purely. He did not want it messed up, and he didn't want people to get in the way of it. So if you got in the way of it he would essentially raise the volume of what he was saying, raise the intensity, and essentially break through your resistance and your defensiveness. So you would learn in a week what otherwise would have taken you five years to learn about yourself. He just did not suffer fools in that regard. So he would make sure that you got what he was saying. And he was invariably correct in what he was trying to tell you. It was valid. I've never known him to get on someone's case when he wasn't right about their ego or whatever. He would get it done. If he called you on something you would go away altering the way you went about things, and you would have the benefit of that for the rest of your life, however it applied to anything in the rest of your life.

So, in retrospect, when I see all the stuff that's going on, all the people who are off track and all the people shooting themselves in the foot and getting in the way of the message—the way Syd went about it minimized that. I'm not saying it didn't happen a little, but it minimized it. And the reason is, he could care less about your feelings and defenses and how it looked to others; all he cared about was the results. And it's not that he was Machiavellian; it's just that he didn't consider that people's personal reactions to things mattered. It was kind of like in basketball, "No harm, no foul." And the people who didn't take it well, like Rick, for example, left. So in a way it was kind of like Darwinism, the survival of the fittest, and he ended up with people who got over themselves and who were, for whatever reasons, willing to put up with their egos getting crushed on a regular basis, and that's the way he wanted it. Like, "That's a good group to work with."

JP: [laughs]

GP: Syd's primary purpose in life was to get the understanding he gained from his experience as close to the mainstream as he possibly could. He knew that this understanding was a missing piece in the world, the ignorance of which was the cause of human suffering. If anybody's frailties got in the way of his work, he let them know about it. Yes, he could be very direct and confrontive. If you didn't hear what he said he would not only raise the volume himself, but he would even get other people to help him get the message across. The downside was being on the business end of that directness, criticism, disapproval. It was tough on the ego and frankly it was a little embarrassing knowing that you were the problem child.

The upside of this dynamic is more visible to me now. First of all, Syd's batting average was unbelievably high. In every instance what he saw in me as problematic turned out to be problematic, not only for him but for me as well. His approach would, in fact, get the point across and it would change me. It might have taken years for me to see that for myself. You might say he was enormously effective as a change agent. This not only benefited me and my colleagues but it benefited the cause. When my personality changed I was no longer in the way. I was part of the solution rather than part of the problem. Everyone close to Syd was at some time part of the problem who was turned into part of the solution by his perceptiveness, intervention and direct manner.

JP: Are you saying the end justifies the means?

GP: No one had more respect for human beings than Sydney Banks! Respecting their personal reactions and their ego is quite another matter. Syd wasn't concerned if we were upset or if our feelings were hurt. He knew we understood enough to get over ourselves, and he was right. Don't get me wrong: Syd did his best to be as gentle and as reassuring to people as he could, but he wouldn't shy away from delivering his message. He hung in there until you heard what he was saying. He understood that people would have their reactions but he didn't see this as a terminal problem, given the Principles.

JP: Are you saying that people not taking other people's feelings into account is a good idea? Are you saying that's the way the world should be?

GP: Here's what I'm saying. Before I met Sydney Banks I had a huge respect for my personal feelings and other people's personal feelings. Growing up professionally in the New Age movement and the Berkeley, California encounter group culture, sensitivity to other people's feelings was the currency at that time, and I bought it hook, line and sinker. I thought that negative emotions like anger and dissatisfaction provided valuable information about me and other people and how I should interface with other people. When I met Sydney Banks in 1976, all this was turned upside down. I saw that our feelings were just information about our thinking in that particular moment. My feelings such as anger, jealousy and dissatisfaction were founded in misunderstanding rather than accurate knowledge of what was happening in the world. As a result of that shift in my understanding, my respect for emotions as a guidance system for relationships went down significantly. I saw that a negative state of mind was something that I would naturally get over, rather than something to be indulged and tiptoed around. In my relationship with Linda and my family we were less precious about hurting people's feelings and more trusting that if we can all get over ourselves, knowing that we could get over our emotional reactions in life, it allowed us the freedom to relax and not have to be so cautious and careful around each other.

Do I think this is a better model for humanity than tiptoeing around each other's sensitivities? I must say that I do. With my family, friends and in my professional life I have the "get over yourself" interpersonal model, and it has worked great for all of us. We are able to be more direct and to the point when we communicate. We know we will be forgiven for any frailties and our transgressions. I know this model only works when people understand the true nature of emotions and see that they have the capability of getting over negative states of mind. I know the world isn't there yet, but that is the potential that the Principles bring to the table.

JP: But when you were estranged from Syd, it was tough for you, wasn't it? What was that like?

GP: When Syd would feel that I was going in the wrong direction and getting in the way he would try to talk to me, but I wouldn't listen. I couldn't hear him. He would raise the volume and get more direct with me. Sometimes I still couldn't hear what he was saying. At some point he would give up temporarily and back off. He was probably thinking, "Pearls to swine," and he was probably right. At that point I wouldn't hear from him much and he would put his energy into other people who he thought were on track and receptive. Don't get me wrong, I could call him up and we would have a good conversation. He said to me, "George, I don't care about you personally. I mean, I do as a friend and you can count on me as a friend, but in terms of your participation in getting this message out, I'm just interested in your level of consciousness and your willingness to put your shoulder to the boulder."

JP: That's interesting.

GP: So there were years when I was out of the picture, and I could still call him and talk with him and he would help me out, and this and that, but in terms of being on his staff, you might say—this is a good way of saying it—I wasn't on his staff at that time.

JP: [laughs]

GP: But when I finally heard what he was trying to tell me I came back and we would be working closely together again. He was on me at times. He was on Roger at times. He was on Christine at times—a lot of people. But he felt that was the way to deal with us, that we had to wake up, that we sometimes had to hit bottom so we could wake up. He said, "Something has to happen in them. I've tried to help them but I can't, and I've got to do my work. And I think the way to help them is to just leave them alone and let them sort it out themselves. If you don't feel that way, then by all means go in there and try to do something." I said, "No, I feel the way you do, Syd." He said, "Then why are you calling me up? Why are you hassling me?" [laughs].

JP: But wouldn't you say there have been at least a few times in this community where some people felt shunned by others when Syd was down on them?

GP: Well, I don't see it that way, Jack. That's another piece of this that I realized. What some people would call shunning was everybody's respect for Syd interfering with their own judgment, in my opinion. In other words, when Syd was down on me about my tapes, he would call up people and talk to them about the damage my tapes were doing, and a lot of people, in deference to Syd, would then be cautious about their affiliation with me. They kind of saw me as, "Well, George is interfering with things here, so I should keep my distance." And they might even talk amongst themselves about me. Whereas, if it was me saying, "Oh, that Jack Pransky is screwing things up here," nobody would take heed, nobody would think it was their problem; they would just blow it off. But when Syd got down about someone, for some reason they took it personally and may have felt like they had to keep their distance from that person. But I have never seen intentional "shunning" in this community. I define shunning as intentionally avoiding someone to deliver a message. It's a behavioral modification technique in some communities. I've never seen that in our community. What some might call shunning I would see as people innocently feeling awkward because Syd has gotten down on the person with whom they are talking. I mean, it's understandable that they might feel awkward around that particular person when Syd would call them up on the phone and tell them that George, Roger or someone else was standing in the way of getting the message out. I think Syd did that to get that person to possibly help get his message across to the "obstructive" person.

JP: Are you suggesting that's a good thing?

GP: I'm suggesting it could have worked out well but it didn't. Syd thought he could get everyone to help him to straighten out whoever was getting in the way. That's not an unreasonable expectation, given the understanding we all have. But ultimately we couldn't pull it off. We were all sensitive people. It created some awkwardness and unpleasant conversation. In retrospect, it made sense that Syd thought we could help him in that way, and it also made sense that we couldn't. If this was an experiment you would have to say it failed.

JP: What about somebody like John Wood [of Western Australia] putting all his wealth into getting Syd's message out, particularly in getting Syd's original tapes out into the world with Syd's blessing, and then getting essentially wiped out? I mean, wasn't that a little extreme?

GP: Well, I personally think John Wood was severely unappreciated, because he did a huge amount for Syd, and Syd didn't seem to appreciate what he did. Syd didn't know all it took to get his tapes out; he thought all you had to do was to take a recorder and duplicate them and that was it. So John duplicated Syd's tapes. And Syd said, "Now he wants all this credit. All he did was duplicate my tapes. Give me a break." That was Syd's attitude about John Wood. He felt totally put out by John's demands and insulted by them. And Syd wasn't receptive to how beyond his depth he was about this. Syd wasn't interested in the details of it. I think John's heart was in the right place, he was in service, he helped things out, and he was unappreciated because Syd was, in my opinion, out of his depth here.

JP: What do you mean by "out of his depth?"

GP: Well, this is just my own subjective viewpoint, Jack. I think that Syd was out of his depth when he was working within a system, like with West Virginia University.

JP: That's interesting. How?

GP: Now, most people don't have that, Jack, because they've paid their dues. They grew up in the system. But here, you're taking an enlightened person and you're dropping him into a system. He has no background, no experience, no trial and error, no learning curve, nothing, totally out of his depth that way. But my opinion about that is just that; I know it's a little of a stretch. I think other people would say, "He knew exactly what he was doing. The system was bullshit, and he was trying to change it," for example. There are a lot of people who would say, "The problem was with West Virginia University, the problem was with John Wood, and they didn't understand Syd. If he had understood Syd he would have gone about it differently and it would have worked out." And that's true too, you know? [laughs].

The other part of it, in my mind, is it's indisputable that there was a method to his madness. It's indisputable to me that the humanness of him and everybody else manifested itself. I don't think anybody would argue with that. I don't think anyone would say, "Oh I didn't take it personally. I didn't feel bad," and this and that.

JP: Would you just chalk it up to blind spots?

GP: I guess. I would call it human frailty, Jack. First of all, there isn't a single leader anywhere who has ever lived that doesn't have some human frailties built into whatever they do. For example, every one of us, at one time or another, has held back the progress of the Principles. Like everyone else, Syd was a human being. When he would go off on someone it was very much the exception, but it did happen, and when that happened it was difficult for me and many others. We were very open to him and very much wanting to do right by him. When he would lose it, it was difficult. To his credit he would often apologize afterwards when he realized that he has lost his bearings. Sometimes he would apologize in the heat of the moment saying something like, "Don't mind my manner. I'm caught up right now, but I mean what I'm trying to say." I guess you could say that dealing with frailty comes with the territory of dealing with human beings.

THE THREE PRINCIPLES GLOBAL COMMUNITY

JP: How did the Three Principles Global Community come about?

GP: In the late stages of Syd's life he became increasingly concerned about the Principles proliferating after his death. A bunch of us were meeting with him when it was suggested that an organization could be formed that would disseminate the Principles. It was suggested that this organization could have a website, a practitioner list and outreach into the community, if not the mainstream. Syd suggested that the organization be run by business people who were grounded in the Principles. David Bekhor and Pritam Singh and myself were the people Syd turned to. We made a list of long-time practitioners and business people for a small retreat in Vermont. We discussed starting this organization, now called the Three Principles Global Community, and organized a second retreat to include three times as many long-time practitioners at that second retreat. Don Donovan was selected as the leader. We formed a Board. Don and others worked very hard to put together a website and build a global organization.

CERTIFICATION?

JP: Speaking of dissemination, what do you have to say about certification, and whether it's a good idea or not?

GP: Back in the early nineties when the Psychology of Mind Training Institute was in existence, we all thought it was a great idea to have a certification program. We reasoned that a certification program would help us develop practitioners and would also protect the public from unqualified practitioners. Each person seeking certification would be assigned two supervisors who were members of the Board of Directors. We would listen to therapy sessions, evaluate the candidate and develop him or her. The supervisors would evaluate the candidates' work after listening to audiotaped sessions of the candidates. If the candidate needed development, the supervisors would then develop the candidate and certify them when they displayed a critical mass of competence.

JP: That didn't work out as well as it sounded.

GP: It sounded like a great plan. But we soon found out that the two supervisors often differed in their evaluation of the candidate. They went to a third person who often offered yet a different opinion. The supervisors couldn't even agree on the criteria, never mind whether those criteria were met. We began to see that this work was all about grounding, and that grounding is hard to evaluate. It's a large, subjective component. There were no techniques that could be evaluated, as in other approaches. The only thing that mattered was the person's understanding, and that was difficult to quantify.

Then, another even more delicate problem reared its ugly head. Some of the people we certified at some later point no longer looked qualified to us. Do we recall them, as they do cars in Detroit? And then there were people who didn't qualify who now looked like they would. It became very complicated. We concluded that this understanding does not lend itself to an objective qualification program. I feel that way to this day. I think that a certification program in the Principles would be fraught with insurmountable difficulties.

JP: I absolutely agree. And what does it mean if a certified person does less of a good job than a noncertified person? And what if a certified person then screws up—what does that mean about the program that certified them? And what about a community person who is great at communicating this stuff who would never get certified?

GP: Yeah.

THE PRESENT AND THE FUTURE

JP: With the Three Principles community growing now so much, where do you think things are at now, and where do you think they'll be in the future.

GP: Well, when I used to talk about the stages this understanding has gone through, I talked about the Pre-Concept stage and the Concept stage, and the Principles stage. [*See Appendix D*] I think that the most dedicated people, the people who are always most looking to learn, are in the stage now where the Principles are simpler and have more clear definitions. I'll tell you what I mean. Like, I think for the longest time in the Principles Stage, people saw *thought* as having a lot to do with people's experience, but in their hearts they really didn't see it as the *whole* story. They just saw it as an absolutely crucial part of the human experience, that people's thoughts are a big part of what they're experiencing, but there are other external things people were teaching that are part of where the human experience comes from. And I think the stage now is that thought is the *only* thing. You know how Vince Lombardi said that "Winning isn't everything; it's the only thing." Thought is the *only* thing! There's nothing else happening but thought. And I think that's the next stage, and it makes it easier to see it as a new paradigm, that there is nothing else out there but thought. Then the subsequent perceptions, feelings, and experience—that one-way flow between thought and the senses—is the essence of the Principles. So this is like the "Distillation stage." And the people who are teaching this are getting people to see that the Principles are purely descriptive— and not prescriptive. They're getting people to see that all you have to do is *understand*, and that's it. And they are getting people to see that the message is simpler than we previously thought. So I see this as the new stage. Now, the community used to move together through these stages—mostly because of Syd. But now it's different because there are some people who are moving together, and there are other people who are out doing other things who aren't really hooked in.

JP: Going back to the "All there is is thought" thing, I see it a little differently than you do. I see it as absolutely true that thought is all there is in terms of it being our *only* experience, but it doesn't address what exists when there is *no thought*. Like, when there's no thought, what's left?

GP: Well, when there's no thought, you're talking microseconds.

JP: But in the microseconds of no thought, what is there? You know what I'm saying? There's got to be "something" else—

GP: Well, there *is* something deeper, Jack—

JP: Yes, that's exactly what I mean! So we have to be careful when we say, "It's only thought." It's only thought that can give us our experience, yes, but we can't say it's only thought, because there's Mind, Consciousness and Thought. In other words, let's say, the Oneness of Mind coming into our pure consciousness, if it were uncontaminated by any thinking, what would it be?

GP: Well, let me think for a second. When I said, "All there is is thought," I didn't pay as much attention to that, now that you're questioning it. If I had to say it more accurately, I would say that the human experience comes from thought.

JP: I buy that 100%.

GP: And behind the human experience is the possibility of the creation of any experience via the Principles. And, to me, that's the way that Mind comes into it, as well: The possibility of new thought at any moment. That's a big part of this message, that anybody can have new thought. And when they do they have new perceptions and new feelings.

JP: I buy that too.

GP: I was a little sloppy in my expression.

JP: So what do you attribute to the fact that this has all happened very slowly, from the time Syd had his experience to now, except now the curve is getting a little steeper.

GP: Oh I don't think it's happened very slowly, Jack, at all. In other words, when you consider how long it takes for any completely new paradigm to reach the mainstream and gain a critical mass, it's been happening pretty quickly. It's been in universities. It's been in business. There are hundreds if not thousands of practitioners. So I think it's been very quickly, given how far it is from the mainstream. And the farther an idea is from the current thinking the longer it takes to reach the mainstream. That it's taken so long to me is how far ahead of its time it is.

I'll give you an example. I have a client who is totally into the Principles—changed his life. Well, his son has struggled psychologically in school, so they were mandated to see the psychologist. The school psychologist described his son's symptoms, and the father says, "You know, in my understanding, my son dwells on his thoughts too much." The psychologist said, "What do you mean by that?" He said, "Well, you know how people think about things and thoughts come and go? Well my son dwells on a lot of different thoughts, and it kind of brings him to his knees because the dwelling really affects him emotionally. That's why he's struggling so much emotionally." The psychologist said, "Well, we can't change his personality." So in her mind his son's personality made him think like that. See? Now, how many years ahead of his time is it between the psychologist and the father? How many iterations of the old paradigm, how much suffering has to happen before this reaches the mainstream? So I don't think it's going slowly at all.

But I do think it's going to go slower now because it's getting contaminated. People are mixing it with other things, and it's going to be harder for people to see that it's something new, and it's going to get discredited when that doesn't produce results. So back in our day no one would say, "I went to see a Three Principles person and there wasn't anything new there." Not everyone got affected, but they knew something was there. They won't be able to say that in the future.

They'll say, "I saw this guy who was certified as a Principle-based person, and it was nothing; it was just like anything else." So I think that is going to slow down the growth. Once people position themselves as Principle-based, if they're very, very superficial and don't get results, it's going to slow down the growth.

JP: What do you see as the future of this understanding going out into the world?

GP: Well, I think that this understanding will change the current thinking in the world. It will find its way into the world, and people will see an internal component to life that they didn't see before. And I think people will begin to see a potential that they didn't see before. So that's the good news. The bad news is I think that it will lose depth or substance of the understanding over time.

JP: You mean because of what you just said?

GP: That and because, for example, to me the depth is represented in the fact that Sydney Banks had this experience where he had seen a vertical dimension to life represented by the notion of levels of consciousness. If you take the original people who learned from Syd, the vertical dimension really affected them. That's getting lost. Many people getting into this understanding now don't understand why we would want to mention Sydney Banks. They are seeing it as the way to manage their thinking better. Some people are very sensitive about bringing Sydney Banks into the discussion. And right now we prevail only because the people who think Sydney Banks is important, and that the vertical dimension is important, outweigh the people who don't. But outside of that it's beginning to lose its origins. It's losing its initial defining moment. And I think losing that is going to hurt the depth. I think ten years from now it will be seen as helping people be more accountable for what they think, rather than your whole life could be changed in a moment!

See, that's the hope, that in a moment your level of consciousness can change, and everything can change across the board. That's the whole point: that can happen! And that's what happens when things change vertically—not horizontally. Like if I'm mad at someone and all of a sudden I see them in a different light. And people say, "Well, isn't that a change of thought?" And I say, "But it's a change of thought in a vertical dimension."

JP: It happens in a flash of new insight, not because someone is trying to get there, and when it happens people jump to a higher level of consciousness.

GP: Yes, otherwise it would be positive thinking or reframing. Those are changing your thoughts on a horizontal dimension. This is a different dimension than that. I've said this to people who were thinking the other way, and they were thrilled. Some of these people have even been at this for six or seven years, they have their businesses and centers and institutes, they are students of all these wonderful teachers, and this is news to them?! So that to me is a statement about the future of the Principles. The vast potential is there for enormous change to happen in the world as a result of this, but will it get watered down so much over time that that potential will be unrealized.

JP: So are you saying one has to have a critical amount of grounding to teach the Principles "right" or properly?

GP: I want to make it clear that our discussion here is exclusively about practitioners. I don't mean to say that there is some line in the sand a practitioner must cross to be qualified to teach. I don't believe that. I know it sounds that way because I am not expressing myself right. Anyone who is touched by the Principles can teach and will help people, as far as I am concerned. Each person will attract people who see that they have something to offer and then they can offer it to those people.

My concern about spreading Syd's message has to do with *how* "his message" is defined. Everyone—including me—significantly understates his message. We are all limited by our grounding, by our own understanding of his message. Many times I thought I had my arms around his message, only to find that it was much more profound and deeper than I thought. After a while I concluded that we all, myself included, misrepresent his message because of the limitations of our personal, limited grounding. One of the things I saw in that first summer in Salt Spring was that the most grounded people would say, "I see a small percent of what Syd says," and less grounded people like me secretly thought that we saw a high percentage of what Syd was saying. If practitioners truly understood and acknowledged that they are misrepresenting Syd's message because of the limitations of their own grounding, then clients would look beyond what we are saying and the integrity of the message would be preserved to that extent.

JP: Okay, I get what you mean. But I can see where some people could get confused.

GP: What I mean is, the teachers and practitioners would say—and really mean—something like, "These Principles are deeper than I see them. I am just teaching my limited understanding of them. You need to experience Syd's material in order to see the depth and breadth of Syd's message." I think every practitioner—if they searched their soul—would say at the very least we all have had defining moments when we saw these Principles way deeper than we normally see them, and then that momentary vision disappears like the will-of-the-wisp.

JP: So how does what you're saying help to spread the Principles?

GP: It will keep people open to the depth of the message. Otherwise the message will spread smaller and smaller as people are limited by the grounding of their teacher. Down the road what people are taught will be a much more diluted, scaled-down version of the Principles, and that is how the Principles will be perceived. If practitioners suggest that there is more depth to be seen than their representation, there will be X-amount of protection from that dilution. Bear in mind that people are already orientated towards seeing what they already know within the current paradigm. They will tend to gravitate towards that. If the practitioner points beyond that and says "I am pointing towards something that I cannot express as well as I'd like," then students will look beyond what they already know.

JP: So back to the question I posed: "How do you see the Principles going out in the world in the future?" Can you summarize?

GP: I see the Principles continuing to spread because they will continue to help people. I also see a dilution, a continued misrepresentation of Syd's message over time. Because the understanding has no techniques or methodology it must, necessarily, be passed on through word of mouth or the written word. It will get diluted and misrepresented the way the message gets misrepresented in the childhood game of "telephone." There are two factors in my opinion that will slow the dilution and misrepresentation process: the use of Syd's materials, and the practitioners pointing beyond their grounding (as I described earlier), and pointing out that their own grounding limitations misrepresent Syd's message, no matter how valuable their message presentation might be.

JP: Why place such an emphasis on Syd's materials, when Syd himself said that what he was saying is not Truth but only a representation of the truth?

GP: To me they point to true north. Yes, they too are limited by the fact that truth cannot be conveyed by the spoken or written word but, that said, there is no doubt in my mind that Syd's materials are the deepest, purest, clearest medium for his message of truth. We are fortunate that a man who had an enlightenment experience like he did lived in a technological age when his teachings could be recorded.

JP: George, thank you! I think this will be very helpful to people, especially in years to come when all the original people who learned directly from Syd are no longer around.

Paradigm Shift

PART II

SOME EVENTS IN THE HISTORY OF THREE PRINCIPLES UNDERSTANDING AND DISSEMINATION

An Attempt to Show the Scope and Sequence of How
'The Three Principles' Rippled Out Into the World

compiled by Jack Pransky*

*with assistance from Barb Aust, Sydney Banks (via resume), Judy Banks, Joe Bailey, Dicken Bettinger, Keith Blevens, Cheryl Bond, Joe Boyle, T. Bruce, Chantal Burns, Chip and Jan Chipman, Cindi Claypatch, Don Donovan, Allan Flood, Milli Gilin, Linda Halcon, Christine Heath, Sandy Krot, Ed Lemon, Rudi and Jenny Kennard, Gabriela Maldonado-Montano, Kathy Marshall Emerson, Diane McMillen, Ami Chen Mills-Naim, Clytee Mills, Linda Quiring, Bill Pettit, Karen Reinecke, Linda Ramus, Judy Sedgeman, Rita Shuford, Elsie Spittle, Aaron Turner

Criteria for Inclusion in this Chronology:

1. Noteworthy events that enhanced or propelled the understanding or dissemination of the Three Principles. [Note: I realize this is subjective. When it seemed unclear whether or not an event fit this criterion I erred on the side of inclusion. The same is true for all other criteria below.]
2. The first in a series of noteworthy seminars or trainings; not all events in the series, with the exception of Sydney Banks seminars and talks. Not all talks, seminars and trainings of all Three Principles practitioners.
3. Published papers and books; not unpublished papers, unless noteworthy for other reasons.
4. Doctoral dissertations; not Masters Theses, unless noteworthy for other reasons.
5. Sydney Banks' dated audios and videos; not audios and videos by other practitioners, unless noteworthy for other reasons.
6. National television appearances; not local TV appearances, not radio interviews, unless noteworthy for other reasons.

7. Establishment of only those private Three Principles-related businesses or nonprofit organizations that had a major impact on Three Principles dissemination; not a list of practitioners' businesses or organizations, unless Centers or Institutes that trained hundreds of professionals who, in turn, teach others.
8. Not personal information on practitioners, except where necessary if an important part of an event.
9. Not individual trainings for organizations that did not result in institutional change.

Notes from the chronicler:

1. This is a difficult historical chronology to record because, especially in the early years, many people have varying recollections, different perceptions, and therefore different experiences of what happened.
2. Formal names and degrees (where applicable) are listed the first time someone's name appears; after that, names are used more informally, except in cases where an event was billed with a formal name.
3. It took much time to compile this. I tried to be thorough and inclusive and show the scope of what has transpired historically with regard to the Three Principles and its dissemination. I tried to get feedback from key people. If I left anyone or anything out that anyone thinks is important, or if there is anything anyone thinks should not be in here, I apologize. In years to come this chronology will likely end up online and other additions and updates can be made at that time. I added detail in places I thought were particularly interesting. Since I compiled it, I also reserved the right to make a few personal comments as I went along (included as "side notes").
4. Although not everyone could be mentioned in this historical chronology, it is not meant at all to minimize the countless contributions of so many other Three Principles practitioners and others who along the way have been touched by this understanding thus far and in turn have affected hundreds, even thousands of lives, and those who will continue to make contributions in the future as this understanding takes hold throughout the world.

It is most important to recognize that none of what appears in this chronology, nor all the lives changed as a result, would have occurred had it not been for what happened to Sydney Banks in the Fall of 1973, and his good grace and willingness to share what he saw with the world. We are forever grateful!

THE THREE PRINCIPLES HISTORICAL CHRONOLOGY

- January 25, 1931. Sydney Banks is born, is adopted, and has a difficult childhood primarily on Duke Street in the Leith section of Edinburgh, Scotland, and later on King Street in the Portobello section. Syd attends the Lochend Road Primary School and the David Kilpatrick Secondary School but leaves school after the 9th grade.

- 1957. Syd moves to British Columbia [hereafter referred to as B.C.], Canada.

- 1962-1974. Syd Banks works as a maintenance welder at the MacMillan Bloedel Pulp Mill in Nanaimo, B.C.

- Fall, 1973. While visiting his in-laws on Salt Spring Island, B.C. after returning from an awareness group Syd has, in his words, "...an enlightening experience and realized the existence of a world that very few people know exists." [Note: Syd's C.V. states: "...I received a spiritual revelation of Three Principles which explain the nature of God."] He begins to talk about what he *saw* and is largely ignored or ridiculed by the people who knew him. The only people who remain friends with him are Ken and Elsie Spittle, and as Syd said, "Even that was touch and go."

- 1974. Syd quits his job and moves to Salt Spring Island. Before long, Linda Quiring, recently released from a psychiatric hospital and told she would need medication and periodic shock treatments for the rest of her life, turns up at his door looking for help. What prompts this is Linda seeing an ad in the "Notice" section of the local paper, *The Driftwood*, on August 21, 1974: "For anyone seeking guidance through self-awareness. I am offering an informal friendly type group situation based on the here and now. This group will be led by someone who himself is enlightened. Contact [the phone number]," which Linda traces to B. Banks on North End Rd. Linda is the only person who shows up. Syd begins talking with her, and she becomes free of all medication and treatments. Following Linda and her husband Bill, Pam and Jim Beck appear within two months, followed by Jim and Judy Wallace. Their lives change. [Note: Not long after Syd's experience, his wife, Barb realizes something profound has happened to her husband, and she begins to listen to him and support him in his work of sharing what he has found.]

- 1975. The first wave of people begin to come over to Salt Spring Island to learn from Syd. Gatherings take place at Syd and Barb's house. [Note: Along with Syd, Barb welcomes people who come to Salt Spring to listen to him. Together they set an example of living with love and understanding in their family life. This example has a powerful impact on the early group listening to Syd.]
- 1975. Syd has Pam Beck be the first to share this understanding with people who come over. Syd goes over to Vancouver Island to talk with others.
- 1975. Syd gives his first major public appearance as keynote speaker at the "Gathering of the Ways" conference in Jericho Beach, Vancouver, B.C.
- 1975. Some "well-meaning people" (as Syd described them) establish the Sydney Banks Spiritual Foundation [Note: Their purpose is to help Syd have money on which to live, since he is doing so much for others. Apparently Syd is not really in favor of this but goes along with it. In October 1977, at Syd's request, its name changes to the Sydney Banks Foundation for Inner Consciousness Development.]
- September 27, 1975. The first known tape of Syd's talks is made on Mayne Island, B.C. A small group of people interested in Syd's understanding begins to form on Mayne Island (including Dave and Carol Simpson, Chip and Jan Chipman, and others).
- 1975. Syd gives a public talk in Victoria, B.C.
- November 22, 1975. Pam and Jim Beck and Carol and Dave Simpson lead a workshop in Vancouver based on Syd's teachings.

Publications:
  o 1975. Linda Quiring and Syd collaborate on the first book written about him, *Island of Knowledge*, authored under

Linda's name and published by the Sydney Banks Spiritual Foundation, Ganges, B.C. [Note: This book is being republished in 2015 by CCB Publishing.]

- January 16, 1976. Syd offers the first workshop for the Victoria group at Larry and Chris Colero's home, Victoria, B.C. A small group interested in Syd's teachings forms with Larry and Chris, Barb and Strick Aust, Shane Kennedy, and others.
- January 17, 1976. Syd gives a public talk at the Unitarian Church, Vancouver, B.C. Nearly 200 people attend. A small group forms there with Edith Sacker, Bob and Christa Campsall, Brian Lercher, Marty Lipsky, Harry Derbitsky, and others.
- January 24, 1976. Syd gives a public talk at Sons of Norway Hall, Nanaimo, B.C. A small group forms with Elsie and Ken Spittle, Richard and Marika Mayer, Sandra Clapham, Robin and Jerry Lee Allen, and others.
- 1976-1977. Many of the people from these and other small groups in Victoria and Vancouver move to Salt Spring, along with others such as Jane and Tommy Tucker and many more (estimates vary from 60-100 people by 1978).
- 1976. Sydney Banks gives a talk to the heads of the Theology and Psychology Departments at the University of British Columbia in Vancouver, B.C.
- March 6, 1976. Syd gives a public talk at Mayne Island Hall, Mayne Island, B.C. [Note: In April, Chip and Jan Chipman move to Salt Spring Island, having met Syd in the summer of 1975.]
- March 12-13, 1976. Pam and Jim Beck and Carol and Dave Simpson hold another workshop at the Unitarian Church in Vancouver, B.C.
- May 6-7, 1976. Syd speaks at the Health Symposium at the New Age Community Center in Vancouver, B.C.
- May 1976. "It's That Simple" by Syd is a tape of a talk held in Courtenay, B.C.
- May 1976. "Beyond Religion" by Syd is a tape of a talk at the Unitarian Church, North Vancouver.
- June 5, 1976. Syd holds a five-day retreat at Seabeck, Washington.
- August 1976. "It's all Thought" by Syd is a tape of a talk at Van Dusen Gardens, Vancouver.
- October 1976. Syd's talks move from his and Barb's house to the

United Church Hall in Ganges, Salt Spring Island, on Friday nights. "The Missing Link" is a tape of the first of these talks.

- 1976. A businessman and "professional seeker" named Val attends one of Syd's talks. He convinces Gestalt psychologist John Enright, Ph.D. to go hear Syd. Enright attends, then tells his partner, George Pransky, M.A., who becomes the first mental health professional to have a conversation with Sydney Banks. George and his wife, Linda convince Dr. Roger Mills, with whom George is a partner in the ARC/Good Neighbor Project under a Federal National Institute of Mental Health (NIMH) Research Grant for the Prevention of Mental and Emotional Disorders through the University of Oregon that Roger had secured, to go hear Syd. [Note: This is not a Three Principles-related grant and does not show results of Three Principles-related programs.] Roger moves to Salt Spring Island for the summer; George and Linda follow later, as do Keith Blevens, Ph.D. and Valda Monroe.

Publications:
  - 1976. The first magazine article is written about Syd (in a Vancouver spiritual magazine), titled, "Awakening on Salt Spring Island: Conversations with Sydney Banks."

- 1976. Sydney Banks begins to consult with George Pransky, M.A., and Roger Mills, Ph.D., to assist them in the development of a new paradigm for their work in the mental health field. George and Roger become the first two mental health professionals to change their practices to deal solely from Sydney Banks' understanding. Keith Blevens, Ph.D. soon joins them.
- 1976. "Seminar on Mental Health" presentation by Syd is made to mental health professionals, psychologists and therapists, co-sponsored by ARC seminars, Sacramento, California (on audiotape).
- 1976. Elsie Spittle, who now works closely with Syd and begins to join him at some of his talks, begins to offer consultation to Dr. Roger Mills [Note: ...and later to Dr. Enrique Suarez.]

- January 4, 1977. Syd speaks to the Nanaimo group at the Kin Hut, Nanaimo, B.C.
- January 8, 1977. Syd speaks to the Vancouver group at the Members'

Lounge, Planetarium, Vancouver, B.C.

- January 16, 1977. Syd speaks to the Victoria group at Holyrood House, Victoria, B.C.
- January 22, 1977. Syd speaks to the Vancouver group at the Planetarium, Vancouver, B.C.
- January, 1977. Syd and Elsie Spittle speak at the University of California Berkeley Faculty Club, Syd's first California presentation. Elsie Spittle becomes the first teacher to give formal talks with Syd.
- April 1977. A talk by Syd is taped at the "Vancouver Marine Museum."
- April 1977. A talk by Syd is taped at "Shawnigan" Lake in B.C.
- 1977. Barb Banks and Elsie Spittle conduct a seminar in Chinatown, San Francisco. [Note: Elsie says, "It was an amazing seminar, as this was the first and only time Barb presented formally. Syd was very keen on the two of us doing this together. He wanted Barb to have the experience of sharing without him there, so she could get a taste of her own power. Barb was such a powerful presence; she could convey such depth with a few words."]
- August 10-12, 1977. Syd gives a talk on "The Spiritual Foundation of Mental Health Treatment and Prevention" co-sponsored by Community Mental Health Consultants in Eugene, Oregon through Roger's NIMH grant at the Cedar Beach Resort, Salt Spring Island, B.C.
- 1977-1981. Syd allows Paul William Fowler of Beaverton, Oregon to put out a series of his audio cassette recordings, including "Shawnigan," "Changing Your Mind"/"Gratitude," "A Spiritual Reality," "Mind and Positivity," and others, and from 1984-1988 including "The Consciousness Within," "Thought and Alcoholism"/"Aloha Consciousness," "Jumping Time," and others.
- 1977. George Pransky sees his first client based upon what he learned from Sydney Banks. [Note: By 1978 the practice consists of George and Linda Pransky, then Amy Crystal, and soon followed by Kimberly Kadoo. Their first business client—a software development firm—occurs in 1979, as does their first mediation, an advertising company.]

- 1978. Syd and Linda Quiring complete a second book, *Beyond Beliefs,* but it is shelved.
- 1978. Syd strongly encourages the people following him on Salt Spring Island to move off the island to live ordinary lives and find out how much they have learned. He ends the Sydney Banks Foundation

for Inner Consciousness.
- 1978. A Syd Banks talk is taped, titled, "Changing Your Mind."
- April 16-17, 1978. Syd offers a seminar, "Innate Mental Health and the Prevention of Emotional Disorders" to mental health professionals, graduate students and faculty at the University of Oregon, co-sponsored by the Lane County Community Health Center and the School of Community Service and Public Affairs at the University of Oregon.
- August, 1978. Syd offers a retreat at the Qualicum Inn in Qualicum, Vancouver Island.
- October, 1978. Syd and Elsie offer a presentation, "Principles of the New Psychology" in Eugene, Oregon, co-hosted by Roger Mills and George Pransky.
- 1978. Syd and Elsie present a "New Psychology Conference" in Portland, Oregon, hosted by Dr. Roger Mills.
- 1978. Roger Mills, George Pransky and Keith Blevens establish New Psychology Consultants, the first organization to spread the message of this understanding professionally.

Publications:
  o 1978. "Psychology: Seeing Beyond Techniques Methods and Approaches" and "A New Framework for Psychology" by Roger Mills, Ph.D., Keith Blevens, Ph.D., and George Pransky, M.A. become the first two psychological papers written about this understanding, put out by New Psychology Consultants [Note: Subsequently these papers are published in the Appendix of George Pransky's 1998 book, *Renaissance of Psychology*].

- 1979. A Syd Banks talk is taped, titled, "Insecurity."
- 1979. George and Linda Pransky hold their first professional training in this understanding.
- March 1979. Syd and Elsie go to the home office of the global company Syd used to work for to meet with the Division Manager and Head of Resources. [Note: This is Syd's first introduction of this understanding to the corporate world. In April Elsie provides follow-up consultation.]
- April 16, 1979. Syd makes a presentation on "The Health of the

Helper: Personal Principles for Effective Helping" for clinical psychology graduate students at John F. Kennedy University, Orinda, California.

- 1979. A Syd Banks talk is taped on "Spirituality and Psychology" at a presentation to the public and mental health professionals, Vancouver, B.C.
- July 10-12, 1979. A Syd Banks talk is taped on "The Wisdom Within" at a presentation to therapists and academics, sponsored by New Psychology Consultants at the University of California faculty club, Berkeley, California.
- August 10-15, 1979. Syd is brought in by George Pransky and John Enright to give a presentation on "The Spiritual Nature of Therapy" at a retreat for psychotherapists from the Gestalt Institute of Munich and U.S. Mental Health Professionals, sponsored by ARC, Lodestar, California. [Note: This retreat is a turning point for teaching to mental health professionals. Enrique Suarez, Ph.D. is in attendance, is touched, and subsequently begins talking with Syd.]
- October 10-15, 1979. Sydney Banks and Dr. Roger Mills provide management consultation and training on "Managing and Motivating Genius" to the U.S. Naval Surface Weapons Center, Department of the Navy, Center for Advanced Weapons Research, Bethesda, Maryland.
- October 18-19, 1979. Syd Banks provides a seminar on "Spirituality, Innate Mental Health and the Prevention of Mental-Emotional Disorders," for the Ph.D. program in the behavioral sciences, Johns Hopkins University, Baltimore, Maryland.
- December 1979. Syd and Elsie run a seminar in Vancouver on "The Power of Thought."
- 1979-1980. Dr. Enrique Suarez spends time with Syd and does more conceptualization of a new psychology.

- February 1980. Syd Banks and Elsie Spittle speak on "Positivity and Proper Mental Health" in San Francisco, California.
- March, 1980. Syd Banks encourages Chip Chipman to go to Hawaii to speak on TV about helping businesses. Chip invites Roger Mills and they are interviewed on two network TV stations in Honolulu. [Note: Jack Hawkins at KITV conducts one of the interviews on April 4, 1980. This is likely the first TV interview about the Principles in business.]

- March 6-9, 1980. Syd speaks on "Our Spiritual Nature and Principles of a Unified Psychology," sponsored by R.C. Mills and Associates and San Jose State University, Center for Organizational and Leadership Development at the Airport Marina Hotel, Burlingame, California.
- July 1980. A Syd Banks talk is taped, titled, "Four Seasons Hotel."
- 1980. The Advanced Human Studies Institute is founded by Dr. Enrique Suarez with Dr. Roger Mills in Coral Gables, Florida. [Note: AHSI becomes the primary center for training in the understanding uncovered by Sydney Banks. Syd is a resource consultant. Kimberly Kadoo is the first staff person hired, followed by Amy Crystal; then Darlene Stewart and Rita Shuford. AHSI begins an externship training program in Coral Gables, where many of the early pioneers come to study for a year.]
- November 14-16, 1980. Syd and Elsie offer a seminar for mental health and health care professionals on "Towards the Elimination of Stress," sponsored by the Advanced Human Studies Institute and the Jackson Memorial Hospital at the Mailman Center, University of Miami, Miami, Florida.
- December 1980. A Syd Banks talk is taped, titled, "Mind and Positivity."

Publications:
  - 1980. "Human Relations Trainers: An Ethnomethodological Exploration of Issues and Effects" by Allan Flood is a Master's thesis through the University of Oregon School of Community of Service and Public Affairs, focused on Sydney Banks and his teachings. [Note: This is notable both for being the first Master's Thesis based on Syd's understanding, and for including a six-page interview with Roger Mills, the first interview given by Roger, as well as others on Salt Spring Island. It also includes a description of how Allan and his team were personally affected by Syd and changed as trainers.]

- September 13-15, 1981. Syd Banks offers a seminar on "The Missing Link: Connecting the Spiritual to Human Psychological Functioning" for staff and administrators of the Jackson Memorial and Veterans Hospitals of Dade County Florida, sponsored by the Advanced Human Studies Institute and the University of Miami Medical School, Miami, Florida.
- November 29-30, 1981. Syd offers a seminar on "The Spiritual Reality

Within" for healthcare professionals and the public, sponsored by the Advanced Human Studies Institute, at the Sheraton River House, Miami, Florida.

- 1982. The Advanced Human Studies Institute holds the first annual Psychology of Mind Conference in Miami, Florida.
- 1982. Enrique Suarez, Ph.D. speaks in Minneapolis at the Arboretum, brought in by Joe Bailey and Christine Heath who had been studying at the Advanced Human Studies Institute in Florida. [Note: Cindi Claypatch attends this session and changes her practice in a Dual Disorder program at the St. Paul Ramsey Medical Center and, as a result, the lives of many of her clients change.]
- 1982. A seminar by Syd Banks is taped on "The Spiritual Reality of Life" at the Richmond Inn, Richmond, B.C.
- 1982. Craig Polsfuss becomes likely the first Licensed Clinical Social Worker (LCSW) to apply Psychology of Mind to social work.
- September 1982. A Syd Banks talk is taped, titled, "Richmond Hotel."

Publications:
  o 1982. *Sanity, Insanity and Common Sense: The Missing Link in Understanding Mental Health* by Enrique M. Suarez, Ph.D. and Roger C. Mills, Ph.D. is the first psychology book published about this understanding. [Note: Its third printing is in 1983, published by Med-Psych Publications.]

- 1983. The Minneapolis Institute of Mental Health is founded by Joe Bailey and Christine Heath and becomes the second mental health organization to help people solely through Psychology of Mind, as this new psychology is called. [Note: This licensed mental health center and addictions outpatient center stays open until 1995, serving over 5,000 patients, training hundreds of professionals, conducting research on outcomes and sponsoring many conferences with Syd Banks in the Twin Cities. Syd consults with MIMH on a regular basis.]
- July 1983. William Pettit, M.D. brings Psychology of Mind into the Galesburg Mental Health Center, a State mental hospital in Galesburg, Illinois and becomes the first psychiatrist to practice psychiatry from this understanding in his position as Psychiatric Consultant. [Note: Bill had been National Program Director and Psychiatric Consultant for Lifespring Experiential Training, San Rafael, California (a

position previously held by Robert Kausen, who goes on to become a teacher and author in this understanding specializing in applications to business). After Bill meets George and attends a Syd Banks workshop in 1983 Bill resigns his position and studies first with George, then at AHSI. At Galesburg, "miracles started to occur." This 700-bed facility closes in July 1984.]

- August 6-7, 1983. A Sydney Banks Conference is held in Richmond, B.C.
- October 1983. Syd establishes International Human Relations Consultants, Inc. (IHRC) to support getting out his message.

Publications:
  o 1983. "A Transforming View of Mental Health" by Donald C. Klein, Ph.D., a well-respected community psychologist, reviews *Sanity, Insanity and Common Sense* for the *Journal of Primary Prevention*. 836, 202-206.
  o 1983. "The Adolescent in the Transitional Family: How the Schools Can Help" by Sandy Krot is published in the journal, *Educational Horizons,* 61, 205-208

  o 1983. *Second Chance* by Sydney Banks is published by Med-Psych publications. [Note: In 1989 it is republished by Duval-Bibb Publishing, and in 2010 its 4th Edition is published by Lone Pine Publishing.]

- 1984. [Editor's Note: No entries of note were brought to my attention for 1984.]

- 1985. A Syd Banks talk is taped, titled, "Vancouver."
- 1985. Rita Shuford, a licensed clinical psychologist, becomes Clinical Director for the Advanced Human Studies Institute, taking over from Kim Kadoo.
- 1985. Sandy Krot opens a second office of the Advanced Human Studies Institute in Tampa, Florida to set up the first clinic there, which subsequently becomes a main site for Psychology of Mind training from 1986-1991. [Note: Reese Coppage provides the seed money to get the clinic started. After about a year Sandy hires Janice Phelps, followed by Jeff Timm.]
- 1985. Sandy Krot begins the first Psychology of Mind-based EAP

(Employee Assistance Program) for Reese Coppage's Duval-Bibb Company in Tampa, Florida.

- 1985. Bill Pettit, M.D. begins The Psychiatric Institute of Florida in Bradenton, Florida, after being encouraged by Dr. Dick Conard. [Note: Bill is joined by Sue Odom, Hazel Foss, and intern Clytee Lally. The Institute closes in July 1988, when Bill becomes Staff Psychiatrist at the Manatee Palms Adolescent Residential Treatment Center, Bradenton, Florida.]

- April 8, 1986. The Hawaii Counseling and Education Center (HCEC) is incorporated in Kailua, Oahu, Hawaii by Christine Heath, Susan Sickora, Karen Miller and Cynthia West, and provides clinical and prevention services. [Note: HCEC is still ongoing as of the date of this chronology and has trained hundreds of professionals and served thousands of clients. Syd provides consultation and probably speaks more at HCEC than at any other center. HCEC provides the location for the next few annual conferences. A psychiatrist, Gordon Trockman, MD, is subsequently hired to work out of this clinic, as are Sharon Usagawa and Sheralynn Emilano.]
- November 29-30, 1986. Syd Banks holds a seminar, "The Spiritual Reality Within" for the public and mental health professionals, sponsored by the Advanced Human Studies Institute at the Sheraton River House, Miami, Florida.
- December 6-7, 1986. Sydney Banks speaks on "Beyond Philosophy, Beyond Psychology, Beyond Humanistic Theory to the Spiritual Reality Within" at a conference in St. Petersburg, Florida, sponsored by the Advanced Human Studies Institute.

Publications:
  o 1986. "An Exploratory Study to Determine the Effectiveness of a Neo-Cognitive Treatment Approach When Utilized in a Clinical Setting" by Rita Shuford is an unpublished doctoral dissertation through the University of Oregon, Division of Counseling and Educational Psychology. It is the first dissertation based on this understanding.

  o 1986. *Understanding: Eliminating Stress and finding Serenity in Life and Relationships* by Jane Nelsen, Ed.D. becomes the first self-help book about this understanding, published by Sunrise, Fair Oaks, California, and later by Prima Publishing. [Note: This book is republished in 2008 as *Serenity: Simple Steps for*

Recovering Peace of Mind, Real Happiness, and Great Relationships by Conari Press, San Francisco, California.]

- 1987. Dr. Roger Mills enters the Modello Housing Project, maneuvering his way into a program that began in Modello in 1986 by Dade County State Attorney Janet Reno, through her chief assistant, Tom Petersen. *[Note: For more information on this groundbreaking effort, see Part III A.]*
- May 1-3, 1987. The 6th Annual Psychology of Mind Conference is held at the Fontainebleau Hotel, Miami Beach, FL, sponsored by the Advanced Human Studies Institute (AHSI).
- May 16, 1987. Syd Banks gives a talk in Tampa, Florida, sponsored by AHSI.
- August 29, 1987. Syd gives a talk in Minneapolis, Minnesota, sponsored by AHSI. This talk is taped, titled, "Minneapolis Institute Talk."
- September 12, 1987. Syd gives another talk in Tampa, Florida, sponsored by AHSI.
- September 13, 1987. Syd Banks gives a taped presentation on "Defining Mental Health" to the staff of the Psychiatric Institute of Florida at the Holiday Inn, Bradenton, Florida, sponsored by AHSI. The taped talk is titled, "Bradenton."
- September 19, 1987, Syd gives a talk in Miami, Florida, sponsored by AHSI.
- October 30-31, 1987. Syd gives a "Management through Understanding" seminar for business leaders and nonprofit agency heads, co-sponsored by the Advanced Human Studies Institute and Vantage Consulting, Inc. at the Pacific Beach Hotel, Honolulu, Hawaii.

Publications:
- o 1987. The monograph, "Dropout Prevention: What We Have Learned" by Nancy Peck, Anne-Marie Law and Roger C. Mills is published by the ERIC/CAPS [Educational Resources Information Center/Counseling and Personnel Services] Clearinghouse.

- o 1987. *Sanity, Insanity and Common Sense* is substantially revised, now coauthored by Darlene Stewart, M.S. and subtitled*: The Groundbreaking New Approach to Happiness,* published by Fawcett-Columbine. [Note: It specifies four principles: Thought, Separate Realities, Levels of Consciousness, Feelings and Emotions.]

o   1987. *Coming Home: A Collection* by Sue Pettit of poetry inspired by this understanding is published by Sunrise Press, Fair Oaks, California.

- March 1988. Bill Pettit, M.D. creates a series of 8 videotapes, titled "The Key to Mental Health." [Note: This is notable as the first videotape to be used in outpatient and inpatient settings.]
- March 12, 1988. Syd Banks speaks in Tampa, Florida, sponsored by AHSI.
- March 19, 1988. Syd speaks in Miami, Florida, sponsored by AHSI.
- April 8-10, 1988. The 7th Annual Psychology of Mind conference is held at the Biltmore Hotel, Coral Gables, Florida, sponsored by the Advanced Human Studies Institute.
- June 12-14, 1988. Syd Banks gives a presentation on "Spirituality, Prevention and Mental Health Treatment: A Principle-Based Understanding" for the Metro Dade Department of Youth and Family Development and the Center for Dropout Prevention at the University of Miami Sheraton River House, Miami, Florida.
- July 1988. Bill Pettit, M.D. becomes Staff Psychiatrist/Medical Director of the Sarasota Palms Hospital, Sarasota, Florida. He and Judy Sedgeman (who manages Bill's practice since late 1986) negotiate to have a section of the hospital devoted to Bill's patients, which becomes the first Psychology of Mind-based Inpatient Program, with staff training assistance from AHSI. [Note: Hazel Foss and Sue Odom are full-time counselors, and Clytee is an intern. Bill creates a series of 12 videotapes, used for years with patients and also shown on the closed circuit TV channel of Blake Memorial Hospital in Bradenton.]
- 1988. The Advanced Human Studies Institute closes its Coral Gables office and moves to Tampa, Florida. Rita Shuford, Darlene and Charles Stewart transfer as staff to the Tampa office. Rick Suarez follows a bit later.
- 1988. "The Art of Leadership" program, aimed at introducing the Principles to business, organizations and leaders begins through the Advanced Human Studies Institute/Florida Center for Human Development in Tampa, spearheaded by Chip Chipman. [Note: After the Center closes in 1992 Chip and Jan Chipman of Vantage Consulting

Group continue to present Art of Leadership courses in organizations throughout the U.S., including to over 30 not for profit organizations in the Tampa Bay area.]

- October, 1988. Syd Banks gives a seminar in Hawaii. [Note: At this event Syd and Rick Suarez have a parting of the ways. After this, Rick Suarez leaves the Advanced Human Studies Institute.]
- November 1988. A Syd Banks talk is taped, titled, "Honolulu Conference."

Publications:
  o 1988 (Fall). "Working with High Risk Youth in Prevention and Early Intervention Programs: Toward a Comprehensive Wellness Model," by Roger C. Mills, Roger G. Dunham and Geoffrey P. Alpert is published in the journal, *Adolescence,* 23 (91), 643-660.
  o 1988. "A Neo-Cognitive Dimension (Reaction)" by Enrique Suarez is published in the journal, *The Counseling Psychologist*. 16 (2) 239-244.
  o 1988. "State-Dependent Learning: The Effect of Feeling and Emotions on Reading Achievement" by Darlene Stewart is an unpublished study. [Note: This study is notable as it shows how state of mind has a greater effect on reading achievement compared with the traditional approach "experts" provide. This paper is eventually put out by the Philosophy of Living Center, Midland, Australia.]
  o 1988. "The Power of Appreciation," by Donald C. Klein is published in the *American Journal of Community Psychology, 16,* 305-323, where he writes of his personal encounter with Sydney Banks.

- 1989. George and Linda Pransky establish Pransky and Associates in La Conner, Washington, which for many years becomes the primary hub for professional training for practitioners of the Three Principles. [Note: As this business quickly grows it takes on three associates: Keith Blevens, Sandy Krot and Dicken Bettinger, each of whom by that time had established their own successful practices. By 1997 additional consulting staff are added: Kara Stamback, Erika Bugbee, Aaron Turner and Mara Gleason, and to meet demand by businesses and organizations it assembles a core of trained, adjunct consultants—Robert Kausen, Cathy Casey, Mark Howard, Annika Hurwitt—who travel to Pransky and Associates' business sites and to La Conner to conduct programs. All consultants and staff also maintain their own private practices.]

- May 20, 1989. Syd Banks gives a talk in Minneapolis, MN, sponsored by AHSI.

- May 12-13, 1989. The 8th Annual Psychology of Mind Conference is held at the Tradewinds Resort, St. Petersburg Beach, Florida, sponsored by AHSI.

- May 27, 1989. Syd gives a talk in Tampa, Florida, sponsored by AHSI. This talk is taped, titled, "Jumping Time."

- June 3, 1989. Syd gives a talk in Miami, Florida, sponsored by AHSI.

- June 10, 1989. Syd gives a talk in San Francisco, sponsored by AHSI.

- 1989. George Pransky, Ph.D. of Pransky and Associates puts out the first of his audiotapes: "Anxiety." [Note: These tapes become a series of "Practical Psychology" audio and videotapes (over 60 tapes on many subjects, then subsequently additional ones, totaling over 100). These are notable in that they are used by and help many hundreds of clients and practitioners understand how Psychology of Mind applies to various mental health issues. In 1995 this evolves into a Monthly Tape Club.]

- 1989. The Advanced Human Studies Institute evolves into the nonprofit organization, Florida Center for Human Development in Tampa, Florida, directed by Elsie Spittle. [Note: Elsie and Chip Chipman already have been in Tampa working with Reese Coppage's company. After Rick Suarez leaves they both become part of AHSI, along with Jan Chipman. Ann Thomas joins the staff. The purpose of FCHD is to provide trainings to mental health professionals, inner city communities, and businesses. The Center closes in 1992.]

- 1989. Syd Banks gathers together people he considers "leaders" in getting this understanding out to the world at the Women's Faculty Club at U.C. Berkeley, California. [Note: At this gathering Syd helps people see that they are not seeing (or teaching) the Three Principles of Universal Mind, Consciousness and Thought at the core of the understanding; it is not about four principles. George Pransky makes his first attempt to share the Three Principles. Also at this meeting the Modello residents, brought there by Roger, meet Syd.]

Publications:

- o 1989. *In Quest of the Pearl*, by Sydney Banks, a sequel to *Second Chance*, is published by Duval-Bibb.

- o 1989. *Customer Satisfaction Guaranteed: A New Approach to Customer Service, Bedside Manner and Relationship Ease* by

Robert Kausen is published by Life Education.

- April, 1990. A *Today Show* (NBC) segment is aired on the Modello/Homestead Gardens Intervention Program, with Bryant Gumbel hosting.
- April 1990. A Syd Banks talk is taped, titled, "Hawaii Conference."
- May 4-6, 1990. The 9th Annual Psychology of Mind Conference is held at the Tradewinds Resort, St. Petersburg, Florida, sponsored by the Florida Center for Human Development.
- 1990. The Foundation for the Advancement of Mental Health, with Joe Bailey founding president, is formed to do research on the Three Principles and sponsor trainings and talks by Sydney Banks. [Note: Many Board members come from the Twin Cities local business community. The Foundation lasts until around 1994.]
- 1990. A Health Realization Leadership Program begins in Riverview Terrace, Tampa, Florida, with Elsie Spittle as Project Director.
- 1990. A Health Realization Leadership Program begins at the Tampa United Methodist Center's YouthBuild Program, with Elsie Spittle and Chip Chipman as project directors.
- 1990. The first set of Psychology of Mind Therapy Audiotapes by George Pransky, Ph.D. is put out by Pransky and Associates. [Note: In 1995 George puts out another completely revised set of audiotapes, "The Practice of Psychology of Mind Therapy," also through Pransky and Associates.]

Publications:
- 1990. "Revolution from within: With the help of determined residents, South Dade's housing projects are changing—for the better" by S. Rowe is published in *The Miami Herald News*, Florida, May 10.
- 1990. "A Neo-Cognitive Model of Crime" by Thomas Kelley is published in the *Journal of Offender Rehabilitation*. 16, 1-26.
- 1990. "Putting the Self in Self-Regulated Learning: The Self as Agent in Integrating Will and Skill" by Barbara McCombs and R. Marzano is published in *Educational Psychologist*, 25 (1), 51-69.
- 1990. "The Thinking Teachers Guide to Self-Esteem: Plus Simple Effective Strategies for Promoting Self-Esteem in the Classroom" by Darlene Stewart and Jeffrey Timm is self-

published. [Note: This is likely the first educational curriculum based on Sydney Banks' understanding.]

- o 1990. *Divorce is Not the Answer* by George Pransky is published by Tab Books. [Note: This book was subsequently republished as *The Relationship Handbook* (see 2001).]
- o 1990. *The Serenity Principle* by Joseph Bailey is the first book about this understanding to be published by a major publisher, Harper and Row. [Note: It applies this understanding to substance abuse.]

- January 23, 1991. Syd Banks puts out a tape titled, "Discussing the Three Principles," the first tape where he talks about Mind, Consciousness and Thought as three universal Principles.
- February 1, 1991. The Vermont Center for Human Understanding is co-founded by Dicken Bettinger and Janice Solek-Tefft, and becomes the first organization in the northeast to provide Psychology of Mind counseling and therapy. [Note: Barbara Jordan joins the staff shortly thereafter, followed years later by Katie Kelley.]
- May 2-4, 1991. The 10th Annual Psychology of Mind Conference is held at the Hyatt Regency Hotel in Minneapolis, Minnesota, sponsored by the Florida Center for Human Development.
- 1991. The University of Minnesota's federally funded Midwest Regional Center in Minneapolis, Minnesota is directed by Kathy Marshall and becomes the first to incorporate Principles of Health Realization and resilience research into U.S. Department of Education Drug Free Schools community-based substance abuse prevention programming. [Note: This leads eventually to the establishment of the National Resilience Resource Center (NRRC) at the University of Minnesota. *For details on this important and extensive effort, see Part III E.*]
- 1991. Joe and Doris Boyle establish Crossroads Counseling and Consulting of Great Falls, Montana, which becomes the first Principle-based practice in the central northwest. [Note: In 1992 they hire Bobbin Maki and in 1994 Janet Breedin as staff. In 2001, Joe and Doris open a satellite office, Crossroads of Jackson Hole, in Jackson Hole, Wyoming, funded by private funders and operate there for four years working with nonprofit organizations, municipal offices, businesses, and underfunded groups needing help developing staff. In 2006 they establish Crossroads Solutions in Great Falls, working primarily with businesses and

organizations, such as Pizza Hut, Pacific Steel and Recycling, Farmers Union, Government, Political Action groups, Health clubs, Medical groups, Restaurants, Artists and Universities.]

- 1991. Informed Families of Miami, Florida takes on Health Realization. Roger Mills of the Community Health Realization Institute puts out an Informed Families Parenting Series (videotape) of Modello and Homestead Gardens residents and other parents talking to Informed Families.

- 1991. Cindi Claypatch introduces Health Realization to the Glenwood-Lyndale Community Center, Minneapolis, Minnesota, where she is hired as staff, supported by the Center's new director, Christian Akale. As a result, the community changes markedly. [Note: In 1994 a formal training center begins as a result of donations from big funders. Glenwood-Lyndale's Board and all staff are trained, and the understanding becomes the operational philosophy in the entire organization. In 1995, a health clinic begins there in partnership with the Hennepin County Medical Center, with all staff trained in Health Realization.]

- 1991. Jim Marshall and Oscar Reed, former Minnesota Vikings football players (Jim's number is retired by the Vikings), and Deb Renshaw establish Life's Missing Link (formerly Professional Sports Linkage). [Note: Its purpose: "to transform the lives of inner-city youth and their families by providing health realization training, case management, role modeling and life skills training, which result in greater success in school, more stable families, healthier youth, and safer, more supportive communities."]

Publications:
  ○ 1991. "The Psychology of Mind applied to substance abuse, dropout, and delinquency prevention: Modello-Homestead Gardens Intervention Project" is a paper by Roger C. Mills presented to the Florida Alcohol and Drug Abuse Association Annual Conference, Orlando, Florida.
  ○ 1991. "A New Understanding of Self: The Role of Affect, State of Mind, Self-Understanding, and Intrinsic Motivation" by Roger C. Mills is published in the *Journal of Experimental Education.* 60:1, and in the same issue "Unraveling motivation: New perspectives from research and practice" with Barbara McCombs. 60: 3-14.
  ○ 1991 (August). "Fostering Resiliency in Kids: Protective

Factors in the Family, School, and Community" by Bonnie Benard is published by the Northwest Regional Educational Laboratory in Portland, Oregon, where she cites the work of Roger Mills.

o 1991. Mention of Roger Mills' work in the Modello/Early Intervention Project and Psychology of Mind is cited in the book, *Prevention: The Critical Need* by Jack Pransky, within the chapter, "Spirituality of Prevention," 337-339, published by Burrell. [Note: This book is subsequently revised and republished in 1995 by 1st Books Library (which becomes Author House) 483-485.] [Side note: What prompts inclusion in this book is Jack Pransky's first exposure to Psychology of Mind, March 22, 1991 at the "Please Stop Our Hurting" conference in Burlington, Vermont, sponsored by the Chittenden County Child Protection Team (Janice Solek-Tefft is a member), where Roger Mills, Cynthia Stennis and Elaine Burns of the Modello project speak.]

o 1991. *Management by Inspiration* by Allan Flood is published by Purgrose Publications.

- 1992. The Psychology of Mind Training Institute (POMTI) is established by a group of highly experienced practitioners of Psychology of Mind [Note: Purpose: "to formalize the conceptual framework of the understanding and create courses of instruction that would ultimately support academic programs and broader availability and acceptance of this model in the field of psychology. It sets forth four goals: 1) Support and develop accreditation program for certifying professionals; 2) Produce an annual conference; 3) Spearhead and encourage publications and disseminate Information about Psychology of Mind; 4) Support and help sustain demonstration projects in Psychology of Mind/Health Realization. The first POM Faculty meets in Victoria, B.C. in 1992. Present are Dr. George Pransky, Linda Pransky, Dr. Roger Mills, Dr. Keith Blevens, Dr. Mark Howard, Dr. Rita Shuford, Christine Heath, Joe Bailey, Jeff Timm, Dr. Gordan Trockman, Dr. Dicken Bettinger, Judy Sedgeman, Dr. Barbara McCombs, and Sandy Krot.]
- 1992. The Comprehensive Community Revitalization Project is started in the South Bronx, New York by Dr. Roger Mills as Director/trainer and Elsie Spittle as Consultant/trainer.
- April, 1992. A letter by George Pransky and Roger Mills spearheads a "POM Documentation Project," coordinated by Judy Sedgeman.

- June 18-21, 1992. The 11th Annual Psychology of Mind Conference is held at the Claremont Hotel, Oakland, California, sponsored by the Florida Center for Human Development.
- 1992. The Hillsborough County Health Realization Train the Trainers program begins with Roger Mills and Elsie Spittle in Tampa, Florida.
- Sept. 4-9, 1992: Syd Banks meets with the Psychology of Mind Faculty at the Dunsmuir Lodge in Victoria, B.C.
- 1992. The Coliseum Gardens Health Realization Community Empowerment Project begins in Oakland, California as a consortium of East Bay Recovery, the City of Oakland, The Oakland Housing Authority, Drug Free Communities, and "Fighting Back." Dr. Roger Mills is Director/Trainer, Elsie Spittle consultant/trainer, and Beverley Wilson primarily makes it happen on the ground. [Note: Police Officer Jerry Williams is assigned to this project to establish a Community Policing Program at Coliseum and Lockwood Gardens, is mentored by Beverley and adopts Health Realization as its foundation.]

Publications:
  o 1992. "The Listening Cure: Psychology of Mind Urges Clients to Heal Old Wounds by Living in the Present" by Ted Furtado is published in the *Utne Reader* (January/February). [Note: The article quotes George Pransky extensively, stating, "The simple secret to Psychology of Mind,' Pransky explains, 'is that therapists who use this approach don't focus on your problems. They focus on your health.'" The author quotes Enrique Suarez: "Applying Psychology of Mind to schizophrenia is like trying to put out a forest fire with a squirt gun." The author says he remains skeptical, but ends with this statement: "But for people such as the Miller's [sic], who feel that their marriage has been given a second chance after a few sessions with Pransky, it doesn't matter if the therapy is 'valid' or not. As to how the larger psychotherapy establishment will receive Psychology of Mind, only time will tell."]
  o 1992. The next issue of the *Utne Reader* (March-April) contains numerous pro and con "Letters to the Editor" about Psychology of Mind.
  o 1992. "Changing Hearts, Changing Minds: The Usefulness of Psychology of Mind in the Treatment of Paranoid Schizophrenia: Two Case Studies" by Carol Ringold is a doctoral dissertation in clinical psychology through the

Minnesota School of Professional Psychology.
- o 1992. "Project Mainstream Hawaii" by Christine Heath, Sherilynn Emiliano and Sharon Usagawa is presented at the American Educational Research Association in San Francisco, California.

- o 1992. The *Self-Esteem is for Everyone (SEE)* Program Student Handbook by Jeffrey Timm is put out by Learning Advantages, Tampa, Florida.
- o 1992. *You Can Feel Happy No Matter What* by Richard Carlson is published by New World Library.

- February 6-7, 1993. A seminar with Sydney Banks and George Pransky, "Deepening Your Understanding of Life and Relationships" is held at the Four Seasons Hotel, Vancouver, B.C., sponsored by IHRC. [Side note: This is where Jack Pransky has a personal encounter with Syd and meets George for the first time (as adults).]
- July 15-18, 1993. The 12th Annual Psychology of Mind Conference is held in Burlington, Vermont, hosted by the Vermont Center for Human Understanding.
- October 1993. A two-day symposium, "Health Realization: An Approach to Personal and Community Empowerment" is held by Roger Mills and Elsie Spittle for housing authority professionals, educators, social service providers, and resident leaders in Palo Alto, California.
- December 1993. An Advanced Training Seminar in substance abuse prevention is held in Tampa, Florida by Roger Mills and Elsie Spittle with the Atlanta Neighborhood Reinvestment Corporation, State of Florida Governor's Office, a Washington consulting group, and educators.
- 1993. The "Commonsense Parenting Series" by George Pransky [a set of six audio tapes] is put out by Pransky and Associates, La Conner, Washington.

Publications:
- o February 1993. "Making Connections: A new foundation-backed experiment gives six well-established South Bronx groups a chance to dream, plan, network, into community

organizing" appears in the magazine, *City Limits*. [The article makes the statement, "But some critics question their grassroots credentials. They called it a self-esteem training program run by Roger Mills. Critics say a proliferation of such programs is a serious concern because they...divert attention from the power structures that reinforce poverty."]

o 1993. "An Advanced Criminology Based on Psychology of Mind" by Thomas Kelley, Ph.D. is published in the *Journal of Offender Rehabilitation*. 19, 173-190.

o 1993. "Neo-Cognitive Learning Theory: Implications for Prevention and Early Intervention Strategies with At-Risk Youth" by Thomas Kelley is published in the journal, *Adolescence*. 28 (110), 439-460.

o 1993. "Psychology of Mind: The Basis for Health Realization: The Founder's Monograph" by Roger C. Mills and George Pransky is put out by the Psychology of Mind Training Institute as an unpublished manuscript.

o 1993. "The Health Realization Primer: Empowering Individuals and Communities" by Roger Mills with Sandy Krot is put out by R.C. Mills & Associates and the California School of Professional Psychology, Community Health Realization Institute in Alhambra, California. [Note: This is later revised with Elsie Spittle as co-author (see 1998).]

o 1993. *Creating the Teachable Moment: An innovative Approach to Teaching and Learning* by Darlene Stewart is published by Tab Books. [Note: This is the first book about this understanding to be applied to education.]

o 1993. *Shortcut Through Therapy* by Richard Carlson is published by Dutton (A Division of Penguin).

o 1993. *You Can Feel Good Again: Common-Sense Therapy for Releasing Depression and Changing Your Life* by Richard Carlson is published first by Dutton and later by Plume/Penguin books.

• 1994. The Ingham Regional Medical Center (IRMC) in Lansing, Michigan embarks on what turns out to be a major inside-out change process over many years, initiated by Marsha Madigan, M.D. and spearheaded by Milly Gilin and Lisa Laughman (Davidson). *[Note: For details on this important effort, see Part III F.]*

- 1994. The Selby Avenue Police Community Storefront in St. Paul, Minnesota takes on Psychology of Mind as its primary focus as a result of Police Officer Ed Lemon's assignment there. It has such a favorable response in fostering community empowerment that it leads to the creation of the "Cops N Kids" program in collaboration with Central High School students and staff. [Note: Ed receives a Minnesota Prevention and Intervention grant to expand and creates this student-based curriculum, including a videotape. Ed begins to teach in elementary, middle and high schools and in 1995 receives grants from Children, Families and Community Initiatives and the Minnesota After-School Enrichment Program to further expand the POM (later called 3 Principles psychology) program by hiring local youth outreach workers and offering classes out of the Selby-Dayton Apartments. In 1996, in partnership with Ramsey County Juvenile Corrections, Ed secures a large grant to create the "First Time Detainee" program, which provides services to juvenile offenders with potential to escalate into criminal behavior through enhanced probation and classes and coaching/counseling in 3 Principle Psychology.]

- February 3-7, 1994. The first Psychology of Mind Core Concepts Course is taught by George Pransky in San Francisco, California, sponsored by the POM Training Institute.

- July 14-17, 1994. The 13th Annual Psychology of Mind Conference is held in Seattle, Washington at the Washington State Convention Center, sponsored the POM Training Institute.

- 1994. The Selah Group begins in West Vancouver, B.C. by June Earle and Sally Wiens, followed by Barbara Burt-Davis, to bring an understanding of the Principles to, primarily, the Lower Mainland (Greater Vancouver area).

- November 5-6, 1994. "Finding Peace of Mind" seminar by Syd Banks is held for mental health and private professionals, sponsored by Life Education Inc., Mills College, Oakland, California.

- 1994. Syd Banks hosts a retreat for business leaders and Three Principles professionals with Chip Chipman in Victoria, B.C.

- 1994. The Community Health Realization Institute begins at the California School of Professional Psychology (CSPP), Los Angeles, California, by Dr. Roger Mills. [Note: Dr. Raymond Trybus spearheads this effort, assisted by Charles Boyd. This program ends around 1997.]

- 1994. Reese Coppage donates and sends countless copies of Syd

Banks' books, CDs and DVDs to individuals, social service agencies, prisons, jails and other correctional institutions in his community of Tampa Bay, Florida, as well as other parts of Florida, California, Michigan, Hawaii and other states. [Note: Reese continues this practice through 2007.]

Publications:
- o 1994. "Can Prevention Be Moved to a Higher Plane?" by Jack Pransky is published in *New Designs for Youth Development* magazine, by Development Associates (William Lofquist) of Tucson, Arizona. [Note: This article was originally titled "Moving Prevention to a Higher Plane" but the publisher changed the title.]
- o 1994. "Crime and Psychology of Mind: A Neo-Cognitive View of Delinquency," by Thomas Kelley is a chapter in *Varieties of Criminology: Reading from a Dynamic Discipline,* edited by G. Barak, published by Prager.
- o 1994. "Helping Students to Understand and Value Themselves" by Barbara McCombs and J. Pope is published as a chapter in *Motivating Hard to Reach Students: Psychology in the Classroom Series* edited by Barbara McCombs for the American Psychological Association, Washington, D.C.

- o 1994. The *Self-Esteem Is For Everyone Handbook* by Jeffrey Timm and Christa Campsall is published by Learning Advantages.

- February 17-18, 1995. The Missing Link between Psychology and Spirituality conference by Syd Banks is held for mental health professionals at the Pacific Beach Hotel, Honolulu, Hawaii, sponsored by the Hawaiian Counseling and Education Center.
- 1995. A Syd Banks talk is taped, titled, "Beyond the Word" in Minneapolis, Minnesota.
- Summer, 1995. The Department of Alcohol and Drug Services (DADS) of Santa Clara County, California begins a process that leads to the creation of a Health Realization Division within DADS. [*Note: For details on this groundbreaking effort, see Part III C.*]
- July 13-16, 1995. The 14th Annual Psychology of Mind Conference is held at the Royal Sonesta Hotel, Cambridge, Massachusetts,

sponsored by the Psychology of Mind Training Institute.

- Aug 25-27, 1995. Syd Banks meets with the Psychology of Mind Training Institute faculty at the Dunsmuir Lodge in Victoria, B.C.
- October 2-4, 1995. Empowering Communities and Families, a seminar with Dr. Roger Mills and Elsie Spittle is held at the Dunsmuir Lodge, Victoria, B.C., sponsored by the California School of Professional Psychology Community Health Realization Institute.
- October 12-13, 1995. Syd Banks holds a seminar at the Richmond Inn in Richmond, B.C., sponsored by International Human Relations Consultants.
- 1995. Syd Banks, with Chip Chipman of Vantage Consulting Group of Tampa, Florida, host a series of retreats for national and international business and not for profit organizational leaders, and sometimes Three Principles professionals. [Note: Retreats are held in December 1995 for business leaders (for the hotel and restaurant industry) at the Dunsmuir Lodge Executive Training & Conference Center, Victoria, B.C.; November 1996 in Hope Town, Bahamas; September 1997 at The Inn at Aspen, Aspen, Colorado; May 1998 at the Osborne Hotel in Torquay, England; November 1998 at the Beachcomber Hotel, Negril, Jamaica; October 1999 (for executives from a U.S. high-tech company) at the Oak Bay Hotel, Victoria, B.C.; May 2000 at the Osborne Hotel in Torquay, England; June 2002 in Longboat Key, Florida; July 2003 at the Salt Spring Spa & Resort, Salt Spring Island, B.C.]

Publications:

- o 1995. "From Risk to Resiliency: A Training Module," a publication co-written by Jack Pransky, Susie Wilson and Scott Johnson, is put out by the State of Vermont Agency of Human Services, and incorporates Health Realization as "internal resiliency."
- o 1995. "Inner Resource Guide: Activity Book," by Christa Campsall is put out by Proactive Training, Inc.
- o 1995. "Common Sense Ethics in Business" by L. Colero appears in *World Business Academy Perspectives*. 9 (1); includes Psychology of Mind.
- o 1995. "Cleaning Out the Clutter" by Sydney Banks, is a chapter in *Handbook for the Soul* edited by Richard Carlson and B. Shield (Eds.). Boston: Little, Brown and Company. pp. 74-77.

-     ○ 1995. *Realizing Mental Health: Toward a New Psychology of Resiliency* by Roger C. Mills is published by Sulzberger and Graham.
-     ○ 1995. "Background Report for the Development of Center for Substance Abuse Prevention's (CSAP's) Prevention 2001 Curriculum" includes recommendations for Health Realization by the Division of Community Prevention and Training, Training and Evaluation Branch, Washington, D.C. Chapter III-12 and III-22, highlights Health Realization as one of ten recommended prevention models for the field. [Note: Jack Pransky served on this national "expert panel." The article, "Can Prevention be Moved to a Higher Plane?" by Jack Pransky becomes one of the recommended articles for "Comprehensive Components of Effective Prevention Programs" and for "Models/Theories/Concepts," and his "Spirituality in Prevention" chapter of *Prevention: The Critical Need* (highlighting Modello) is a recommended article for "Spirituality."]

- 1996. Cathy Casey and Beverley Wilson bring Health Realization into a Santa Clara County, California jail. [Note: At one point Syd visits the Elmwood Jail in Milpitas and speaks to over 100 inmates and at least one county supervisor. *For further information on the effort in the Santa Clara County correctional system, see Part III C.]*
- 1996. Kristen Mansheim brings Health Realization into the Mariposa Lodge, the largest residential women's treatment facility for substance abuse in Santa Clara County. [Note: *For further information, see Part III C.]*
- 1996. Psychology of Mind Training Institute develops "core concepts": Mind, Consciousness and Thought; Thought processes; Conditioned thinking/thought systems; Moods; Original thought; Levels of Understanding; Healthy Psychological Functioning. [Note: Later the concepts are revised to Two Types of Thought; Feelings and Emotions; Moods; Thought Systems; Healthy Functioning; Levels of Understanding; Innate Health.]
- 1996. Psychology of Mind Training Institute announces its faculty to teach the Core Concepts Courses. [Note: The teaching faculty includes Joe Bailey, M.A., Dicken Bettinger, Ed.D., Keith Blevens, Ph.D., Christine Heath, M.S., Mark Howard, Ph.D., Sandy Krot, M.A., Roger Mills, Ph.D., George Pransky, Ph.D., Linda Pransky, Carol Ringold, Ph.D., Judith Sedgeman, M.A., Rita Shuford, Ph.D., Gordon Trockman, M.D. Later Bill Pettit, M.D.

becomes a faculty member from 1993-1994. In 1997 Ken Manning, Ph.D., Leslie Miller and Elsie Spittle join the faculty.]

- Feb 17-18, 1996. Syd Banks gives a seminar on "The Missing Link between Psychology and Spirituality" in Honolulu, Hawaii, sponsored by the Hawaii Counseling and Education Center, Honolulu, Hawaii. This presentation is audiotaped, titled "Hawaii."

- May 9-12, 1996. The 15th Annual Psychology of Mind Conference, "The Logic of the Cure" is held at the Red Lion, San Jose, California, sponsored by the Psychology of Mind Training Institute.

- June 7-9, 1996. Syd Banks and Roger Mills offer a conference titled "Empowerment and Leadership through Respect for the Individual" at the Dunsmuir Lodge in Victoria, B.C., sponsored by Texaco, Quality of Work Institute, and the California School of Professional Psychology. [Note: Syd kicks off this conference; others then share their experiences about how their lives and work have been affected, which is put out as a double VHS videotape.]

- October 6-10, 1996. The first Psychology of Mind Core Course Training of Instructors is held by George Pransky of Pransky and Associates in La Conner, Washington.

- October 12-13, 1996. Syd Banks gives a seminar on "The Missing Link in Psychology" for mental health professionals, sponsored by Pransky and Associates at the Richmond Inn, Richmond, B.C.

- October 1996. "Fellows" gathering is held by Pransky and Associates in La Conner, Washington, by invitation only, to help practitioners gain conceptual clarity.

- 1996. The newsletter/magazine, *Communiqué* is started by John Wood through his Psychology of Mind Resource Center of Midland, Western Australia. [Note: Subsequently the center's name is changed to the Philosophy of Living Center with a branch in Bend, Oregon with Allan Flood. David Bodman and Rolf Clausnitzer also are staff in Western Australia.]

- 1996. Ken Manning, Ph.D. begins a professional training center in Belmont, Massachusetts to train psychotherapists, counselors and consultants in Psychology of Mind, running 6-9 month training programs. [Note: In 1999 this center moves to Sudbury. In 2003, Ken co-creates an international executive coach training program called Coaching from Within. In 2006, he teams with Robin Charbit to cofound Insight Principles, a global consulting firm to bring the human dimension provided by the Principles into businesses and Fortune 100 and Fortune 500 companies. Over the years Ken trains hundreds of Three Principles professionals.]

- 1996. Kathy Marshall begins long-term systems change coalition projects primarily within the communities of St. Cloud, Minnesota and Menomonie, Wisconsin. *[Note: For information on this important and extensive effort, see Part III E.]*
- November 1996. Dr. William Pettit wins the Outstanding Health Care Professional Award given by the Mayor's Committee of People with Disabilities, Aberdeen, South Dakota.
- December 1996. The NorthEast Health Realization Institute is established by Jack Pransky in Cabot, Vermont to provide training, consultation and publications in Health Realization to the fields of Prevention, Human Services and Education, with the intent to shift at least 50% of practice in those fields to the inside-out paradigm. [Note: In 2008 its name is changed to the Center for Inside-Out Understanding in Montpelier, then Moretown, Vermont. While its intent is not remotely close to being realized, hundreds of professionals in these fields are trained in the inside-out paradigm.]
- 1996. A seminar by Syd Banks titled, "Sharing Wisdom and Hope" is presented by The Foundation for Advancement of Mental Health and the Glenwood-Lyndale Community Center, St. Paul, Minnesota.

Publications:
- o 1996. "Musings II: Rethinking How We Do Prevention" by Bonnie Benard appears in the *Western Center News* (March); includes Health Realization.
- o 1996. "The Foundation of the Resiliency Paradigm" by Bonnie Benard appears in the journal, *Resiliency in Action* (winter); includes Health Realization.
- o 1996. "Research Report: Roger Mills: A Community Psychologist Discovers Health Realization" by Bonnie Benard appears in *Resiliency in Action*. 1(3).
- o 1996. "A Critique of Social Bonding and Control Theory of Delinquency Using the Principles of Psychology of Mind" by Thomas Kelly is published in the journal, *Adolescence*. 31 (122), 321-337.
- o 1996. "At-risk youth and locus of control: Do they really see a choice?" by Thomas Kelley is published in the *Juvenile and Family Court Journal,* 47, 4, 39-54.

- o 1996. *You Can Be Happy No Matter What* by Richard Carlson is published by New World Publishers.
- o 1996. *Turned on: Eight vital insights to energize your people, customers and profits* by Dow and Cook, published by HarperCollins, and *The Quickening of America* by Lappe and DuBois, published by Jossey-Bass both mention Psychology of Mind.

- 1997. The Health Realization Institute is co-founded by Roger Mills and Elsie Spittle in Saratoga, California. [Note: This occurs after Roger leaves his position at the California School of Professional Psychology.]
- February 4-7, 1997. George Pransky begins a Rigor Correspondence Course. [George wrote, "Rigor is nothing more than clarity and precision in one's thinking...We are drawing a sharp distinction between what you are trying to say and how you say it—your message and delivery. The message is the essence point you want to make. The delivery is the constructs, explanations, metaphors and stories you use to make those points. Rigor has to do with getting your essential message clear and delineated in your mind so that it comes out clear and delineated." A 24-hour course is held at the Sheraton Palace Hotel in San Francisco. A certification program is announced consisting of core concepts courses, introductory therapy course, an advanced therapy concepts course, and a supervised internship.]
- February 6-9, 1997. The first Psychology of Mind Training Institute Therapy I course is held in Kailua, Hawaii.
- April 17-20, 1997. The 16th Annual Psychology of Mind Conference, "The feeling of Aloha and Innate Mental Health" is held at the Turtle Bay Hilton, Oahu, Hawaii, sponsored by the Hawaii Counseling and Education Center and the Psychology of Mind Foundation. Syd Banks comes in to give the closing presentation, his first at an annual conference.
- May, 1997. Health Realization training of professionals begins in Bemidji, Minnesota with Jack Pransky and, in October, also Cynthia Stennis, sponsored by Mary Marchel, Director of Beltrami County Public Health Nursing, and Susan Smith, psychotherapist. [Note: These trainings are noteworthy as they became the basis of study for Jack Pransky's Ph.D. dissertation, the first qualitative follow-up study on the effects of Health Realization (see 1999 publications).]
- Oct 18-19, 1997. Syd Banks seminar, "The Relationship Between the

Psychological and the Spiritual" is held at Metro State University, St Paul, Minnesota.

- 1997. John Wood of the Psychology of Mind Resource Center, Midland, Western Australia puts out Sydney Banks' original tapes [Note: These had been initially put out by Paul Fowler], and publishes a *Psychology of Mind Handbook* listing POM resources, with an Introduction by Judith Sedgeman.

Publications:

o 1997. A chapter titled, "An Emerging Paradigm for Brief Treatment and Prevention" by George S. Pransky, Roger C. Mills, Judith A. Sedgeman, and J. Keith Blevens appears in *Innovations in Clinical Practice: A Sourcebook, Volume 15*, Edited by Vandecreek, Knapp and Jackson, published by Professional Resource Press, Sarasota Florida.

o 1997. "Realizing Mental Health in the Classroom: A Practical Guide for Teachers" by Roger Mills and Jeff Timm is published [Editor's Note: I could not locate the publisher.]

o 1997. "A Framework for Practice: Tapping Innate Resilience" by Bonnie Benard and Kathy Marshall is published in *Research/Practice* through the University of Minnesota, Center for Applied Research and Educational Improvement, Spring, 9-15. [Note: This was the first publication combining an innovative approach to youth prevention grounded in resilience research and Health Realization that challenged prevailing risk-focused prevention practices. This special issue also included articles by Dr. Richard Holt, "Resilience and Health Realization: An Administrator's Perspective," and Roger Mills (also see entry below).]

o 1997. "Tapping Innate Resilience in Today's Classrooms by Roger Mills is published in *Research/Practice*, 5 (1), 19-27, the same publication and issue as above.

o 1997. Roger Mills of R.C. Mills and Associates puts out an unpublished monograph, "Psychology of Mind-Health Realization: Summary of Clinical, Prevention and Community Empowerment Applications; Documented Outcomes." [Note: This is notable for being the first time the outcomes of many Health Realization efforts were documented in one place.]

- o 1997. "The Impact of Training in the Health Realization Model on Affective States of Psychological Distress" by Mark Borg is a doctoral dissertation through the California School of Professional Psychology, Los Angeles, CA.

- o 1997. *Don't Sweat the Small Stuff...And It's All Small Stuff* by Richard Carlson is published by Hyperion and becomes a New York Times #1 best seller. [Note: This book is loosely based on the Three Principles and makes no mention of Sydney Banks. It spawns a series of "Don't Sweat the Small Stuff"-related books on various topics, including *What About the Big Stuff?*, published in 2003.]

- o 1997. *Falling in Love with Life: A Guide to Effortless Happiness and Inner Peace* by Thomas M. Kelley, Ph.D. is published by Breakthrough Press.

- o 1997. *Slowing Down to the Speed of Life: How to create a More Peaceful, Simpler Life from the Inside-Out* by Richard Carlson and Joseph Bailey is published by Harper San Francisco. [Note: This book becomes a best seller in the U.S. and Japan and is reprinted in 26 languages. As a result of this book, in the Fall Joe appears on the NBC nightly news with Brian Williams and is written up in *USA Today*. As of the date of this chronology Joe Bailey's books have sold over a half-million copies worldwide.]

- o 1997. *Parenting from the Heart: A Guide to the Essence of Parenting from the Inside-Out* by Jack Pransky is originally published by NEHRI publications. [Note: It is slightly revised and republished in 2012 by CCB Publishing, British Columbia, Canada.]

- 1998. The Psychology of Mind Training Institute creates "Foundations I & II Courses" taught by the POM faculty. [Note: The intention is to eventually train others to teach these courses.]
- 1998. Pransky and Associates starts work with a high tech electronics company in the Defense and Aerospace industry that leads to the first large-scale corporate Three Principles application in a Fortune 50 corporation. *[Note: For more detailed information on this groundbreaking effort, see Part III D.]*
- 1998. Ed Lemon establishes the City-wide Gun Violence prevention program in St. Paul, Minnesota, hired by the City Council, working via a POM/3 Principles psychology approach. [Note: Ed begins working with

incarcerated youth and youth assigned to alternative high schools, then expands to work with youth in the Ramsey County Juvenile Detention Center and Boys Totem Town correctional facility. (A study of the latter shows significant results from admission to discharge in moving from "abnormal" to "normal" range in asocial behavior and social maladjustment, compared with years prior to program.) Ed is responsible for receiving a large Federal School-Based Partnership grant in collaboration with the alternative high school, Face to Face Academy, to provide POM to students, parents, administrators, teachers, and run parenting classes through the East Side Family Center. In 2000 Ed is responsible for the St. Paul Police Department receiving a larger State Incentive Grant in collaboration with the school district and County to expand the 3 Principles program to more offenders, juvenile corrections and probation officers, school teachers, support staff and police department members. Ed also teaches POM in the Juvenile Detention Center sexual offender program (START). When the grant ends in 2003 Ed is reassigned as a juvenile investigator, but before the program ends over 1,000 people receive 3 Principle training by Ed, Roger Leonard, Mike Johnson, Sherry Schaffer, Sharon Nelson, Errol Johnson, Abbey Caitland, Joe Bailey, Mavis Karn and Pam McCreary. To quote Ed: "For goodness sakes, we had severe sex offender juveniles teaching the Minneapolis/St. Paul Catholic Archbishop the Principles."]

- 1998. The Los Angeles Drop-In Center in Skid Row, a part of Volunteers of America (VOA) inner city program, adopts Health Realization as its operating philosophy in dealing with its homeless population. [Note: Training is provided by Roger Mills and Elsie Spittle and affects people throughout the VOA, from Bob Pratt, President of VOA Los Angeles, to Jim Howat, VOA Drop-In Center Director, through VOA Case Managers David Williams, Katheryn Seissert-Jones, Leslie Brackins and others. This effort ends around 2012. Another Health Realization-based homelessness effort also begins in San Francisco, California by Andrew Hayes.]

- January 13, 1998. A curriculum committee of the Psychology of Mind Foundation is established, spearheaded by Judy Sedgeman, POM Foundation chair, and Sandy Krot, Curriculum Committee chair. [Note: The first meeting is scheduled for February, 1998, "The charge...from the Foundation is to develop a course or courses that present the basic understanding of POM which everyone, no matter what the particular application, must learn to become grounded in POM. A second charge is to develop teachers to teach these fundamental POM courses. Related to these two tasks are questions on the essence of teaching and the evaluation of course participants and/or teachers to determine whether a person has grasped what has been taught." Four committees are established: 1. Grounding Committee (Elsie Spittle, Linda Pransky, Bill Pettit, Melinda Calkin); 2. Teaching Process Committee (Sandy Krot, Kristen Mansheim, Jolene Parrish, Christa Campsall, Jack Pransky); 3) Evaluation Committee (Kathy Marshall, Beverley Wilson, Cathy Casey, Sharon Usagawa; 4) Teaching of Teachers Committee (Dicken Bettinger, Mark Howard, Janice Solek-Tefft.) (Cindi Claypatch is also on the faculty.) This meeting is postponed on January 16 "because it seemed wise to address the more essential questions facing POM, such as, 'What is the best strategy to get POM out in the world?' before we begin to discuss a new POM curriculum. A meeting is being organized by Roger Mills and Elsie Spittle in consultation with Syd Banks to address this and other fundamental issues."]

- February 1998. A Psychology of Mind Foundation meeting is held in La Conner, Washington. [Note: Mission: "to tell the simple and meaningful story of the human spirit unleashed by the power of understanding... Undertake national and international effort to increase the impact and visibility of Psychology of Mind. Purpose: ...to change the mental landscape of our world...; reach major institutions in society...; actively seek funds; thorough training of teachers and leaders who wish to bring Psychology of Mind into their life and work; leverage impact of teaching currently available; support research into the results of POM to provide a base of evidence...[beyond the] remarkable anecdotal results that POM practitioners have observed for two decades.]

- February 1998. An E-Newsletter Forum for the POM/HR community begins, spearheaded by Gordon Trockman.

- March 8-12, 1998. Syd Banks runs a seminar at the Richmond Inn, Richmond, B.C., sponsored by the POM Foundation.

- March, 1998. Psychology of Mind meeting. [Note: It is informative to see the issues discussed at this time in the evolution of this understanding. *For a summary of these issues, see Appendix A.*]

- April 2, 1998. A letter from Sandy Krot to update the Curriculum Committee announces that Judy Sedgeman joins the faculty of West Virginia University, which eventually leads to the establishment of the Sydney Banks Institute of Innate Health (see September 2000). [Note: The letter states, "There is a solid foundation of POM–trained at WVU who are excited to lend support to POM." *For details on this groundbreaking effort, see Part III B.*]

- 1998. The Psychology of Mind Foundation moves from Bradenton, Florida to Morgantown, West Virginia. Chair: Judy Sedgeman; CEO: Alix St. Paul.

- June 11-14, 1998. The 17th Annual Psychology of Mind Conference is held in St. Paul, Minnesota at the St. Paul Hotel, sponsored by the Glenwood-Lyndale Center and Psychology of Mind Foundation.
- June 16-17, 1998. A Syd Banks seminar, "Changing Lives from the Inside-Out" seminar is held at the University of Minnesota, St. Paul, Minnesota, sponsored by the Foundation for the Advancement of Mental Health.
- July 15-18, 1998. The Psychology of Mind Foundation Curriculum Development Committee meets at West Virginia University, Department of Community Medicine in Morgantown, West Virginia. Dean Bob D'Alessandri and Professor Dr. Jamie Shumway meet and interact with the POM group. [Note: It is informative to see the issues involved in decisions about creating a curriculum based on this understanding. For a summary of the invitation letter by Judy Sedgeman, Adjunct Assistant Professor at West Virginia University, which presents these issues, see Appendix B.]
- July 16, 1998. Chip and Jan Chipman host a Three Principles Symposium for leadership and staff of the St. Petersburg Police Department at Tradewinds Resort on St. Petersburg Beach, Florida, assisted by Ed Lemon, Jerry Williams, Cynthia Stennis and Lloyd Fields.
- August, 1998. Robert Kausen, Roger Mills and Elsie Spittle write an open letter to POM/HR practitioners/teachers. [Note: It states, "We feel the time has come to announce to the world the miraculous results of Psychology of Mind/Health Realization. We are preparing a major PR campaign and need testimonials to back up our release. We are asking people who feel they have benefited from this understanding to provide a statement of results."]
- September, 1998. Marilyn Fedewa becomes CEO of the Psychology of Mind Foundation.
- November, 1998. John Wood of The POM Resource Center of Midland, Australia puts together the first POM/HR practitioner website listing to assist people seeking contact with a POM/HR practitioner, teacher or consultant, as well as a listing of people in POM/HR teaching and consulting organizations, and a listing of POM/HR resources [Note: It states, "...looking for a book or tape that addresses a particular area of interest or concern has become a bit like looking for the proverbial 'needle in a haystack.'"]

- 1998. The first long-term professional Psychology of Mind/Health Realization trainings begin in New England—in Massachusetts by Ken Manning, and by Annika Hurwitt and Jack Pransky. [Note: A number of these are held over the next decade, with Ken Manning teaming with Dicken Bettinger and others, and Jack Pransky teaming with Lori Carpenos in Vermont and Connecticut.]
- 1998. Chip & Jan Chipman begin providing Three Principles training to leaders of the Jordan Park public housing neighborhood in St. Petersburg, Florida, under the jurisdiction of the St. Petersburg Housing Authority. [Note: Training is provided through 1999.]
- 1998. David "Tully" LeBaron of the Nevada Department of Corrections begins a series of 13-week groups teaching the Principles to prison inmates, after being inspired by attending the annual POM conference. [Note: By the time the prison closes in 2000, about 200 men complete the groups, the atmosphere of the yard changes to calm and self-determination, many men claim their group experience pivotal for getting them out of the criminal thinking cycle, terminating their drug use and settling down with families, something they never thought they'd be able to do. For example, Wayne Bridge, an inmate clerk, becomes Director of the Sin City Chamber of Commerce, and with Tully (who begins Phoenix Counseling) and David Brady, facilitate a volunteer group at an inpatient county substance abuse program. This group runs for 2 1/2 years until a new administrator says what they are teaching is not compatible with their 12-step model of treatment.]
- 1998. The health clinic at the Glenwood-Lyndale Community Center in Minneapolis receives the prestigious American Hospital Association Nova Award, one of the five clinics selected from 200 clinics nationwide. The Health Realization Model is pointed to for its results.
- 1998. Health Realization-trained police officer, Jerry Williams, wins the California Peace Prize from the California Wellness Foundation for his work in the Coliseum Gardens Housing Project in Oakland, California.

Publications:
  o 1998. "Reculturing Systems with Resilience / Health Realization" by Kathy Marshall appears as a chapter in *Promising Positive and Behaviors in Children* by The Carter Center (48-58) and is presented at the Fourteenth Annual

Rosalynn Carter Symposium on Mental Health Policy in Atlanta, Georgia.

o 1998. "Integrating Metacognition, Affect, and Motivation in Improving Teacher Education" by Barbara McCombs is published as a chapter, 379-407, in *How Students Learn* edited by Nadine Lambert and Barbara McCombs for the American Psychological Association, Washington, D.C.

o 1998. "Adolescents and the Myth of Peer Pressure" by Mavis Karn is an unpublished paper put out by Mavis Karn and Associates, Minneapolis, Minnesota. [Note: This is the first paper to deal with adolescents from this perspective.]

o 1998. *The Missing Link: Reflections on Philosophy and Spirit* by Sydney Banks is initially published by International Human Relations Consultants and distributed by Lone Pine Publications. [Note: Later it is republished by Lone Pine Publications, Shane Kennedy's publishing company (Shane was originally on Salt Spring Island), which eventually takes on publication and distribution of most of Sydney Banks' books, and also Elsie Spittle's. It then begins Lone Pine Media, which publishes the first videotapes of Syd.]

o 1998. *The Renaissance of Psychology* by George Pransky is published by Sulzburger and Graham.

o 1998. *Modello: A Story of Hope for the Inner-City and Beyond: An Inside-Out Model of Prevention and Resiliency in Action* by Jack Pransky is originally published by NEHRI Publications. [Note: It is subsequently republished in 2011 by CCB Publishing, British Columbia, Canada.]

o 1998. *The Health Realization Primer: Empowering Individuals and Communities* by Roger Mills and Elsie Spittle is put out by R.C. Mills & Associates. [Note: This is a revision of the 1993 version Roger wrote with Sandy Krot. In 2000 it is published by Lone Pine Publishing.]

• January 1999. The first seminars are held for the Health Realization Prevention Certification Program by Roger Mills and Associates, taught primarily by Elsie Spittle.

• January 1999. The Center for Optimal Living is started by Annika Hurwitt, sponsoring year-long trainings for Three Principles practitioners around Boston and Martha's Vineyard. [Note: Subsequently Annika sponsors 3P Practitioners Programs available virtually through online meetings, coaching and webinars; and Women's Leadership Programs in Boston and NYC, training hundreds of 3P practitioners.]

- January 24-26, 1999. Sydney Banks meets in a private session with AEquanimitas Foundation (the new name given to the Psychology of Mind Foundation) faculty at the Richmond Inn in Richmond, B.C.

- March, 1999. The Health Realization Institute is co-founded by Roger Mills and Elsie Spittle.

- March, 1999. Police officer Jerry Williams is formally cited for his community policing work by Attorney General Janet Reno and President Clinton.

- April 1999. The Psychology of Mind/Health Realization Resource Center in Midland, Australia creates an Editorial Advisory Board for the *Communiqué*: [Note: Board members are John Wood (editor), Rolf Clausnitzer, Allan Flood, Carol Ringold, Gordon Trockman, Jack Pransky, Janice Solek-Tefft, Joe Bailey, Robert Kausen, David Bodman.]

- 1999. Mavis Karn writes "The Secret" to youth as her Principles-based class closing celebration letter gifted to participating juvenile males incarcerated at the State of Minnesota correctional facility in Red Wing. [Note: Mavis and Willie Lee voluntarily facilitate this group on Sundays. By 2002 the National Resilience Resource Center, with Mavis' permission, disseminates this letter as a self-published laminated poster extensively in its school and community organizations serving youth.]

- June 24-27, 1999. The 18th Annual Psychology of Mind/Health Realization conference, "Illuminating the Human Spirit," is held at the Fairmont Hotel, San Jose, California, sponsored by the AEquanimitas Foundation. Syd Banks gives the closing presentation. [Note: This is the first Annual Conference Syd attends as a participant.]

- 1999. A management retreat, "Creating Leadership from Within" is held in Shepherdstown, West Virginia, sponsored by the West Virginia University School of Medicine.

- August 1999. AEquanimitas Foundation letter from Judy Sedgeman to the Foundation's faculty. [Note: It announces to "undertake a research project that will be an enormous step towards global evaluation of the impact of the understanding of the principles of mind, consciousness and thought on the state of mind and experience of well-being of diverse populations. The research instrument we will use has been designed at West Virginia University with the help of foundation faculty members, including Dr. Keith Blevens and Jack Pransky, and POM/HR advisors with a strong interest in this work, such as Dr. Tom Kelley and Dr. George Pransky. We have tested it and analyzed it, and we feel, starting in January 2000, that it will be ready to roll out officially and that we can begin a short term, midterm and long-term study of thousands of people who go through Foundations I and II courses."]

- August 1999. AEquanimitas Foundation spearheads a meeting to put together Objectives for Foundations I & II Courses, and to establish a Faculty mentoring committee. [Note: It consists of John Wood, Cindi Claypatch, Cathy Casey, Marsha Madigan, Judy Sedgeman, Sandy Krot, Carol Ringold, Christa Campsall, Ann Thomas, Christie Winkelman, George Pransky, Dick Bozoian, Janice Solek-Tefft, Christine Heath, Reese Coppage, Joe Boyle, Bob Gunn, Bob Ford, Beverley Wilson, Darlene Turner, Jack Pransky, Rolf Clausnitzer, Patty Shackleford, Rita Shuford, Annika Hurwitt Schahn, Lori Carpenos, George Patterson, Helen Neil-Pore, Elena Mustakova-Possart, Melinda Calkin, David Bodman, Bruce Duncan, Jolene Parrish and Frances Cox. (*For an informative listing of objectives, see Appendix C.*) Also, Sarah Quesen of the AEquanimitas Foundation establishes a faculty website.]

- September 17-19, 1999. Syd Banks runs a seminar at the Richmond Inn, Richmond, B.C., sponsored by International Human Relations Consultants.

- October 1999. A Psychology of Mind Association is established from an idea started at the Annual Conference, organized by Rita Shuford, Susan Sickora, Pat Billington, Joe Boyle, Lynn Keyes and Ken Spittle. [Note: By December it becomes a membership organization of 52 charter members and 31 founding members. At the July 2000 Annual Conference, the Association holds its annual meeting, changes its name to the Association for the Advancement of Human Understanding (AAHU), decides to maintain its incorporation status but become inactive, and the remaining balance of membership dues is given over to the AEquanimitas Foundation.]

Publications:

- o 1999. "*D is for Dreaming, Pictures of Peace and Unity*" by the Children of Riverview Terrace, Tampa, Florida, in conjunction with Jan Chipman, coordinator, editor and Three Principles Youth Leadership Trainer at Riverview Terrace Public Housing Project. Preface by Roger Mills.
- o 1999. "The Experience of Participants after Health Realization Training: A One-Year Follow-Up Phenomeno-

logical Study" by Jack Pransky is a doctoral dissertation in community psychology through The Union Institute, Cincinnati, Ohio. [Note: Based on research from Jack Pransky's Bemidji, Minnesota Health Realization trainings (see May 1997).]

- o 1999. *Perfect Misfortune: Hope Healing & Happiness* by Allan Flood is published by the Psychology of Mind Resource Center.
- o 1999. *The Speed Trap: How to Avoid the Frenzy of the Fast Lane*, by Joseph Bailey is published by Harper San Francisco.
- o 1999. *Inner Resources Guide* by Christa Campsall is published by Proactive Training, Inc., Salt Spring Island, British Columbia.

- January 2000. A faculty mentoring committee is established, dedicated to assisting the AEquanimitas Foundation faculty to do their best in facilitating Foundation Seminars and to act as a liaison between the faculty and Board of the AEquanimitas Foundation. [Note: Tasks: matching faculty with Foundation seminar teaching opportunities; mentoring/coaching faculty by being co-facilitators in Foundation seminars or by phone; helping faculty preparation for seminars; debriefing teaching experience after seminars; providing a support and sounding board for faculty concerns.]
- March 3-5, 2000. Syd Banks gives a seminar at the West Coast Long Beach Hotel, Long Beach California, co-sponsored by Health Realization Seminars and IHRC. It is videotaped by Lone Pine Media and put out as a series of four talks (later combined into three DVDs) as *The Long Beach Lectures,* the first full-length video of Syd Banks.
- 2000. A Health Realization Division within The Department of Alcohol and Drug Services (DADS) of Santa Clara County, California is officially created by Bob Garner, Director, with Barbara Faye Sanford as Coordinator, Gabriela Maldonado, Sister Margarita Tran and Linda Ramus as primary staff and Billy King as a rehabilitation counselor from another division assigned to Health Realization; also supported by a cadre of Roger Mills-trained contractors/facilitators. *[Note: For details on this groundbreaking effort, see Part III C.]*
- July 13-16, 2000. The 19th Annual Psychology of Mind conference is held at the Hyatt Regency Hotel in Washington, D.C., sponsored by

the AEquanimitas Foundation. Syd Banks gives the closing presentation on "The Power of Mind."

- September 20, 2000. The Sydney Banks Institute of Innate Health (SBIIH) is established at the Robert C. Byrd Health Sciences Center, West Virginia University School of Medicine, Morgantown, West Virginia, with Judith Sedgeman Director. At the Vision for Humanity dedication ceremonies, Sydney Banks gives two presentations on "The Power of Wisdom." [Note: A series of presentations is also made to Medical School staff, students and faculty directed toward furthering the research goals of the SBIIH. In June 2002 William Pettit, M.D. becomes Medical Director for the Sydney Banks Institute for Innate Health and is appointed Assistant (later Associate) Professor of Behavioral Medicine and Psychiatry at the West Virginia University School of Medicine in 2002 and 2008, respectively. [*For details on this groundbreaking effort, see Part III B.*]

- November, 2000. The first Midwest Regional Conference, titled MIND: Moving in New Directions, is held in the Twin Cities, Minnesota, hosted by Alice Poulter and Cindi Claypatch of Glenwood-Lyndale Community Center. [Note: A second Midwest Regional Conference is held in 2002.]

- 2000. Linda Halcon, Ph.D., Cheryl Robertson, Ph.D., and Cindi Claypatch, M.A. begin a successful Health Realization intervention and study in an East African refugee community of Somali and Oromo women. [Note: A Park Nicollet Foundation grant provides Health Realization training to Somali and Oromo staff, who find it an approach that resonates with their communities and culture. In 2002 a University of Minnesota grant enables an instrument to be developed to measure resilience. In 2003-2004 small pilot projects incorporate the Three Principles along with parenting education and Yoga. In 2004-2005 an NIH grant allows for feasibility-testing of 3P training of Somali and Oromo refugee women, many of whom had been tortured. In 2010-2013 an NIH/NINR study (R21) of 3P training vs. an alternative intervention (nutrition education vs. nothing) among Somali women in three communities shows significant results (not published, as of this chronology). In 2012 a small youth resilience project training mothers/caregivers and teen girls in the 3Ps begins.]

Publications:

- o 2000. "Thought Recognition, Locus of Control, and Adolescent Well-Being" by Thomas Kelley and Steven Stack is published in the journal, *Adolescence,* 25, 139, 531-550.

- o 2000. "Peace from the Inside Out," a story about Cindi Claypatch's work in public housing is published in the book, *Compassionate Rebel,* by Bert Belowe. [Note: Cindi also worked in the Chaska, Edina, Wayzata, and Eden Prairie school districts in Minnesota.]
- o 2000-2003. Judith Sedgeman writes a series of inside-out-related articles on many subjects for the Sydney Banks Institute of Innate Health, which she sends via email to her WVU students and the Innate Health community.

- o 2000. *Insight Inspirations: Messages of Hope* by Jane Tucker is a booklet put out by Inner Change Consulting, Middletown, Maryland. [Note: This is republished in 2013.]
- o 2000. *Healthy Thinking/Feeling/Doing from the Inside-Out: A Middle School Curriculum and Guide for the Prevention of Violence, Abuse & Other Problem Behaviors* by Jack Pransky and Lori Carpenos is published by Safer Society Press.

- 2001. Roger Mills and Elsie Spittle begin the Visitacion Valley project in San Francisco, California. LaThena Clay and Barbara Glaspie are hired as staff. [Note: This multi-million dollar community revitalization project includes Wells Fargo Bank, Charles Schwab Corporation Foundation, Charles and Helen Schwab Foundation, Isabel Allende Foundation, Pottruck Family Foundation, McKesson Foundation, Richard and Rhoda Goldman Fund, S. H. Cowell Foundation, San Francisco Foundation, Evelyn and Walters Haas, Jr. Fund, Milagro Foundation, *Dresdner* RCM Global Investors. The coordinators and staff work with residents, police, schools, housing authority and others.]
- 2001. The book, *Modello: A Story of Hope for the Inner-City and Beyond* by Jack Pransky is awarded the *Martin Luther King Storyteller's Award* by the Minister's Alliance of Rhode Island for the book best exemplifying King's vision of "the beloved community."
- 2001. The Poco Way Community Project in San Jose California, with support from Gabriela Maldonado and Sister Margarita Tran, secures prevention funds from the Department of Alcohol and Drug Services in collaboration with the Housing Authority of Santa Clara County. [Note: First a weekly parenting class is held in Spanish, followed by Vietnamese and Cambodian classes. Community residents apply for and receive funds to provide community services. Residents visit museums,

organize community events focusing on children and celebrate cultural holidays, work with San Jose Police Department resulting in a greater police presence and higher trust, work with the Housing Authority to improve living conditions, and develop a sense of community among neighbors that transcends language and cultural differences.]

- April 15, 2001. Syd gives a talk on "Our Spiritual and Psychological Nature: The Wisdom Within," to a select group of Psychology of Mind and Health Realization practitioners, therapists and educators at the Inn at Saratoga, Saratoga, California, sponsored by the Health Realization Institute. [Note: At this talk Syd insists this understanding is only about the Three Principles of Mind, Consciousness and Thought.]

- April 17, 2001. Syd Banks gives a talk on "Discovering the Nature of God" to inmates in the Regimented Corrections Program and County and correctional system supervisors at the Elmwood Correctional Facility, sponsored by the Department of Alcohol and Drug Services, and the Santa Clara Valley health and hospitals system, Milpitas, California.

- June 14-17, 2001. Sydney Banks presents a seminar on "The Three Principles and Releasing the Power in Health" in Pittsburgh, Pennsylvania, sponsored by the Sydney Banks Institute of Innate Health and the West Virginia University School of Medicine. [Note: This presentation includes a series of talks to faculty, students and staff of WVU to promote the research goals of the Sydney Banks Institute for Innate Health.]

- October 2001. Louie Pavao and Christine Heath present outcomes of their Ke Ala Pono Domestic Violence Cessation program on Oahu, Hawaii at the National American Association of Marriage and Family Therapists conference. [Note: In 1997 the Family Peace Center initiates an outcome study of the different models for perpetrator groups. Chris and Louie provide a 24-week Ke Ala Pono group for batterers, which are assessed using three instruments and show significant decreases in depression, physical conflict and nonphysical conflict.]

- October 11-14, 2001: Sydney Banks offers a retreat on "The Three Principles: A Spiritual Understanding" at the Turtle Bay Hilton, Oahu, Hawaii, sponsored by the Hawaii Counseling and Education Center. This is videotaped and released by Lone Pine Media as *The Hawaii Lectures* (2001) and includes, "Secret to the Mind," "Oneness of Life," "The Power of Thought" and "Going Home."

- 2001. The "Inner Life of Healers" Program begins at the University of Minnesota, Medical School Center for Spirituality and Healing, to teach medical healers how to be resilient, using the Three Principles. Joe Bailey and Dr. Henry Emmons are the primary teachers. [Note: This program ends in 2004.]
- 2001. *The Washington Lectures* by Syd Banks, including "The Three Principles" and "Separate Realities" are videotaped at a conference in Washington, D.C. and released by Lone Pine Media.
- 2001. "The Great Spirit: Reflections on Native American Spirituality," is a CD recording by Sydney Banks put out by Lone Pine Media, Alberta, Canada.

Publications:
- o 2001. "Mind Over Matter: You Create Your Own Reality—At Least That's What Some Therapists Say Using The Three Principles of Mind, Thought and Consciousness" by Regina Reitmeyer is published in *Counseling Today* magazine (August). [Note: The article quotes Judith Sedgeman, William Pettit, Robert D'Alessandri of the School of Medicine at West Virginia University, Morgantown, WV), followed by an interview with Sydney Banks.]
- o 2001. "Mind Over Matter? Critics Say A New Institute at West Virginia U. Pushes Junk Science; Supporters Insist That It Be Given a Chance" by S. Smallwood is published by *The Chronicle of Higher Education*, Dec. 7.
- o 2001. "Health Realization as a Psychotherapeutic Intervention with Children in a Multicultural Environment" by P. Grenelle is a doctoral dissertation through the American School of Professional Psychology, Hawaii Campus, Honolulu.
- o 2001. *Bringing Out the Best in Our Kids* by Kathy Marshall is a booklet put out by the School District of the Menomonie Area, Menomonie, Wisconsin.
- o 2001. *Insights in the Moment: Messages of Peace* by Jane Tucker is a booklet put out by Inner Change Consulting, Middletown, Maryland. [Note: This is republished in 2014.]
- o 2001. *Resilience Research for Prevention Programs* by Kathy Marshall and Bonnie Benard presents a series of seven scholarly research reviews for the federally-funded Center for Prevention and Technology "Literature Reviews," which

bridges the gap between research and practice and points to the inside-out nature of prevention, resilience, and youth development.

o 2001. "The Need for a Principle Based Positive Psychology" by Thomas Kelley is published in *American Psychologist*, 56(1), 89-90

o 2001. *The Enlightened Gardener* by Sydney Banks is published by Lone Pine Publishing.
o 2001. *The Wisdom Within* by Roger Mills and Elsie Spittle is published by Lone Pine Publishing.
o 2001. *The Relationship Handbook: A Simple Guide to Satisfying Relationships* by George S. Pransky is published by Pransky and Associates. [Note: Former title: *Divorce is Not the Answer.*]

- September 2002. Christie Binzen, Director of Woodbury College Prevention and Community Development (PCD) Program of Montpelier, Vermont makes the decision to place equal emphasis on inside-out (as well as traditional outside-in) prevention, where Health Realization is taught as an integral part of its curriculum. [Note: The PCD Program within Woodbury College is "the first comprehensive college level program to focus on initiatives to preemptively address systematic violence and substance abuse issues." Christie Binzen becomes PCD Program Director in Spring, 2001 and is exposed to Health Realization independently by Patty Toth and Jack Pransky, a consultant and Health Realization instructor for PCD. Woodbury College President, Larry Mandell approves the inside-out focus. When Christie leaves, Assistant Director, Kelly Young, who is equally enthusiastic about Health Realization, becomes Director. In 2008 Woodbury College closes and becomes the Woodbury Institute of Champlain College, which ends the Prevention and Community Development Program shortly thereafter.]
- November 2002. Nancy Lopin begins a Health Realization Program at the Suffolk County House of Correction in Boston, first as a volunteer and in July 2006 as an "Independent Contractor." [Note: As of the date of this chronology this program has been running for 12 years, helping scores, perhaps hundreds, of inmates.]
- 2002. Kathy Marshall Emerson creates and begins teaching a "Spirituality and Resilience" course at the University of Minnesota,

focusing on the Three Principles. [Note: This course is able to be used as part of the Center for Spirituality and Healing graduate minor, in many professional disciplines. Dr. Linda Halcon from the UM School of Nursing assists with early development.]

Publications:

- o 2002. "Clinicians' Reported Experience of Integrating the Psychology of Mind Paradigm into Clinical Practice" by D. Carino is an unpublished doctoral dissertation through the Saybrook Graduate School and Research Center, San Francisco.
- o 2002. "The Role of Health Realization Training in Enhancing Managerial Everyday Creativity and Co-Creative Processes" by Celestine McMahan-Woneis is an unpublished doctoral dissertation through The California School of Professional Psychology, Alameda, California.
- o 2002. "The Avalon Gardens Men's Association: A Community Health Psychology Case Study" by Mark Borg is published in the *Journal of Health Psychology*, 7(3), 345-357.

- 2003. Gabriela Maldonado begins a Health Realization program in Santa Clara County Juvenile Hall, running numerous groups, assisted by others such as Ami Chen Mills, Azra Simonetti and Celestine McMahan-Woneis. [Note: A study is conducted on this successful effort: See Publications 2007, last entry; *see also Part III C*; and for an inside look into this program see *Somebody Should Have Told Us!* by Jack Pransky (last section of Chapter VII).]
- 2003. Christine Heath establishes the Minnesota Counseling and Education Center (MCEC) in Minneapolis, Minnesota as a branch of the Hawaii Counseling and Education Center (HCEC).
- 2003. Gilly Chater conducts the first Training of Trainers in New Zealand. [Note: Gilly attends her first training at Pransky and Associates in October 1997, and is mentored by Linda Pransky, Judy Sedgeman and Elsie Spittle. In November 1999 Gilly, with Leanne Tane, brings Judy Sedgeman to New Zealand to teach the Principles to Child Youth & Family (CYF) in Auckland, Rotorua, Wellington, and Christchurch, where 80-120 attend in each location, several outside CYF. Judy also runs a Wisdom at Work workshop for business people, which David Lewis attends (see 2010). Gilly begins to specialize with businesses and in 2012 wins the National Speakers Association of New Zealand (NSANZ) Inspirational Speaker of the Year. Also,

in 2011, Tanya Kennard-Campbell moves to NZ to open her own 3P consulting business. (Previously, in 1995 Jack Pransky had introduced Health Realization to New Zealand through the Mental Health Foundation of New Zealand, with Dr. Barbara Disley, and the University of Aukland Department of Psychiatry and Behavioral Sciences, with Dr. John Renbourne, but it didn't take hold.)]

- June 19-22, 2003. The 21st Annual Three Principles Conference is held at The Hayes Mansion, San Jose, California.
- October 4-5, 2003. Syd Banks holds a seminar on "Discovering the Spiritual Side of Life" in Richmond, B.C.
- 2003. Chip & Jan Chipman of Vantage Consulting Group begin Three Principles Training for the City of St. Petersburg, Florida, which includes the Mayor and executive staff and managers of all city departments, including the Police and Fire Departments. [Note: This training extends through 2005.]

Publications:
- o 2003. "Preventing Youth Violence through Health Realization" by Thomas Kelley is published in the journal, *Youth Violence and Juvenile Justice*, 1, 4, 369-387.
- o 2003. "Health Realization: A Principle-Based Psychology of Positive Youth Development" by Thomas Kelley is published in the journal, *Child and Youth Care Forum*, 32, 1, 47-72.
- o 2003. "A Strengths-Based Practice Model: Psychology of Mind and Health Realization" by S. A. Wartel is published in the *Families in Society: Journal of Contemporary Human Services*, 185-191. 84(2).
- o 2003. "'Miracle survivors': Promoting Resilience in Indian Students by Iris HeavyRunner and Kathy Marshall is published in the *Tribal College Journal of American Indian Higher Education*, 14(4) Summer (May).

- o 2003. *We've Got to Start Meeting Like This: How to Get Better Results with Fewer Meetings* by Robert Kausen is published by Life Education.
- o 2003. *Prevention from the Inside-Out* by Jack Pransky is published by AuthorHouse. [Note: Includes extensive interviews with Helen Neal-Pore, Beverley Wilson, Kristen Mansheim, Elsie

Spittle, Judy Sedgeman, Desi Shebobman and Barbara Glaspie. It is used as a textbook in a number of colleges and universities.]

- 2004. The Center for Sustainable Change (CSC) is founded in Palo Alto, California by Roger Mills (President) and Ami Chen Mills-Naim (Executive Director), with help from Jim Barry, Don Carlson, and the Shinnyo-en and San Francisco Foundations. [Note: In 2011 Gabriela Maldonado-Montano joins Ami Chen Mills-Naim as Co-Director of CSC, and in 2012 Dave Nichols takes over as Executive Director, the Center becomes based in Charlotte, North Carolina; Gabriela becomes Senior Trainer and Ami Education Director.]
- 2004. Roger Mills provides Health Realization training in the U.K., sponsored by Margaret Opio of the Blue Balloon Foundation, then begins the first Trainer of Trainers program in the U.K. Roger then brings Syd over. [Note: These sessions are attended by Dean Rees-Evans (who later brings the Principles to Eastern Australia), Rudi Kennard (who later co-establishes Three Principles Movies with Jenny), Sue Pankiewicz (who later co-establishes Space for Connection) and others, who help to initially spread the Principles into the U.K.]
- 2004. Principles-based trainings in Des Moines, Iowa are conducted primarily by Kristen Mansheim, which subsequently evolves into a project partnership with the Center for Sustainable Change (CSC) National Community Resiliency Project (NCRP) (see 2008 entry). [Note: This initial training by Kristen, assisted first by Cathy Casey then Chris Heath, leads to an initiative directed by Mary Webb Martin with interested community members, where over the next four years trainings occur with numerous national Innate Health facilitators, and which leads to a Training of Trainers (TOT) program funded by United Way of Central Iowa. By 2007 it becomes a model where a network of Des Moines' organizations align around the Innate Health paradigm: United Way of Central Iowa (Corrine Lambert), Carver Community School (The National Community Resiliency Project trains teachers and parents), Callanan Middle School (Success Case Manager Aisha White brings the understanding to her staff), West Des Moines Youth Justice Initiative (Claudia Henning; in which the Principles are integrated in all its young offender problems and includes the West Des Moines Police Department), Iowa Health-Des Moines which in 2013 becomes UnityPoint Health (Connie Ziller brings Innate Health training into three hospitals), Des Moines Public Schools Success Program, Iowa Department of Human Services (Tony Wilson), Department of Corrections (Marlene Turner and Connie Ziller run classes at Mitchellville Women's Prison), the community-based health clinic La Clinica de la Esperanza or

Clinic of Hope (Social Worker Karen Reinecke implements a program to address patient depression and anxiety and offers individual counseling, primarily in Spanish, with an Innate Health perspective). Outcomes of two years of this effort are chronicled in *Awakening the Beloved Community: Report on Year 2 of the National Community Resiliency Project*, by Ami Chen Mills-Naim, NCRP Project Director, assisted by Corinne Lambert, *http://cscmediacenter.org/read.html*. Further, this effort showed results could occur in an average mid-western community, not merely a distressed community.]

- January 16-17, 2004. A Health Realization Training of Trainers begins in Columbus, Ohio conducted by Jack Pransky through the Ohio Resource Network for Drug-Free Schools and Communities. [Note: This training, meeting one weekend a month for seven months, is an effort to bring Health Realization into the mainstream in the State of Ohio. Results are documented of changes in the lives of prospective trainers (unpublished). The First Lady of Ohio visits. Jack brings in different co-trainers each month to assist, including Lori Carpenos, Kristen Mansheim, Cynthia Stennis, Beverley Wilson, Sandy Krot and Gabriela Maldonado.]

- June 2004. Washburn University social work professor Dr. Diane McMillen begins a sabbatical, embarking on a cross-country study of Health Realization. [Note: On her journey she meets in Vermont with Jack Pransky; Cheryl Santacaterina (St. Johnbury); Principal Don Schneider and teacher Amy Kahofer Dalsimer (Thatcher Brook School, Waterbury); Christie Binzen and Kelly Young (Woodbury College Prevention and Community Development Program, Montpelier); Nancy Lopin (Suffolk County House of Correction, Boston, MA); Ohio Training of Trainers with Jack Pransky and Beverley Wilson (Columbus, OH); Bill and Linda Pettit and Judy Sedgeman (West Virginia Institute for Innate Health, Morgantown, WV); Sheila North (DePaul Treatment Centers, Portland, OR); Pransky and Associates (La Conner, WA); Roger and Clytee Mills and the Visitation Valley project (San Francisco, CA); and Linda Ramus, Cathy Casey, Kristen Mansheim, Gabriela Maldonado, Billy King, Carlos Hankins, Sister Margarita Tran and Bob Garner (Department of Alcohol & Drug Services, San Jose, CA). By 2002 Dr. McMillen assigns *Modello* in her Prevention and Human Services class, after using Jack Pransky's *Prevention: The Critical Need* as a major textbook. In 2005 she begins an "Advanced Prevention" class, teaching Health Realization to more than 100 students, as of this publication.]

- October 2004. Dr. Diane McMillen gives keynote speech on "A New Model of Prevention: Health Realization" at the National Conference of the National Organization for Human Service Educators in Houston, Texas. [Note: This begins a series of national, regional and state

Keynote and major speeches by Diane on inside-out prevention and human services, including National Organization of Human Services Annual Conferences (Milwaukee WI, Tucson AZ, Portland ME, Portland OR, Atlanta GA, San Diego, CA); Midwest/North Central Organization of Human Services Annual Conferences (Indiana, Wisconsin, Illinois, Michigan, Iowa and Kansas); Governor's Conference for the Prevention of Child Abuse and Neglect (Kansas), Kansas Correctional Association, Child Welfare Excellence in Supervision Conference, Kansas National Guard Family Programs, and many more.]

- 2004. Judith Sedgeman teaches the first on-line graduate course on Innate Health at West Virginia University.
- 2004. George Pransky and Aaron Turner conduct the first Principle-based sales training at Adams Outdoor Advertising. [Note: Adams is headquartered in Atlanta but extends throughout mid and east U.S.]

Publications:
- o 2004. "Resilience Research and Practice: National Resilience Resource Center Bridging the Gap" by Kathy Marshall is a chapter in H. C. Waxman, Y. N. Padron and J. Gray (Eds.). *Educational Resiliency: Student, Teacher, and School Perspectives*. Greenwich, CT: Information Age Publishing (63-84). [Note: This book is the first volume in the series *Research in Educational Diversity and Excellence* supported by the U.S. Department of Education, Office of Educational Research and Improvement. Marshall introduces Principles of Health Realization as fundamental to tapping natural resilience in students.]
- o 2004. "Positive Psychology and Adolescent Mental Health: False Promise or True Breakthrough?" by Thomas Kelley is published in *Adolescence*, 39, 154, 257-278.
- o 2004. "Insight and Wisdom: Insight for Leaders" by Robin Charbit and Charles Kiefer is published in *Reflections, The Sol Journal*, 5 (9). www.reflections.solon.org
- o 2004. *Insights of the Spirit: Messages of Love* by Jane Tucker is a booklet put out by Inner Change Consulting, Middletown, Maryland.
- o 2004. *Dear Liza* by Sydney Banks is published by Lone Pine Publishing.
- o 2004. *Slowing Down to the Speed of Love* by Joseph Bailey is published by McGraw-Hill.

- o 2004. *O.K. Forever: A Book of Hope* by Helen Neal-Ali is published by Life Changing Consulting, Tampa, Florida. [Note: This book is republished in 2007.]

- March 2005. The "Second Chance" program begins in the Hillsborough Correctional Institution in Tampa, Florida, conducted by the Vantage Consulting Group (Chip and Jan Chipman). [Note: This occurs as a result of Syd Banks being contacted and touched by an inmate the Chipmans met while conducting staff training at Tampa Crossroads, a women's transition house. Syd asks Chip and Jan to visit her in prison, where she asks if they can start a class there. Syd strongly encourages them to "share a spiritual understanding of the Principles" with inmates. With help from Reese Coppage's charitable foundation the Second Chance program serves hundreds of inmates and is made mandatory when the prison Chaplain sees its impact on inmates. The Warden then has them provide in-depth training to all corrections staff, which impacts how staff interact with inmates. As some inmates move out to work release programs, they spread the word about Sydney Banks, the Three Principles and the Second Chance program. As a result, additional Second Chance classes begin in major correctional programs including a Florida State work release program, a large Pinellas county drug and alcohol treatment center with Goodwill Industries. The Chipmans also teach a Second Chance class for youthful offenders in the Hillsborough County Jail. Additional drug and alcohol rehabilitation programs start by trainers developed during the Second Chance program which, in turn, offer "train the trainer" opportunities for Second Chance graduates returning to the community who wish to give back.]

- Summer 2005. YES (Youth Empowered for Success) of Tucson, Arizona takes on Health Realization as the foundation for its five-day summer Teen Institute (TI), sponsored by Community Partnership of Southern Arizona (CPSA) (the Regional Behavioral Health Authority for five counties), which adopts Health Realization as a basis for its substance abuse prevention programs. [Note: This comes about as a result of The Tucson Resiliency Initiative Coordinator, Pam Parrish, initiating a two-day Health Realization workshop conducted by Jack Pransky in August 2002. She then transfers to CPSA in September 2004, as CSPA develops YES, a youth leadership and community development project in which high school students work with school staff to create a positive school climate, and take back what they learn at the TI to their schools and communities. Youth TI participants become mentors and paid staff for subsequent TIs. (As of this chronology YES celebrates its 10th anniversary, and past youth participants comprise 80% of TI leaders and staff.) In addition, in January 2005 CPSA hosts a two-day Health Realization training, which leads in April 2005 to a long-term professional training in Tucson, conducted by Jack Pransky. From these trainings Diana Jiminez-Young takes Health Realization into Child & Family Resources Inc., and Annamaria Flannigan and Anne Rego take it into Southeastern Arizona Behavioral Health Services (SEABHS).]

- October 1-2, 2005. Syd Banks seminar, "Unlocking the Mystical Secrets of Mind, Consciousness, and Thought" is held in Richmond, B.C.
- 2005. Judith Sedgeman begins the first on-line public course on the Three Principles, a Continuing Education course offered through West Virginia University Distance Education.

Publications:
- o 2005. "Parenting with Heart" by Kathy Marshall is a booklet put out by the School District of the Menomonie Area, Menomonie, Wisconsin.
- o 2005. "Health Realization/Innate Health: Can a Quiet Mind and Positive Feeling State Be Accessible Over the Lifespan Without Stress Relief Techniques?" by Judith Sedgeman is published in *Medical Science Monitor*, 11, 47-52.
- o 2005. "A Principle-Based Psychology of School Violence Prevention" by Thomas Kelley, Roger C. Mills and Rita Shuford is published in the *Journal of School Violence,* 4, 2, 47-73.
- o 2005. "Sustainable Community Change: A New Paradigm for Leadership in Community Revitalization Efforts" by Roger C. Mills is published in the *National Civic Review*, 94(1), 9-16.
- o 2005. "Mental Health and Prospective Police Professionals" is published in *Policing: An International Journal of Police Management and Strategies*, 28(1), 6-29
- o 2005. "Natural Resilience and Innate Mental Health" by Thomas Kelley is published in *American Psychologist*, 60(3), 265.
- o 2005. "Resilience in Our Schools: Discovering Mental Health and Hope from the Inside-Out" by Kathy Marshall appears in D. L. White, M. K. Faber, and B. C. Glenn, (Eds.), *Proceedings of Persistently Safe Schools 2005*. Washington, D.C.: Hamilton Fish Institute, George Washington University, for U. S.

Department of Justice, Office of Juvenile Justice and Delinquency Prevention. [Note: This was a federally funded national conference. The solicited presentation outlines a new prevention perspective with Principles for Health Realization grounded in resilience research.]

o   2005. *The Enlightened Gardener Revisited: A Wise Old Gardener Teaches Life's Principles of Mind, Consciousness and Thought* by Sydney Banks is published by Lone Pine Publishing.

o   2005. *Somebody Should Have Told Us!: Simple Truths for Living Well* by Jack Pransky is published by Burrell, Inc., and subsequently revised and published in 2011 by CCB Publishing, B.C., Canada. [Note: In 2012 this book is translated into Spanish by Antonio Gomez Molero and edited by Gabriela Maldonado-Montano as *Los Tres Principios*, and in 2014 into Italian by Alessandro Saramin as *Qualcuno Avrebbe Dovuto Dirtello!*, with versions in French and Dutch by Veronique Pivetta, in German by Katja Symons, in Russian by Maria Dunaeva, and also coming in Danish by Mette Louise Holland and in Swedish.]

o   2005. *Wisdom for Life: Three Principles for Well-Being* by Elsie Spittle is published by Lone Pine Publishing.

o   2005. *The Spark Inside: A Special Book for Youth* by Ami Chen Mills-Naim is published by Lone Pine Publishing.

o   2005. *On the High Wire: How to Survive Being Promoted* by Robert W. Gunn and Betsy Raskin Gullickson is published by AB.C.-CLIO. [Note: "At the heart of the book is the notion that productive and fulfilling management is not simply a collection of skills and techniques, but a mindset," although this book is not primarily Principles-based.]

• 2006. The Army Aquisition Corps Executive Leadership Development program for colonels and one and two-star generals includes the Three Principles as a core theme, designed and taught by Aaron Turner, Barry Frew and Jeanne Frew. [Note: This program runs until 2013.]

• February 23, 2006. Syd Banks gives a talk for women from Chip and Jan Chipman's Second Chance Program at Hillsborough Correctional Institute. [Note: On February 24 Syd makes a surprise appearance at a Second Chance session in a prison classroom and on the 27th makes a second surprise appearance; and on September 8 Syd gives a talk for the women from the Second Chance Program at Hillsborough Correctional Institute.]

- July 2006. The Tikun Centre of London, England, a not for profit organization takes on Innate Health/Well-Being through Three Principles as the means to help people find their own well-being. [Note: This effort is initiated by Rabbi Shaul Rosenblatt who becomes exposed to the Three Principles by Pransky and Associates in 2002. Tikun exists to provide education focused on the Jewish community but open to everyone and based on the ancient Jewish mission on being a shining moral example of responsibility to improve their world.]

- October 2006. A Kansas Health Realization Long-Term Professional Training (LTT) conducted by Jack Pransky and Diane McMillen begins in Topeka, Kansas. [Note: Included are staff from Shawnee County Prevention and Recovery Services (PARS), Washburn University students of Dr. McMIllen, and community human services professionals. This stems from a day-long training for PARS in March 2005. A participant in the LTT offers Health Realization-based alcohol and drug prevention groups to Topeka public housing residents; the Topeka Housing Authority (THA) social services director wants to know what methods she is using to help residents become more calm and clear-headed. Dr. McMillen meets with the director of THA, John Johnston, and provides training and consultation to THA, involving students in presentations and running groups in public housing resident halls. Jack Pransky, Cynthia Stennis and Barbara Glaspie are brought in for training; later 20 Topeka area Social Services Professionals participate in a five-month LTT June-October, 2008, with Jack Pransky and Diane McMillen. In March, 2009, a 5-month LTT for Parents as Teachers staff from USD 501 and social services professionals is held by Diane and Melinda Kline, who also run trainings in Wichita, Kansas, where Pastor David Fulton subsequently creates many Three Principles-related efforts.]

- October 21-23, 2006. Syd Banks holds a special invitation seminar in Richmond, B.C.

Publications:

- o 2006. "The Effect of Health Realization/Innate Health Psycho-Educational Seminar on Stress and Anxiety in HIV-Positive Patients" by Judith Sedgeman and A. Sarwari is published in *Medical Science Monitor*, 12(10), 397-399.
- o 2006. "Bringing Hope: A conversation with Kathy Marshall" by C. Auer with S. Blumberg is Chapter 7 of *Parenting a Child*

> with *Sensory Processing Disorder: A Family Guide to Understanding and Supporting Your Sensory-Sensitive Child* by, S. Oakland, CA: New Harbinger Publications.
>
> o 2006. *Life Happened Here* by Marilyn Wendler is published by InnerCircle Publishing of Yakima, Washington.

- March 31, 2007. Syd Banks talks to the Second Chance graduation class at Goodwill Industries substance abuse rehabilitation and work release program in St. Petersburg, Florida, where Chip and Jan Chipman establish a Second Chance program.
- April 2007. The *3 Principles-Building Resiliency in Children and Youth* program/curriculum is developed by Quinn Cashion (Vosburgh) for Jessie's Hope Society, a provincial non-profit organization of Vancouver, B.C., as one of their initiatives to prevent eating disorders. [Note: The focus of this 10-week program is to reach students in schools (mostly in grades 5-6, but also grades 1-10). Quinn begins a Train the Trainers program for this curriculum and offers workshops for parents, where within a 3-year period about 700 people come through the program. Jasmine Alexander conducts an independent, controlled research study on the efficacy of this curriculum for her Master's Thesis both for high schoolers, age 15-18, in San Jose, California, and elementary school students age 10-12 in Des Moines, Iowa. Significant positive effects are found, which later develops into a research paper (see publications 2014; papers under review.) Quinn gives a speech on this program at the March 2009 Federal (Canadian) Mental Health Commission conference in Toronto, Ontario.]
- April 17, 2007. Syd Banks speaks at a reception held for him at Macdonald Training Center, a not for profit organization serving people with disabilities in Tampa, Florida. [Note: At the time Chip and Jan Chipman of Vantage Consulting Group are training the staff in the Three Principles. The event is also attended by not for profit leaders and staff from the Tampa Bay area who are trained in the Principles by Vantage Consulting Group.]
- October 19-20, 2007. Syd Banks offers a seminar in San Jose, California.
- October 27, 2007. Syd Banks talks to all the residents at Goodwill Industries, St. Petersburg, Florida. [Note: A video is made of this talk and of interviews with staff and residents. Earlier that day, Syd also makes a surprise visit to a Second Chance class there.]

- November 14, 2007. *The Enlightened Gardener* by Syd Banks is showcased in a drug court in Pinellas County, Florida. [Note: Before Syd's October seminar in San Jose several graduates of the Second Chance Program at Goodwill Industries, now on probation, are given dispensation by the judge to travel outside Florida to attend the conference in California. Because the judge had been so moved by their changes since they began the Second Chance program she asks them to take pictures of the event with cameras donated by court staff so they can do a presentation on their return. The probationers do their presentation at their next drug court session on Nov. 14, telling about their experience at the conference, including being asked by Syd to present on stage. The judges give a heartfelt talk to the whole drug court session about the changes she has seen in those attending Second Chance. She holds up a copy of *The Enlightened Gardener* for all drug court charges to see, saying how we could all learn from this book.]

- 2007. The Cypress Center for Well-Being (The Cypress Initiative) begins in Tampa, Florida as a result of Chip and Jan Chipman's work and Reese Coppage's charitable foundation, with Syd Banks' "unwavering support and guidance."

- 2007. Jonathan Pounder begins and directs Six Dimensions Counseling, an adult outpatient chemical dependency treatment program in Minneapolis, Minnesota "based on the Three Principles: Mind, Consciousness, and Thought." [Note: In 2014 Josh Augst takes over as Director.]

- 2007. Linda Quiring reports that Syd comes to her and says, "I'm not going to be around forever, and someday my story will have to be told, and you are the only one that can do it!" [Note: Linda assumes this means the early years on Salt Spring Island, with which she has direct experience.]

Publications:

- o 2007. "An Examination of the Principle-Based Leadership Trainings and Business Consultations of a Group Private Practice" by Alan Roy is a doctoral dissertation through the Massachusetts School of Professional Psychology, Newton, Massachusetts.

- o 2007. "Leadership Training, Leadership Style and Organizational Effectiveness" by Cheryl Bond is a doctoral dissertation through the Boston University School of Education, Boston, Massachusetts.

- o January 20, 2007. "'I don't read... I write': Writer-Philosopher Sydney Banks Has a Huge Following, But He Rarely Reads," by D. Todd is published in the *Vancouver Sun*. 2-4. [Note: This interview is reported by the Vancouver Sun to be Syd Banks' first and only interview with the mainstream media.]

- o 2007. "Comparison of Health Realization and 12-Step Treatment in Women's Residential Substance Abuse Treatment Programs" by K. Banerjee, Mark Howard, Kristen Mansheim and M. Beattie is published in *The American Journal of Drug and Alcohol Abuse*, 33: 207–215.

- o 2007. "A Theoretical Framework for Using Health Realization to Reduce Stress and Improve Coping in Refugee Communities" by Linda Halcon, C. L. Robertson, K.A. Monsen and Cindi Claypatch is published in the *Journal of Holistic Nursing*, 25(3), 186-194.

- o 2007. "Keys to Wellness: Resilience, Spirituality, and Purpose" by Kathy Marshall is published in *Wellness Works*, 1, (2), 12-13 (Spring).

- o 2007. "Toward a Peaceable Paradigm: Seeing Innate Wellness in Communities and Impacts on Urban Violence and Crime" by Roger Mills and Ami Chen Mills-Naim is published in *National Civic Review*, 94 (4), 45-55.

- o 2007. "Finding the Strength Within: Helping Refugees Deal with Stress" by N. Guiguere is published in *Minnesota Nursing,* Spring/Summer, 7-9.

- o 2007. "The Relationship between Social Decision Making and Health Realization Program among Delinquent and Detained Youth" by Brett Johnson Solomon is published in *The Journal of Juvenile Court, Community, and Alternative School Administrators of California*. Vol. 2007, Spring. 46-56.

- January 2008. Syd Banks strongly encourages people to no longer use the name "Health Realization." [Note: This is much to the chagrin of some prevention and human services practitioners and researchers who had worked hard to build this name recognition in the prevention and human services fields. On January 11, 2008 Roger Mills sends a letter to Health Realization practitioners clarifying why he is requesting a name change: "... I feel that inadvertently, in the quest for legitimization by the fields in which we work, I and others created a 'form' and then got stuck there. To me, it now appears that we were trying too hard to get an understanding of the principles out, and did not recognize that the world was taking our efforts as just another 'strength-' or asset-based 'model' offering less than what the principles explain about the nature of life. The name Health Realization originated with our work in communities and schools. Health Realization is now out in the research, but not purely as the principles of Mind, Consciousness and Thought."]

- May 17, 2008. Syd gives a talk for all residents at Goodwill Industries in St. Petersberg, Florida.

- Spring 2008. A grant is awarded to the Center for Sustainable Change to initiate the National Community Resiliency Project (NCRP) by the W.K. Kellogg Foundation, to fund Three Principles-based projects in low-income communities in Des Moines, Iowa, Lakewood and Charlotte, North Carolina, and the Mississippi Delta region. [Note: Ami Chen Mills-Naim is Project Director, followed by Dave Nichols in 2012. The grant is renewed and funded for four years. In Lakewood, Dave Nichols, Director of the Lakewood Community Development Corporation (CDC) in Charlotte, North Carolina, after reading *Modello* then speaking with Roger Mills, Ami Chen Mills-Naim and Mary Martin of the Des Moines project, begins implementing a Three Principles approach in the Lakewood area, exposing up to 75 residents, then greater Charlotte community members and agencies and schools in neighboring communities. Larry Williams, Director of the Delta Citizens Alliance in Greenville, Mississippi, meets Roger Mills and Ami Chen Mills-Naim at a Kellogg Foundation seminar in San Francisco and begins a Three Principles program in the Delta region. Williams introduces the Three Principles at the first annual DCA conference, with a workshop presented by Ami Chen Mills-Naim, Cynthia Stennis and Lloyd Fields from Modello. This work inspires Gloria Dickerson, formerly with the W.K. Kellogg Foundation, to integrate the Principles into her newly-founded non-profit, We2gether 4 Change, working with youth "at risk" in the Delta region. Principles-based work there continues as of this publication date and inspires interest of the Common Health Action Agency in Mississippi, which in the spring of 2014 conducts a two-day parenting workshop incorporating the Principles.]

- August 14-17, 2008. The first session of "The Three Principles School," founded by Chip Chipman and Elsie Spittle "at the request of Sydney Banks to ensure that the teachings of the Three Principles as taught by Sydney Banks continue," is held in Victoria, B.C. [Note: Other sessions of the School taught by Chip Chipman and Elsie Spittle and offered by the Three Principles Foundation occur November 13-16, 2008, March 26-29, 2009, March 24-27, 2011, Sept. 29-Oct. 2, 2011, May 31-June

3, 2012, November 8-11, 2012, May 30-June 2, 2013, November 7-10, 2013, June 5-8, 2014, and continue to be held.]

- November 13-16, 2008. Syd Banks speaks at the Three Principles School in Victoria, B.C.
- December 2008. Sydney Banks contacts Keith Blevens, Ph.D. and asks him to write a book. [Note: Syd gives his last unpublished writings to this project but states it will be Keith's book. Syd writes an endorsement for its cover. They work together on this project for the next several weeks. The writings begin with an interview between Syd and Keith that subsequently expands to include the rest of the text.]

Publications:
  - 2008. "Effects of a Mind-Consciousness-Thought (MCT) Intervention on Stress and Well-Being in Freshmen Nursing Students" by Judith Sedgeman is an unpublished doctoral dissertation through West Virginia University, Morgantown, West Virginia.
  - 2008. "Principle-Based Correctional Counseling: Teaching Health versus Treating Illness" by Thomas Kelley is published in *Applied Psychology in Criminal Justice*, 4(2), 182-205.
  - 2008. "Three Principles Psychology: Applications in Leadership Development and Coaching" by Craig Polsfuss and Alexandre Ardichvili is published in *Advances in Developing Human Resources*, 10 (5), 671-685.

  - 2008. *Unleashing Genius: Leading Yourself, Teams and Corporations* by Paul David Walker is published by Morgan James Publishing.

- March 26-29, 2009. Sydney Banks gives his last public talk at The Three Principles School in Victoria, B.C.
- 2009. Michael Neill, a well-known international coach, Hay House author and radio host, begins building the Three Principles into his Supercoach Academy. [Note: By 2010 the Three Principles becomes one of its modules, and in 2011 he creates Coaching from the Inside-Out, purely based on the Principles, to which the entire Supercoach Academy evolves. Michael Neill and Jamie Smart, both well-known coaches and trainers of Neuro-Linguistic Programming (NLP) who switch to the Three Principles, bring greater numbers of people into the Three Principles than almost

anyone. As an example, in Sweden alone, a number of well-known Swedish coaches shift to the Three Principles, such as Anders Haglund, David Andersson, Tommy Olausson, Börje Olsson, Rasmus Carlsson, Martin Järnland, Peter Karlén, Svetlana Golubeva and others (most from Michael Neill); Peter and Svetlana in turn introduce the Principles in Russia.]

- May 2009. Syd hosts in his bedroom approximately one week before his death a group of several Israeli veterans, wounded and with PTSD, who have been profoundly affected by his work. [Note: These 21-23-year-old veterans tell Syd they thought their lives were over before they learned this understanding. As Judy Banks says, "As Syd and the vets interacted, the mutual respect was enormous and delightful. The air in that room crackled, the energy was so high." Rabbi Chaim Levine and David and Callie Bekhor help these veterans get there.]

- May 2009. In Syd's hospital room, Syd asks businessmen David Bekhor and Pritam Singh to establish an organization to spread the Principles globally; a major element of which would be to bring his books and recorded materials to a major publisher for world-wide distribution. To Chip and Elsie he says, "You run the school."

- May 25, 2009. Sydney Banks passes away.

- July 18, 2009. A memorial service is held for Syd in Victoria. About 200 people attend.

- July and September 2009. Pritam Singh and David Bekhor host two small gatherings of key people in Vermont to discuss future direction, with the charge: "We can't let this die with Syd." [Note: Invited attendees are Judy Banks, Cally Bekhor, Keith Blevens, Dick Bozoian, Erika Bugbee, Cathy Casey, Jan Chipman, Chip Chipman, Don Donovan, Kevin Gleason, Mara Gleason, Christine Heath, Annie Johnston, Simi Johnston, Ed Lemon, Chaim Levine, Roger Mills, Clytee Mills, Ami Chen Mills-Naim, Linda Pettit, Bill Pettit, George Pransky, Linda Pransky, Linda Ramus, Pritam Singh, Rita Shuford, Elsie Spittle, Kara Stamback, Aaron Turner and Sandy Krot. Many options are discussed, including a "Mind Café" to be held in Key West where various practitioners would reside for periods of time and people would fly in to be with them. It subsequently leads to the development of what becomes the Three Principles Global Community.]

- June 24, 2009. Dr. Diane McMillen and Melinda Kline kick off a Topeka Housing Authority (THA) project, which begins a year-long project with THA staff and residents.

- November 12, 2009. The Three Principles Global Community is incorporated originally as Understanding the Human Experience, Inc. and receives its tax exempt (501(c)(3)) status March 18, 2010. Don

Donovan assumes leadership in a voluntary capacity. [Note: Its stated purpose: "The Three Principles Global Community (3PGC) is a non-profit organization that is committed to bringing an understanding of *The Three Principles* to people throughout the world. Our mission is to increase the number of people who are teaching, sharing and learning *The Principles*, and to enhance and facilitate professional collaboration in this field."]

- December 2009. Rudi and Jenny Kennard from the U.K., make a trip to the U.S. and begin filming for what becomes "Three Principles Movies." [Note: Touched by their own insights and with the hope to create world-wide accessibility, Rudi and Jenny commit their time and their own resources to film interviews with key Three Principles practitioners. They begin in Vermont with Jack Pransky, followed by Keith Blevens, Dicken Bettinger, Linda Pransky, George Pransky, Sandy Krot, Aaron Turner, Mara Gleason, Ami Chen Mills-Naim, and then many more over the years. They create a resource that benefits many people across the globe.]

Publications:
- o August 3, 2009. Sydney Banks Obituary by Douglas Todd appears in the *Vancouver Sun*, commemorating Sydney Banks' life. http://blogs.vancouversun.com/2009/08/03/sydney-banks-obituary-full-version/
- o 2009. "Exploring the True Nature of Internal Resilience: A View from the Inside-Out," by Jack Pransky and Diane P. McMillen appears as a chapter in the well-respected social work book, *The Strengths Perspective in Social Work Practice,* Fifth Edition, by Dennis Saleebey. [Note: This chapter is substantially revised for the 6th Edition (see 2013 publications).]
- o 2009. "State-of-Mind as the Master Competency for High-Performance Leadership" by Craig Polsfuss and Alexandre Ardichvili is published in *Organizational Development Journal,* Fall, 27: 3.

- o 2009. *Fearproof Your Life* by Joseph Bailey is published by Conari Press.

- February 2010. Three Principles Movies, created by Rudi and Jenny Kennard, goes on-line with the first version of its website, which becomes the first time anyone, anywhere in the world can access a comprehensive resource on the Three Principles, including research, footage from TV shows, interviews (multi-language) and transformational stories. [Note: Since its beginnings through the date of this chronology it has literally millions of views and opens the understanding to a much wider audience, and completely for free. 3P Movies offers teleconferences beginning in 2011, the first being Dicken Bettinger, and webinars via computer beginning in 2013 for "immersion retreat" participants.]

- 2010. David Lewis begins the "Foundation Thinking" programme for students at the distance learning/home-based "the Open Wānanga" of Te Wānanga o Aotearoa in New Zealand. [Note: The programme is in two forms: 1) a set of 42 cards with an idea about thinking on one side and on the other a short story to illustrate the idea, with some thinking exercises; 2) a paperback book version of the cards. These are included in four home-based programmes as a resource to raise the life skills of the students. It goes out to approximately 2,400 students every year and is part of staff induction training across Te Wānanga. In the first three years 350 staff are exposed to the cards and a presentation.]
- May 3, 2010. Roger Mills passes away. [Note: Roger leaves behind a legacy of being one of the first two mental health professionals to turn what Syd Banks was talking about spiritually into a viable psychology, and the first to model applying this understanding for community empowerment and prevention.]
- May 2010. Tikun holds its first Annual Conference, "New Horizons: A Vision for the Principles of Wellbeing" in London, England. [Note: Attendance 180 people.]
- September 23-25, 2010. The Three Principles Global Community (3PGC) holds an organizational conference in Key West, Florida, at the Tennessee Williams Fine Arts Center at Florida Keys Community College, with lodging at Pritam Singh's Parrot Key Hotel and Resort.
- 2010. Elizabeth Alameda, a retired Santa Clara County Probation Manager, begins work with San Benito County delivering Domestic Violence classes, establishes Connecting Principles, and expands services in the county to serve "perpetrators" and "victims." [Note: Elizabeth's classes become approved and listed by the State of California in its resource database.]
- 2010. The "Enlightened Success Monthly Mastery Series" is a series of extensive Three Principles practitioner audio interviews conducted by Jamie Smart with Aaron Turner, George Pransky, Linda Pransky, Jack Pransky, Dicken Bettinger, Keith Blevens, Ami Chen Mills-Naim, Mara Gleason and Sandy Krot. [Note: Later interviews are conducted with Michael Neill, Cathy Casey, Linda Ramus, Shaul Rosenblatt, Terry

Rubenstein, Sue Pankiewicz, Rita Shuford, Garret Kramer, Cheryl Bond and Kimberley Porter. This series is originally put out under Jamie's NLP company, Salad, Ltd., but when Jaime sells that company the interviews become temporarily unavailable, while being edited to conform to his new company, Jamie Smart, Ltd. Meanwhile, Jamie shifts his focus to what he calls the principles of Innate Thinking®.]

Publications:

- o 2010. "Evaluating Health Realization for Coping Among Refugee Women" by Linda L. Halcon, C. L. Robertson and K.A. Monsen is published in the *Journal of Loss and Trauma,* 15, 408-425.

- o 2010. *Our True Identity. . . Three Principles* by Elsie Spittle is published through 3 Principles for Human Development. Inc., Salt Spring Island, B.C., with CreateSpace Independent Publishing Platform.
- o 2010. *Success is a Mind Game: How to Improve Consistency and Results in Golf and Business* by Steve Sharpley is published by Channel View Publications.

- March 2011. The 3 Principles Professional Institute is launched in London, England, with its first cohort of students, by Aaron Turner and Mara Gleason. [Note: Inaugural graduates include Chantal Burns, Janet Lindsay and Julian Fraser. In March 2013, The 3 Principles Professional Institute becomes The One Thought Institute.]
- March 25, 2011. Elese Coit's radio show, "A New Way To Handle Absolutely Everything" becomes a solely Three Principles-based broadcast. [Note: This show originally begins in 2008 on Contact Talk Radio, Friday mornings on KRWM in Seattle, iTunes, and internationally, and begins transitioning to the Three Principles in January 2011. The show runs until April 2012 and, according to CTR monthly statistics, over ¼ million people subscribe to its iTunes podcast. In June 2011 Ami Chen Mills-Naim joins as co-host until April 2012. In September 2011 the show becomes sponsored by the Center For Sustainable Change, a new show hosted by Ami in this time slot. Ami then takes over the Friday radio slot independently with "On the Front Porch with Ami Chen: Spiritual Dialogues for the 21st Century," also a Principles-based radio show, sponsored by Green Power Installers and The Gulf Breeze Recovery Center. By 2014 this show gathers nearly 200,000 global subscribers. All above show archives may be listened to and

downloaded free at: http://www.elesecoit.com/radio-archive.html or iTunes podcast: http://itunes.apple.com/podcast/a-new-way-to-handle-absolutely/ id294291371 In January 2013 Elese teams with Gabriela Maldonado-Montano to form TrueChange Consultants.]

- May 2011. Janet Lindsay begins the first-in-Europe Three Principles group work programme for female offenders in Birmingham, England, supervised by Warwickshire Probation Trust, with excellent results.
- December 4-6, 2011. Tikun, in association with One Thought, holds its Second Annual Conference, "Roots of Potential" in London, England. This conference becomes the U.K. equivalent of the Annual Three Principles conferences. [Note: Attendance 300 people.]

Publications:
  o 2011. "Thought Recognition and Psychological Well-Being: An Empirical Test of Principle-Based Correctional Counseling" by Thomas Kelley is published in *Counseling & Psychotherapy Research*, 23, 112-123.

  o 2011. *Stillpower: Excellence with Ease in Sports and Life* by Garrett Kramer is published by Atria Books/Beyond Words.
  o 2011. *Realizing Life. Inspiration in Verse: Insights on the 3 Principles as Taught by Sydney Banks* by Marilyn Wendler is published by Bookstand Publishing, Morgan Hill, California.

- January 2012. Chantal Burns introduces the first Three Principles training to social care (social workers) in the U.K., within a large county council. [Note: With the support of Linda Ramus, Chantal conducts the first formal evaluation of a U.K.-based Three Principles training demonstrating how the workers' 3P understanding generated statistically significant changes in wellbeing, resilience and improved performance. By 2009 Chantal had shifted her ten-year-old Star Consultancy business to a Principles-based business. In March 2012 Chantal introduces the Principles to Japan where she teaches entrepreneurs, coaches and therapists through a large Japanese training company in Tokyo.]
- June 2012. Elisabeth Karlehav of Sweden begins the on-line "The Three Principles Weekly" to create easy access to articles and blogposts on the Three Principles. [Note: As her concept of the Weekly becomes clearer Elisabeth aims it to "host" articles and blogposts from the most experienced 3P facilitators. As of 2014, while still operational,

Elisabeth stops editing or monitoring it and has only a few blog or website streams tied to experienced 3P practitioners.]

- June 2012. Elaine Hilides begins the first weekly Three Principles wellbeing group for people in recovery from Drug and Alcohol addiction and mental illness diagnosis in the U.K. through Kingston RISE (Recovery Initiative Social Enterprise). [Note: This is in collaboration with RISE, Kingston University, and the Royal Borough of Kingston.]

- July 2012. Steve Adair and Tony Fiedler facilitate the first Three Principles programme in the U.K. for people experiencing homelessness, "Less Stress, More Joy," held in Brighton and Hove, England. [Note: These combined cities have an above average homeless population, and course participants also experience mental ill-health, criminal convictions and substance misuse. Over the course, participants report positive changes in seeking employment, finding and setting up tenancy, in substance misuse and in managing anxiety, and they take it upon themselves to hold follow-up gatherings.]

- August 3-5, 2012. "Space for Connection" is started by Sue Pankewicz, Sheela Masand and Katja Symons in Colchester and Marks Tey, England as a way for the Three Principles community members to connect and deepen their understanding, without the structure of a conference. [Note: Additional sessions are held August 2-4, 2013, February 28-March 2, 2014, August 8-10, 2014, all at the Best Western Hotel in Marks Tey, with the intent to continue regularly.]

- 2012. Ami Chen Mills-Naim and Chantal Burns begin work on the R. C. Mills Memorial Library through the Center for Sustainable Change to disseminate material relevant in support of "the Three Principles and Truth in general, as related to Dr. Roger C. Mills, Ami Chen Mills-Naim and close colleagues." [Note: The Library is where to go to find the many unpublished original papers of Dr. Roger Mills, and includes original works, letters and custom audio tapes by Sydney Banks that he sent to both Roger and Ami. As of the date of this chronology this Library is a work in progress, with limited access, although future work will be scanning and getting documents online through CSC. To gain access please email Ami directly about intent and purpose to visit the Library. Copies can be made of documents, but some documents will not be allowed off premises. A donation to the CSC is requested to visit.]

- November 5, 2012. The Three Principles Global Community (3PGC) launches its website. [Note: It includes a listing of 3P practitioners (who fit certain criteria), webinars, blogs and more.]

- November 2012. Tikun, in association with One Thought, holds its Third Annual Conference: "The Missing Link - Unlocking The Simplicity of Life" in London, England. [Note: Attendance: 400 people].
- 2012. "The Principles of Transformation in Recovery," a DVD by Joe Bailey is published [Note: Joe Bailey also puts out about 20 audio tapes on a variety of topics.]

Publications:

- o 2012. "Mindfulness as a Potential Means of Attenuating Anger and Aggression for Prospective Criminal Justice Professionals" by Thomas Kelley and Eric Lambert is published in the journal, *Mindfulness*, 3(4), 261-274.

- o 2012. *Do Nothing! Stop Looking, Start Living: A Simple Way to a Fantastic Life* by Damian Mark Smyth, is printed by Bell and Bain.
- o 2012. *101 New Pairs of Glasses: Essays on Perspective and Why Seeing is Everything* by Elese Coit is published by Las Brisas Publishing, Ventura, California.
- o 2012. *Up the Mood Elevator: Your Guide to Success Without Stress* by Larry Senn is published by Larry Senn. [Note: This book only has a part dedicated to the Three Principles.]

- 2013. Innate Health Connection, 3 Principles for Transformative Solutions (IHC) is a nonprofit organization formed by a small group of Santa Clara County-certified Three Principles teachers (including retired Three Principles Division Director, Linda Ramus) after the Three Principles Division of Drug and Alcohol Services closes its doors and stops teaching classes. [Note: For more information, see Part III C.]
- 2013. The Gulf Breeze Recovery treatment center in Pensacola, Florida becomes the first inpatient addictions program based solely on the Three Principles, founded and directed by Barnett Gilmer. [Note: Joe Bailey is program design consultant and trainer of the staff. Debbie Trent becomes Counseling Director and Leona Hamrick Aftercare Specialist.]
- February 10, 2013. Mark Jones (U.K.) begins and hosts a Blog Talk Radio show, "Ice Cream 4 the Soul," consisting of interviews with 3P practitioners. [Note: As of the date of this chronology, shows are available on iTunes. www.icecream4thesoul.com].

- May 2013. Ian Watson launches Insight Space as a vehicle for Three Principles work [Note: This is notable in that his efforts spread the Three Principles into the countries of the Czech Republic, Finland, Croatia, Serbia, Bulgaria, Greece and Egypt. Ian begins his three principles consultation work in 2011.]
- June 2013. Tikun, in association with One Thought, holds its Fourth Annual Conference, The Annual Principles conference in the U.K., "Change Through Understanding." [Note: Attendance: 420 people].
- September 2013. 3PGC holds its "First Annual" Conference in St. Paul, Minnesota at the St. Paul Hotel.
- September 2013. Erika Bugbee, Kara Stamback and George Pransky of Pransky and Associates create *Insight: The Principles of a Fulfilling and High-Performance Life*, the first public online course on the Principles. [Note: The course consists of eight multi-media video lessons accessible through a private online learning platform. Its vision: to develop a way to spread the Principles that is affordable, instantly available to people around the world, and achieves the level of depth and impact of in-person programs. Lessons include a mix of lectures, animation, graphic illustrations and a private online discussion forum. The lessons build on each other and include interviews with some top practitioners in the Principles field. Each one-hour lesson requires 40-60 hours of preparation and production. As of this chronology, the course has been viewed by 250 people in 19 countries.]
- September 13, 2013. Tomas Lydol begins and hosts "What if life is WOW!" radio show based on the Three Principles, which the show states is "the biggest discovery of mankind!", on Radio WOW! Blogtalk radio, out of Stockholm Sweden. [Note: Shows can be found on www.radiowow.se.]
- November 10-14, 2013. Sheela Masand hosts the first Three Principles global telesummit on "Transforming Communities from the Inside-Out," co-sponsored by the Center for Sustainable Change, where 19 Three Principles speakers over five days speak about various aspects of the title. [Note: Speakers include Ami Chen Mills-Naim, A.M. Stewart, Bill Pettit, Cynthia Stennis, Courtney Alexander, Dave Nichols, Debbie Trent, Ed Lemon, Gabriela Maldonado-Montano, Jack Pransky, Janet Lindsay, Joe Gonzales, Kimberly Porter, Linda Sandal Pettit, Liz Alameda, Nate Moore, Steve Adair, Tony Fiedler and Wil Montano. A second show is held in November 2014 with other speakers.]
- 2013. Tom Kelley and Jack Pransky collaborate on creating a measurable "path" from Three Principles exposure to Improved Mental Health. With it they create a "Three Principles Understanding

Inventory (3PUI)" instrument to be used in conjunction with standardized psychological measures, with the intent to have the Three Principles community use the 3PUI as a consistent means of measuring effectiveness of Three Principles programs and build a body of research data helpful to the entire community. [Note: The 3PUI is tested at the 2013 Three Principles Conference, feedback is gathered from key players and participants. At the 2014 conference the 3PUI is finalized with assistance from Judy Sedgeman and Linda Ramus and is ready for use.]

- 2013. Dave Nichols, Executive Director of the Center for Sustainable Change receives the Martin Luther King Jr. Medallion Award for his work in CSC's National Community Resiliency Project, Charlotte, North Carolina.

Publications:

o 2013. "Principles for Realizing Health: A New Vision of Trauma and Human Resilience" by Thomas Kelley and Jack Pransky is published in the *Journal of Traumatic Stress Disorders and Treatment*, 2, 1. doi:10.4172/2324-8947.1000102

o 2013. "Exploring the True Nature of Internal Resilience: A View from the Inside-Out," by Jack Pransky and Diane P. McMillen appears as a chapter in the well-respected social work book, *The Strengths Perspective in Social Work Practice, 6th Edition*, by Dennis Saleebey, published by Pearson. [Note: This chapter is substantially revised and improved from the 2009, 5th Edition.]

o 2013. *What Is a Thought? (A Thought Is a Lot)*, a children's picture book by Jack Pransky and Amy Kahofer is published by Social Thinking Publishing, San Jose, California. [Note: A sequel, *What is Wisdom (And Where Do I Find It)?*, by these coauthors is awaiting publication as of the date of this chronology.]

o 2013. *Beyond Imagination – A New Reality Awaits* by Elsie Spittle is published through CreateSpace.

o 2013. *Clarity: Clear Mind, Better Performance, Bigger Results* by Jaime Smart is published by Capstone Publishing Ltd., Oxford, England.

o   2013. *The Inside Out Revolution* by Michael Neill is published by Hay House, London, England.

o   2013. *The Essential Curriculum: 21 Ideas for Developing a Positive and Optimistic culture* by Barbara Aust is published by CreateSpace.

o   2013. *Life Beyond Money: Living to Earn? Or Yearning to Live?* by Julian Freeman is published by 3P Publications as a Kindle e-book.

o   2013. *Social Anxiety Inside Out: How to Rise Above the Chatter and Live Life with Clarity* by Steve Light is published as a Kindle e-book.

o   2013. *The Gentle Path to Definitive Weight Loss* by Rachel Norwood is published as a Kindle e-book. [Note: The psychological aspects of this book are Three Principles-based.]

o   2013. *Mind-Fullness: The No-Diet Diet Book* by Elaine Hilides is published as a kindle e-book about diets and relationship with food from a Three Principles perspective.

o   2013. *Inner-Directed: Ten Keys to Fine Tune Your Gut Instincts* by Elese Coit is published by Las Brisas Publishing, Ventura, California. [Note: A copy is available free at www.truechangeconsultants.com/resources.]

- February 28, 2014. Jack Pransky embarks on a Three Principles European goodwill Tour, teaching the principles in England, France, Belgium, Denmark, Sweden, Germany, Switzerland, Italy, Spain, Portugal and Scotland over a two-month period.

- May 2014. Tikun and One Thought hold their Fifth Annual Conference: "Building Blocks for a New Foundation." [Note: Attendance: 550 people.]

- June 2014. A weekly Three Principles podcast begins by Lian Brook-Tyler (Hertfordshire, U.K.) and Jonathan Wilkinson (Yorkshire, U.K.) of Born Happy. [Note: The podcast is released Thursdays on http://www.bornhappy.co/podcast/ and is also on iTunes, in the top 5 for "happiness." https://itunes.apple.com/gb/podcast/id900114017.] Born Happy also features regular articles, 'fly on the wall' coaching sessions by highly regarded coaches and trainers, and a Principles-based "Happy School" course, as well as providing local and global meet-ups, forums and groups.]

- June 25, 2014. Michael Neill performs a Ted talk titled, "Why Aren't We Awesomer?" where he mentions the influence of Sydney Banks.
- September 2014. A weekly Three Principles radio show begins on Contact Talk Radio called "Waking Up: The Neuroscience of Awareness" by Jeanne Catherine-Gray of Divine Play, Charlottesville, Virginia. [Note: Divine Play, which opens in December 2011, evolves into solely a Three Principles training center, serving primarily women and their families and businesses, also with associates John Catherine-Gray and Jen Lucas. The radio show is aired before a live audience, Mondays, 9:00 AM U.S. Eastern Time, and found on http://ctrnetwork.com/profile/wakingup.]
- 2014. The Zetter Group in the U.K. agrees at their leadership retreat and publicly announces that "State of Mind" is a core company value. [Note: Aaron Turner and Mara Gleason's organization, One Thought Ltd. provide training since 2012, and, because of this value The Principles is made the central training in the company.]
- 2014. Brett Chitty establishes Three Principles Supermind as an on-line educational effort for new global learners to interact with experienced Three Principles teachers. [Note: Its purpose: to achieve real results in changing the world.]
- September 2014. Central Working, a U.K. business committed to developing start-ups and entrepreneurs as clients, and major corporations including Barclays and Microsoft, announces on its website partnership with One Thought. [Note: The partnership and announcement puts clarity of mind at the centre of business performance and the Principles at the heart of achieving clarity of mind. www.centralworking.com]

Publications:
- 2014. "Three Principles for Realizing Mental Health: A New Psycho-Spiritual View" by Jack Pransky and Thomas Kelley is published in the *Journal of Creativity in Mental Health*.
- 2014. "Principles for Realizing Resilience in Trauma Exposed Young Offenders: A Promising New Intervention for Juvenile Justice Professionals by Thomas Kelley, Jack Pransky and Judith Sedgeman is published in the *Journal of Child and Adolescent Trauma*.
- 2014. "A New Framework for Easy Effective and Sustainable Leadership Development" by Aaron Turner, and "What Determines State of Mind? by J. Holroyd, K. Brown and Aaron

Turner are two chapters in the social work leadership book, *Self Leadership: Building Personal Resilience and Relationships that Work within Health and Social Care,* edited by J. Holroyd, K. Brown. Bournemouth University, Learn to Care. Publication No. 28 ISBN 978-0-9572896-4-2.

o 2014. "Outside-In or Inside-Out: Understanding Spiritual Principles, or Depending on Techniques to Realize Improved Mindfulness/Mental Health" by Thomas Kelley, Jack Pransky and Eric Lambert is accepted by the *Journal of Spirituality in Mental Health*. [Note: This will likely have a 2015 publication date.]

o 2014. *Being Human: Essays on Thoughtmares, Bouncing Back, and Your True Nature* by Amy Johnson, Ph.D. is a self-published book.

o 2014. *State of Mind in the Classroom: Thought, Consciousness and the Essential Curriculum for Healthy Learning* by Ami Chen Mills-Naim and Roger Mills (posthumously) is self-published.

o 2014. *Instant Motivation: The Surprising Truth about What Really Drives Your Performance* by Chantal Burns is published by Pearson.

[Note: The following papers under review by peer-reviewed journals as of this publication date:]

o 2014. "A Path from Exposure to the Principles of Mind, Consciousness and Thought to Improved Mental Health," by Thomas Kelley, Jack Pransky and Eric Lambert is under review at the *Journal of Creativity in Mental Health*.

o 2014. "The Three Principles: A New View of Mindfulness and Mental Health associated with Mindfulness-Based Intervention" by Thomas Kelley and Jack Pransky is under review at the *Journal of Mental Health Counseling*.

o 2014. "Understanding Fundamental Causal Principles and Flourishing Mental Health: Will Positive Psychology Listen?" by Thomas Kelley, Jack Pransky and Eric Lambert is under review at *The Journal of Positive Psychology*.

- o 2014. "The Three Principles Building Resilience in Youth Program: An Empirical Test of a Promising New Intervention," by Thomas Kelley, Jasmine Alexander and Jack Pransky is under review at the *Journal of Adolescent Research*.
- o 2014. A pre-post controlled study is being undertaken as of this chronology through the Center for Sustainable Change: "Coming Home to Peace" with veterans experiencing PTSD, developed by Nate Moore, Program Manager, with assistance from Dave Nichols, Director CSC, and consultants William Pettit, Judith Sedgeman, Thomas Kelley and Jack Pransky

Editor's Note: It was my intention to end with 2014, and I do, except a groundbreaking event occurred in 2015 that seemed to bring it all full circle. I could not resist ending with this one.

- May 26, 2015. Jacquie Forde, founder and CEO of the Wellbeing Alliance, organizes a presentation titled, "Tackling Public Health Prevention from The Inside Out" for Members of the Scottish Parliament, the Scottish Government, Scottish charities and other health and public sector organisations. This event is chaired by Murdo Fraser, MSP, and conducted by herself, Dr. Jack Pransky, Dr. Aaron Turner, Chip and Jan Chipman and Elsie Spittle (and Syd Banks by video), as a first step in developing interest in public health and resiliency via the inside-out paradigm / State of Mind / the Three Principles. [Note: As part of this, Jacquie separately meets with a number of health committees within the Parliament to bring Three Principles understanding into the Scottish government and public health.] This event also serves to honour the continuing legacy of Sydney Banks and his achievements, and to bring the extended community of Syd back to his home town of Edinburgh, from whence he came.

Editor's Note: *It had been my idea to place the following comments on the back cover of this book. But no matter how careful I tried to be at explaining that these comments pertained only to the chronology section I became persuaded that it may give the wrong impression that they were meant for the entire book. George Pransky was so surprised at the appreciation that came in from so many of the key and long-time members of the Three Principles community that he suggested I add these as quotes at the end of the chronology. Placed here I wasn't so sure, but I accepted his suggestion. So I asked those who sent them if they had objections to their quotes and names being used, and only two or three raised objections, so those were removed. What follows is what came into me, unsolicited, from the rest. I admit it shows how supportive the Three Principles community is for this historical record. Plus, for me their responses are personally gratifying. I also find it somewhat interesting and amusing that the same words were used again and again to describe what people felt.*

Amazing job! Like you..., once I saw how much has been shared with the world, based on Syd's profound experience, I found the information stunning.
- Elsie Spittle, Co-Founder, Three Principles School, Salt Spring Island, BC, Canada

You are a genius. I cannot believe the magic you have done with this project. It is fantastic.
- Clytee Mills, Psychiatric Nurse Clinical Specialist, CA

Amazing what you and George have put together. Wow, great idea and job of capturing so much heartfelt work done over the years.
- Rita Shuford, Ph.D., Turning Corners Group, Kailua, HI

I have to congratulate you on an AMAZING undertaking! Well done! Historians in the future thank you.
- Judy Sedgeman, Ph.D., Three Principles Living, Bradenton, FL

I can't thank you enough for taking on this task!!
>	-	Dicken Bettinger, Ed.D., Three Principles Mentoring, La Conner, WA

What an awesome service you have created, can't believe no one has done it before!
>	-	Rudi Kennard, Three Principles Movies, UK.

I would like to start by THANKING YOU Jack for taking the time and energy to put all this together...
>	-	Gabriela Maldonado, TrueChange Consultants, San Diego, CA

Awesome job. It looks really great.
>	-	Aaron Turner, Ph.D., Founder/CEO, One Thought, U.K.

I am in awe as I write this because you have done such an amazing job with SO MUCH INFORMATION!
>	-	Ed Lemon, Supervisor, St. Paul Police Department Training Professional Development Institute, St. Paul, MN

Well, you did it!! Congratulations, it's quite an accomplishment! It was especially good to read about the work in recent years, most of which I was unaware of, particularly the global work.
>	-	Sandy Krot, Human Dimension Consultant, Pransky & Associates, Insight Principles, Greater Seattle area, WA

I congratulate you on a herculean accomplishment!!
>	-	Bill Pettit, M.D., Family Counseling and Children's Services, Adrian, MI

Amazing, all your hard work!
>	-	Ami Chen Mills-Naim, Co-Founder, Center for Sustainable Change, San Francisco Bay area, CA and Charlotte, NC

Absolutely amazing job on this. What an accomplishment. I'm reading every word. What memories. How time passes!!!
- Tom Kelley, Ph.D., Wayne State University, Detroit, MI

This is one heck of an **amazing** piece of work... It will help SO many people.
- Elese Coit, TrueChange Consultants, San Diego, California

Woo hoo! That is so much better than the first one. You have a lot of Syd in there and that is where it all came from for sure. Well done Jack.
- Barb Aust, Consultant, Salt Spring Island, BC

We...are amazed at how comprehensive it is.
- Jan and Chip Chipman, Co-Founder, Three Principles School, Salt Spring Island, BC

The amount of work on this is simply amazing...can't believe the great detail you went into...it is fascinating to see the part we were not involved in...as I am sure it must be for everyone, seeing the history we were not part of...I believe Syd would have been really grateful that you took this on, and did such a great job!
- Linda Quiring, Salt Spring Island, BC

PART III

BRIEF WRITE-UPS
ON A FEW IMPORTANT HISTORICAL EVENTS
THAT CREATED SYSTEMS CHANGE
WITHIN THE MAINSTREAM
FOR AN EXTENDED PERIOD OF TIME

A. The Modello low-income housing project, serving as the model for inside-out community change and for taking this understanding into other housing projects and low income areas, as a result of Dr. Roger Mills' pioneering efforts
- *summary by Jack Pransky and Diane McMillen, and referral to detailed resources by Jack Pransky*

B. The West Virginia University Medical School and the Sydney Banks Institute for Innate Health
- *by Judith Sedgeman*

C. Santa Clara County, California, Department of Alcohol and Drug Services Health Realization/Three Principles Division
- *by Linda Ramus, Gabriela Maldonado-Montano, Ami Chen Mills-Naim and Barbara Faye Sanford*

D. A Major Defense Contractor
- *by Aaron Turner, Cheryl Bond, Dick Bozoain and a former major executive*

E. National Resilience Resource Center of St. Paul, Minnesota
- *by Kathy Marshall Emerson*

F. The Michigan Story: Beginning in Ingham Regional Medical Center
- *by Milly Gilin and Lisa Davidson Laughman*

PART III A

The Modello Community Empowerment Program as the model for taking Three Principles understanding into low-income housing projects and other areas, as a result of Dr. Roger Mills' pioneering efforts

Excerpt from Pransky, J. and McMillen, D. (2013). "Exploring the True Nature of Internal Resilience: A View from the Inside-Out," in D. Saleeby [Ed.]. The Strengths Perspective in Social Work Practice, 6th Edition, *followed by a personal note from Jack Pransky and referral to detailed resources.*

The precipitating event in the evolution of this understanding in the fields of prevention and human services occurred in the autumn of 1987 when Dr. Roger Mills walked into the Modello (Public) Housing Project for the first time. Modello was a community beset with all the problems associated with poverty and racism. Dr. Mills arrived with this inside-out perspective and hope, buoyed from having had deep personal insights about his own life after being exposed to the philosophy of Sydney Banks... Despite his initial skepticism Mills personally became affected and his life improved markedly. Because of his earlier training as a community psychologist Mills wanted to translate what he understood from Banks into a completely new, inside-out approach to community empowerment and change...

Most who sincerely wanted to change this inhospitable and troubled housing project near Miami, Florida considered Mills' approach crazy. They said his ideas would never work. They said he was approaching the task backwards. "Dr. Mills," they argued, "with all due respect, what does self-esteem or people's thoughts have to do with the fact that their roofs are falling in, that they're dodging bullets on the way home, that their kids are involved with drugs, that their old man is beating on them and sleeping with their daughter. All these terrible things are going on in their lives. What does this have to do with 'thought', or anything you're talking about?" (Pransky, 2011, p. 20).

These objections seem correct, of course, but only on the surface. The Modello Housing Project was replete with substance abuse, drug gangs, shootings, domestic violence, child abuse, addiction, welfare dependency, school failure, truancy, and more. Police officers would not even enter Modello unless they were "three deep." Homestead Gardens, a neighboring low-income housing project, was not far behind. Yet, something remarkable happened in these communities. Dramatic changes began to occur in the residents' lives, in their families, and in the community—changes of a magnitude most of us only dream possible. Three years after Mills introduced this inside-out approach, for the 150 families and 650 youth served by the program, household use or selling drugs dropped from 65 percent to less than 20 percent; the overall endemic crime rate decreased by 70–80 percent; the teen pregnancy rate dropped from 50 percent to 10 percent; school dropout rates dropped from 60 percent to 10 percent; endemic child abuse and neglect decreased by more than 70 percent; households on public assistance went from 65 percent to negligible; and the parent unemployment rate dropped from 85 percent to 35 percent (Pransky, Mills, Sedgeman & Blevens, 1997).

Modello: A Story of Hope for the Inner-City and Beyond (Pransky, 2011b) chronicled in detail how residents' lives were affected. For example *[Note: The names were changed for the book]*, Thelma was a severe alcoholic violently abused by her crack-addicted boyfriend and, in turn, she abused her kids. But after experiencing Mills'…ideas she ended up stopping her alcohol dependency without going into treatment, halted her physical abuse and her own abuse of her children, and completely turned her life around. Ruby was a crack-addicted, extremely violent woman who, through gaining this understanding, came to see enough self-worth to enter treatment, and her life completely changed. Miss Cicely was an extremely withdrawn mother of some of the project's main drug dealers and of a daughter so severely addicted to crack that her weight dropped to 80 pounds and she prostituted herself to support her habit. Yet when Cicely's new insights turned her own life around, she then helped her daughter break her addiction, and Cicely became president of the project's residents' council. Lisa was suicidal, with no self-confidence, welfare dependent, continually being put down by her partner, yet through her insights ended up rising above it all, received her GED, then secured a good job in which she flourished. Lenny was a teenage drug dealer whose life turned around to such an extent that with his gang he began a "crime watch" to keep out all drug dealers, graduated from high school (he had been failing and truant), and went on to college. These are but a few examples of the profound individual, family, and neighborhood changes that took place in Modello.

As "Three Principles"/"Health Realization"/"Innate Health" projects spread into other communities, equally impressive findings were reported. For example, one year after introducing this approach into the Coliseum Gardens housing project in Oakland, California, once known as "the murder capital," the murder rate plummeted to zero and there had not been another homicide in at least seven subsequent years. In addition, violent crimes were reduced by 45 percent, drug assaults with firearms were reduced by 38 percent, and gang warfare and ethnic clashes between Cambodian and African-American youth ceased (Pransky, Mills, Sedgeman & Blevens, 1997). Such results subsequently led to broad application in a number of other settings...[and]... documented significant reductions in crime, delinquency, violence, drug use, child abuse and neglect, and unemployment of these principle-based, community empowerment projects in other crime-ridden areas.

Personal note from Jack Pransky:

For the first time Dr. Roger Mills was able to prove that what Sydney Banks was saying could truly be helpful to humanity, even with people in the depths of despair. The courage it took for Roger to undertake what he did is almost unfathomable, though Roger, himself, did not see it that way. He simply had complete faith in humanity; that once people *saw* what was already part of their innate mental health they would naturally rise to the occasion and overcome their problems, no matter how bad those problems appeared.

Dr. Mills provided the model for community change from the inside-out. He demonstrated how that model could be replicated and produce results (some better than others) in other housing projects and low income communities; first in neighboring Homestead Gardens; then in the South Bronx, New York; Coliseum Gardens in Oakland, California; Riverview Terrace in Tampa, Florida; the Glenwood-Lyndale community of Minneapolis; Visitation Valley in San Francisco, and on and on, changing so many lives for the better, making communities into healthier places and demonstrating the reduction of many social problem behaviors. The approach that began in Modello also became the genesis for the community work of the Center for Sustainable Change, started by Roger Mills and Ami Chen Mills-Naim (and as of this chronology directed by Dave Nichols) at the Lakewood Community Development Corporation (CDC) in Charlotte, North Carolina and the Delta Citizens Alliance in Greenville, Mississippi.

For detailed information on how the Modello Community Empowerment Project unfolded from beginning to end, both in Modello and Homestead Gardens, refer to the book Modello: A Story of Hope for the Inner-City and Beyond *by Jack Pransky (1998). And for detailed information on how this inside-out approach was applied successfully in other areas, see* Prevention from the Inside-Out *by Jack Pransky (2003); specifically, the Coliseum Gardens interview with Beverley Wilson, 199-206 (also 43-54); Riverview Terrace interview with Elsie Spittle, 206-213; Visitation Valley interview with Barbara Glaspie, 317-327 (Elsie also speaks about Visitation Valley in her interview).*

PART III B

The West Virginia University Medical School
and the Sydney Banks Institute for Innate Health

written by Dr. Judith Sedgeman

I went to West Virginia University (WVU) in June, 1998 and was made an Assistant Professor in the Department of Community Medicine, which is where Prevention is taught. Dean Robert D'Alessandri felt that our work fell most gracefully into the area of Prevention, and because of pushback from the Behavioral Sciences Department there is no way I would have been able to receive a faculty appointment there. After a couple of years I enrolled in a Psychology doctoral program at WVU, and once I had done that and was successfully pursuing the degree, people stopped arguing about my credentials. I was qualified to offer prevention courses to students in the Master's in Public Health with my Master's Degree; I did not start teaching Ph.D. students until I had my doctoral degree.

The Dean and I spent 1999 creating a long-term plan for the work and trying to raise money. There was real pushback from the few people who supported Syd's work who had money because they really couldn't wrap their minds around making a substantial donation to WVU. We decided, after consultation with Syd, that if we formed an Institute to which donations could be made it might be possible to gain the support we needed to become a permanent part of the Medical School (we knew we weren't going to get National Institutes of Health grant money with no pilot research or researchers in our field). Normally, university-based Institutes need a minimum of $6-million to be established. Once we announced that we were going to establish the Sydney Banks Institute of Innate Health we received $1.6-million in donations, and a lot of people from around the country accepted our invitation to the big opening ceremony. So the Dean allowed us to form the Institute on the strength of the appearance that more significant support would be forthcoming once it was real.

We had a fabulous opening celebration, and Syd and his family were there, and people outside of WVU were thrilled. Syd did a lecture to a full auditorium (more than 450) during the opening weekend. So we were filled with hope. I still couldn't hire anyone because we needed to bring in more money to do that, but at least we had a name and an identity and a website and Syd's involvement.

We undertook a major effort, with a lot of support from the WVU Foundation, to raise the rest of the money. Interestingly, we were swamped with small donations from community people ($5 to $25), but aside from a couple of gifts we never received any further substantial donations. So there we were with a half-formed Institute, and no hope for much expansion or growth without additional major funding. So we undertook the strategy to try to develop enthusiasm around the community for working with us on research and for getting some research done, in hopes we could develop some grants and then hire our own researcher. We held a big research conference that backfired because the faculty from WVU who had given their time with it all felt that the Principles people who attended had very little respect for rigorous research. I had hoped it would result in collaborations, but it didn't.

We had a lot of pushback from Behavioral Medicine and other departments on campus as we tried to get research going. I didn't know enough about it—I was taking as many research courses as I could as soon as I could while working on my doctoral degree, but I was always behind the 8-ball in a sophisticated research institution. None of the established researchers would work with us. It was an uphill struggle and it increasingly annoyed Syd that the University was pushing us in the direction of research, although he never lost his love for the Dean and he always supported Bill and me. He felt that it was not helping us and was hurting him to have his name associated with the Institute. This was exacerbated when we spent almost two years being investigated by Fundamentalist Christians for being "anti Judeo-Christian values"; it cost the University considerable legal fees to defend against this onslaught and generated a lot of bad PR and further polarization on campus. I offered to leave at that time, but the Dean called a meeting of all the Department Chairs and Deans of the Medical School and they voted 100% to ask me to stay and fight the Fundamentalists. To them it was an academic freedom issue. Bill Pettit and I had done a lot of work with departments and helped resolve a lot of interpersonal issues in the school, and those who knew us well in the Medical School honestly believed in what we were doing. So we changed the name to the West Virginia Institute of Innate Health and hired Bill Pettit, M.D., full-time, in the midst of this chaos — prior to that he had been a consultant to us.

We were able to bring Bill in because he was willing to be a Psychiatrist assigned to the Department of Behavioral Medicine and see a full load of patients, so he essentially was self-supporting as far as the University was concerned. He had an appointment in Behavioral Medicine, which was seriously understaffed and trying to recruit doctors, and he was also assigned to the Institute. Meanwhile, Bill and I were increasingly integrated into Faculty Life. He served on the Med School Ethics Committee; I was elected to the Faculty Senate, where I served two terms and was elected from within the Senate to the Senate Executive Committee. I was on a lot of other University committees, and also worked with the group that founded what has turned into a model Faculty Development program. We continued a lot of public programs and internal consulting. My courses were very popular with students. I was named to the very prestigious Academy of Excellence in Teaching and Learning at the Health Sciences Center. So we felt pretty good about getting through the rough patch and started to hope we could turn the research corner. But government funding for research was being cut year after year and the research environment and competition for dollars was becoming increasingly dog-eat-dog. We didn't have enough money in the Institute to support major research/researchers.

The Dean was promoted to VP Health Sciences and someone else (also our friend) was named Dean, but he was not as strong and well-established as Dr. D'Alessandri, and the situation was becoming increasingly political on campus for a lot of reasons totally unrelated to us. That Dean was forced out, and his departure marked the end of the

D'Alessandri era—he had been Bob's protégé. Bob left WVU to start a medical school in Pennsylvania. We were old news, just perking along teaching, and in Bill's case also working a killer schedule seeing patients and taking calls. We tried to get a research project on PTSD going with the VA, but the hospital administrator who was working with us sent our proposal for review to the Hospital Chaplains, who were doing a lot of the individual mentoring of PTSD patients, and they freaked out and demanded that the VA drop it. We tried to collaborate with some people at Pitt, but they were struggling, too, to get grant money. We just never had much support from the Principles community generally, except that people did come to our conferences. I think the perception was that we had money, but we didn't.

So, finally, Bill and I decided we had had about as much fun as we could stand. We announced that we would close WVIIH. After 10+ years, there was $175,000 left from our original donation, which we eventually got donated to 3PGC. The Medical School had a lovely farewell party for us; individually, by that time, we had a lot of friends and were very well liked and respected, but people just couldn't step up to the risk of getting 100% behind an unproven approach. My Department continued (and to this day still continues) to support my courses on line. And that's the story. Bill and I worked very hard as faculty members and he also as a physician. We left with a good feeling, and we are still Mountaineers — WVU fans through and through.

[See also extensive interview with Judy Sedgeman in Prevention from the Inside-Out *by Jack Pransky, 216-227.]*

[For some history on how this effort began initially, see the George Pransky interview in Part I of this book.]

PART III C

SANTA CLARA COUNTY, CALIFORNIA, DEPARTMENT OF ALCOHOL AND DRUG SERVICES, HEALTH REALIZATION/THREE PRINCIPLES DIVISION

Jack Pransky compiled the following from an informal interview with Linda Ramus by Jack Pransky, and write-ups by Barbara Faye Sanford, Gabriela Maldonado-Montano, Ami Chen Mills-Naim, some input from Mark Howard, plus a compilation from Linda Ramus and Cathy Casey on County-provided Three Principles services.

Gabriela Maldonado-Montano: At times life brings you the opportunity to be a part of something special that not only impacts your life in ways you did not know was possible, but it allows you to be part of a greater effort to better your community. In hindsight I've realized no amount of planning could have brought on all the right conditions to create this situation... Unbeknown to me there was a Department of Alcohol and Drug Services (DADS) of Santa Clara County that was funding prevention services.

Barbara Faye Sanford: In 1994, Robert Garner, Director of Santa Clara County Department of Alcohol and Drug Services, was introduced to the Three Principles (then referred to as Health Realization).

Ami Chen Mills-Naim: Penny Rock, who worked with the Senn-Delaney Consulting Firm at the time and was married to Bob Garner, first heard of the Principles through her work. She then encouraged Bob to attend a workshop on it conducted by my father, Dr. Roger Mills.

Faye: Bob was so inspired by it that he enrolled himself in a year-long program to learn more.

Ami: He attended my father's year-long training through the California School of Professional Psychology—a class that also included (I believe) the police officer Jerry Williams.

Faye: He saw its potential to inspire others and to help people in all walks of life to improve their well-being, as well as to prevent them from creating more life problems. He saw the potential that this had for his department, for both staff and clients.

Gabriela: As I remember the story, told by him, there was a sense of hope he heard at this training. Inspired by this and due to his visionary nature, he funded large trainings.

Linda Ramus: This inspired him in the summer of 1995 to bring in Joe Bailey and Dr. Mark Howard to provide the first introductory training in the Principles for the County, which turned out to be the kick-off training for the entire effort.

Faye: Bob offered an introductory session for his Department and invited other County Departments that offered human services, such as Social Services, Mental Health Services and Public Health Nursing. Then he offered a full four-day training, and Bob invited anyone interested from those departments to attend.

Gabriela: The trainings were open to anyone in the county: employees, contractors, administrative staff, other county departments, non-profits, schools, etc. Hundreds of people attended these trainings.

Faye: I was introduced to Health Realization at a program I attended in San Francisco. It was just a short introduction, but something within me clicked as I heard about it and I couldn't wait to get home to read the article they distributed about it. I was more excited after I read the article and even more when I first heard that the Department where I worked was planning a training in it.

Linda: I was hiking the Appalachian Trail at the time so I didn't hear about it until I got back. Cathy Casey, who had attended, told me about what had happened and went on and on about it. I attended the second training, which Roger Mills conducted in October or November 1995.

He had "on stage" with him a few people from the county who had caught on most from the first training: Cathy Casey, Kristen Mansheim and Carlos Hankins.

Mark Howard: After talking with Bob, I formed the first group applications training class, which met twice monthly. The first year of training included 12 participants. That group continued for 18 years.

Ami: From that group Barbara Faye Sanford, Cathy Casey, and Kristen Mansheim sort of "rose to the top" and began a training-of-trainers program with my father—along with others.

Faye: The training resonated with me as potentially more helpful than the psychological models I learned about in graduate school because it basically teaches people how to get the best use out of their minds, and since everything we do begins in our minds it gets to the root of life's "problems." I saw how it could be helpful to people in all walks of life, both personal and professional. Because the Three Principles function the same way within everyone, everyone is treated as equal and whole, not broken. There is no greater joy than to see the shift in people's perspective of life as their consciousness rises to new heights. Bob saw my interest and excitement about Health Realization and asked me to coordinate the breakout facilitators to assist Dr. Roger Mills. Bob contracted with Dr. Mills to facilitate the trainings and to set up a Trainer of Trainers Program.

Gabriela: After seeing the response, Bob developed a new vision to continue and expand Health Realization services. Synchronicity brought Dr. Roger Mills to Bob's life. He became a contractor and the leader of the TOT for DADS for the first wave of trainees. Some of the people who attended these trainings had personal shifts that gave their lives a renewed sense of hope and possibility. Faye had a sense of excitement because she realized "this was something that was not only for those being served, 'the clients,' but also for the servers."

Linda: Enough interest was generated from these trainings for Bob to decide to take this on and put money into it. He asked Faye Sanford to manage this Health Realization effort for the Department. Faye was the obvious person to coordinate all the training, get all the contracts together and all that. Faye coordinated all this full-time from the beginning, for years when there really was no Division, per se. Bob put all the management of it in her hands.

Faye: I had been an employee of the County in the Department of Alcohol & Drug Services since 1990.

Gabriela: Faye was enlisted by Bob to find people who were interested in becoming trainers. From my perspective the TOT was a way to create sustainability and expansion of services—after all, Joe, Mark and Roger couldn't go around teaching by themselves.

Linda: At the time Cathy [Casey] and I were on contract with the Department doing a federal research project collecting data on drug use, and Bob wanted Cathy to do something with Health Realization because she was so excited about it. He thought about getting her on as a counselor, but she didn't want to do that. But because she had a connection with criminal justice systems she said she would love to take this into the jails, and Bob said. "Okay, I'll fund you." So Cathy and I got together and we wrote up the proposal for the program, and then through some various troubles I almost gave up on it—it's so hard to get something new into these places; people don't have time for anything. But Cathy connected with one person and got us in. It's really funny because when we were doing the proposal Cathy still had some thinking about her ability to pull this off at that time, so she said we should write Beverley [Wilson] into it. "We've got to have Beverley!" [laughs.] So we went into the County Jail in 1996, and we started working with the women.

At the same time Kristen Mansheim was working at the Mariposa Lodge, a drug and alcohol residential facility, and she took it into Mariposa. Kristen was part of the Training of Trainers program from the very beginning. She brought the Principles into Mariposa Lodge in about 1996. You know what happens—as soon as people start hearing this as a counselor working someplace, you start to share it. [Note: In

2000, under the leadership of director Shirley Wilson, an entire dorm at the facility is dedicated to Health Realization as addictions treatment, with the objective: "to enhance the life of the individual by teaching the understanding of the psychological principles of Mind, Thought and Consciousness, and how these principles function to create our life experience…to enable them to live healthier and more productive lives so the community becomes a model of health and wellness." For more detailed information, see interview with Kristen Mansheim in the book, *Prevention from the Inside-Out* by Jack Pransky]

Ami: I came into the training program just as my father was leaving, so my trainers were this first group of three, and I was trained along with Gabriela Maldonado, Linda Ramus, Billy King, Pam Whisnant, Linda Castaldi, Minoo Koushan, and many others. This was a very intensive training program that involved big quarterly county staff and contractor trainings of two and three days, and all of us getting up to speak in large and small groups.

Gabriela: I was part of the second wave of trainers (being trained by the first wave). It has been 18 years since I went to my first training so I don't recall everyone's names who were involved, but there were many people involved, touched and grateful to be part of this program. Some have become best friends and business partners; others went on to live their lives and moved to different countries, but all involved wanted to contribute to the wellbeing of "our" community. So there were people from treatment programs, schools, social services, probation, non-profits, counseling and therapy practices, hospitals, jails, and churches learning how to share what they have found so helpful, understanding the inside-out nature of life. Some of us were allowed to join this program by our employers during working hours and others asked for vacation time. Some of us were local and others were not so local. Some of us were new to the field and others had been serving people for a long time. All training was sponsored by DADS. The Health Realization Services Division was created somewhere in the middle of all these classes—a government agency dedicating funding to promote the wellbeing of the people in Santa Clara County through the understanding of the Principles! Bob was the unpretentious flame underneath.

Faye: In 1997 Bob decided to create a new division based on the Three Principles and appointed me as the Manager. I developed the Health Realization Services Division as a division, while giving full credit to the many who initiated the various programs and services. It was beautiful how it came together and reached out to so many.

Linda: Bob just decided, "I'm going to do this." He had federal prevention money and he said, "I'm going to use some of this money to do this work and provide these classes," then he pretty much left it up to Faye. The first person Faye hired as a trainer was Gabriela [Maldonado], and then I was hired as an Analyst. I could do the reports and all that stuff. Then the next person she hired was Sister Margarita [Tran]. So Gabriela and Margarita gave her the Spanish and Vietnamese language capabilities she needed. In Santa Clara County those were the primary languages. In terms of forming the Division that's kind of how it worked. So I was hired in April 2001.

Also, Billy King was on staff, assigned to Health Realization, but not through our program. Besides creating the Health Realization Program Division, Bob also created a rehab counselor position within the Treatment Division to be staffed by somebody who operated by the Principles, and that ended up being Billy. How that happened was Gabriela and Billy had been working together in a community-based program called Community Solutions, and they had a contract with Alcohol and Drug Services to provide some treatment and probably some prevention. Bob had offered to all his contract staff and service providers to come to these trainings on this new thing, and Gabriela and Billy showed up around 1996. So they both got hired. But Bob already had had a position that he transitioned over from treatment, a woman named Mireya [Vaamonde], and I'll tell you, it didn't go over very well with the traditional treatment managers and supervisors because they didn't really even understand what was going on. So Billy was sort of imposed on them, and they weren't really too thrilled with it. So Billy had to do a lot of rapport-building down there with those people.

Gabriela: Some of the people who were part of the TOT became contractors and others like myself became employees. Our mission was to share the Principles. DADS funded services in the following places and with the following populations: Santa Clara County (SCC) Correction Department of Corrections (inmates and staff), SCC Probation Department (clients and staff), SCC Social Services (clients and staff), SCC Office of Education (students and teachers), SCC Clerk of the Board of Supervisors, SCC Public Health Department (clients and staff), SCC Health and Hospital System, SCC Housing Authority-Poco Way Apartments (clients and staff), Mariposa Treatment Center (clients and staff), InnVission and Montgomery Street homeless shelter (clients and staff), Gardner Community Out Patient services (clients and staff), Eastside Unified School District (students and staff), Morgan Hill Unified School District (students and staff), Center for Employment Training (students, and staff) to mention a few...phew! Out of these classes some people were profoundly touched and experienced a sense of wellbeing that inspired them to share the Principles with others. "Students" became "teachers" and we all had the opportunity to learn from each other.

Linda: So we just built a program with all of the services. We were in the jails. We expanded to work with the men. Then it expanded to where at one time we had about a dozen different weekly classes going on. I eventually managed the whole program. Cathy did the classes for women, first with Beverley, then on her own. Then when we added classes Beverley had her own class, Cathy had her own class, then Kristen was doing a class, and Gabriela was doing a class in Spanish, and Sister Margarita was doing a class in Vietnamese. Then Cathy expanded out to do a class with Probation and Work Furlough programs for the men and the women. Then we expanded to do classes in what was called Phase 2, where people were not incarcerated but still had to show up every day—kind of like a day reporting program. Then Gabriela took it into Juvenile Hall in about 2003 or 2004. We had a whole bunch of classes going on. [Note: In 2007, Cathy and Linda Ramus bring the Principles into San Quentin Prison, in California.]

Ami: Looking back, it was remarkable how much funding Bob was able to put into the program and how big it got. The first "division" became a part of the overall DADS budget. Faye hired me after I graduated the certification program there, and hired many others—we were all running around to the jails, juvenile hall, the county youth correctional ranches, and, with Faye, we started the first school-based program at Camden School. Cathy Casey, Carlos Hankins and I started those trainings, with the support of then Principal Jim Baker, and then Gabriela came in in the second year. Jim secured funding to produce the first video there: "Our Thoughts on Thought," and a lot of the stories in *The Spark Inside* and *State of Mind in the Classroom* came from this school project, and working in juvenile hall.

I initiated the first class in Men's Work Furlough in Santa Clara County, at the request of the Supervisor there and Barbara Faye. There was also a "Leadership Team" created at some point that started small and then included Cathy, Linda, Gabriela, Mark Howard (who taught applications classes throughout the whole history of the county), Billy King (if I am remembering right), myself, and others I am probably forgetting. There must have been up to a dozen or so independent contractors teaching in the jails and work furlough programs, including Carlos Hankins, Beverley Wilson, Azra Simonetti, Kristen Mansheim, Pam Whisnant, Gabriela Maldonado, Marilyn Wendler, Walter Pederson, Andreine Golden, myself and others (I may be forgetting people!). People were running all sorts of projects, the Mariposa project, prevention services, social services, and the executive correctional programs that Cathy and Gabriela did. There were special topics workshops, everything from dealing with difficult people to working with challenging youth. There was an "academy" and then an Internship program run originally by Cathy and Kristen, and then myself and Kristen, and then Gabriela and Billy.

Ami: Then Faye left for Atlanta to be with her kids.

Linda: Faye retired probably seven months after I had been hired, and I took over as Manager. Bob basically said to me, "Here's the money. Do what you want." You never hear that kind of thing! But that's what he said. Besides the staff, the whole Division was supported by a cadre of

Roger Mills-trained contractors/facilitators. The stated objective for the Division was: "To increase the mental health and psychological well-being of individuals and the communities they reside in by providing trainings for the County's staff and for the consumers of DADS." In 2012 the name of the Division was changed to the Three Principles Service Division.

Gabriela: At its peak the department had 45 classes a week and more than 15 contractors in addition to staff. In the 18 years that DADS funded services many formats were created to fit the needs and schedules of people: There were 5-day trainings, 1-day trainings, half-a day trainings, 2-hour trainings, 1.5-hour trainings, "advanced" trainings, monthly trainings, and of course the TOT. We shared the Principles Monday-Friday and even on the weekends; in the morning, afternoon and evenings; in English, Spanish, Vietnamese and Cambodian (with an interpreter). We would go to conferences and present what we were doing and also brought in speakers from far and away.

Ami: There were so many classes happening in the County when the economy was booming. At one point I would drive from Santa Cruz to work at Camden School in Cupertino, then leave Camden and drive to Milpitas to work in the county jail, and then over to Mountain View to work in the Men's Work Furlough Program. At one point there was even an evening class in Women's Work Furlough added that day and I would go from men's to women's work furlough in San Jose. Four classes/four cities/one day! At one point I stopped accepting classes because I felt like I was burning out.

But the stories were amazing. What we all witnessed in the jails and juvenile hall, what we were doing—showing Syd Banks' videos, getting his books in the jails (I think Cathy was in charge of this), talking about *Mind, Consciousness* and *Thought*. It was a lot of fun; it was very, very profound. It was remarkable, really, when you think about it. I think it shows what can happen when the right person or people "get touched" by the understanding and can control and allocate funding. I would be walking around town and see a guy from a jail class, driving a pizza delivery car or something—this actually happened—and he'd stick his head out the window and say, "Hey! It really works!" Some of the stories brought tears to your eyes.

Gabriela: For more than a decade people from all over the country and the world looked at the Department as a resource to establish programs and services in their own communities. We welcomed visitors into our classes from all over the state, country and world. We got calls asking for technical support and insight to get programs started in other places. Bob would get feedback from people who had taken the training at one point or another and thanked him for funding these services. Staff and contractors with unique strengths, passions, and personalities were united by a sincere desire to relieve suffering.

Linda: Then Bob and I both retired and Gabriela left, I was replaced by Betty Nelson, and a new DADS Director replaced Bob who didn't really understand what we were doing, and there were budget cuts, and the Three Principles Division closed in March 2013.

Gabriela: Many factors contributed. DADS was preparing to merge with another large county department, Bob retired, funding sources changed their focus and life took many of us in different directions. For eighteen years DADS funded services that served thousands of people, many of them in dire circumstances.

Linda: I'm not sure how many people were served from the time it started until it closed. All I know is from 2000 until I left in 2012 I think it would be safe to say on average we were serving from 1,000 to approximately 2,000 people a year. We were in schools. We were in Juvenile Hall. We were in the community. We trained and educated staff, clients, community members, trained former clients who, in turn, reached participants in numerous programs and agencies and through weekly on-going classes, which at one point numbered around 45 per week. Also, administrators of many social service agencies, mangers and staff of medical groups, judges, attorneys, probation and parole officers, members of the local homeless shelters, and residents of the local communities were reached. We were all over the place. It's huge.

Everybody who has done this for any length of time in any significant way has their own book to write.

Gabriela: As more people went through training, they got inspired to share in their own way and in settings of their own interest. It was the same story over and over again: People got a sense of hope, they experienced wellbeing, they wanted to help their communities. The transformations we all saw invigorated our hearts and spirits which reinforced our commitment to share…it was a real treat, a gift.

Ami: For all of the good the county did for so many, for all of the thousands and thousands of people that program touched, it also incubated many of us to go out and do our own things later with confidence and experience. Many more people were trained and worked as trainers and I'm sure a lot happened, too, after I left the County to found the Center for Sustainable Change.

Gabriela: Today many of the people involved continue the efforts of trying to promote wellbeing through the understanding of the Principles in their communities. New organizations have been founded, new partnerships have formed, new paths are being created and more stories of hope are being written. The thing about hope is that it touches our hearts and souls; and it inspires us to share in ways we never thought possible.

Note: *In 2013 when DADS ended its Three Principles Program Division and stopped its classes, a small group of Santa Clara County County-certified Three Principles teachers (including Linda Ramus) began the nonprofit organization, Innate Health Connection (IHC): 3 Principles for Transformative Solutions. These teachers came together because they observed that Three Principles understanding has been the basis for profound shifts in human understanding and wanted to continue to provide community-based workshops, supportive mentoring, professional trainings, and a network of practitioners with the focus to share the understanding that Sydney Banks knew was the basis to end all human psychological suffering.*

Linda: The following is a list Cathy and I put together of the programs and classes provided by the Department of Alcohol & Drug Services (DADS) from 1996–2013 when the new director discontinued funding programs. Today, the classes are provided by Innate Health Connections, and Cathy is still doing the jail. Between 1996 to 2013 the following services were provided:

Department of Correction: Elmwood RCP women, men, PC, Spanish, Vietnamese, Vets; Main Jail – 7A maximum; Breaking Barriers gang unit; DOC Day Reporting Phase2 men and women; Re-entry parolees and probations. Average 8 classes per year x 56 weeks = 448 classes; Average 1,800–2,000 individuals served annually.
Probation: Men and women work furlough (for about 6 years: 56 x 2 = 112 classes annually, average attendance).
Juvenile Probation: Juvenile Hall boys and girls (2 classes/week x 56 = 112 classes annually); average annual attendance (7 x 112 + 184); James Ranch and Muriel Wright Ranch (boys & girls, 3 classes/ week).
Residential Drug Treatment: Mariposa – women (various weekly classes-1 class per week of various types); Pathways – men and women
Poco Way Community Development Program (2 years)
Shelters: Julian Street Inn; Montgomery Street Inn; Emergency Housing Consortium
Community: Monday, Wednesday, Thursday and Friday classes
Parenting Classes: both in English and Vietnamese
Schools: Camden; Evergreen High School (1 weekly class, 1 year); Independence High School (Margarita); Cadet Academy – continuation school
Special Project: MIOCR (mental health project)
County In-take Department Training: Probation Staff (3); Probation Administrative (Chief, Deputy Chief, Business Administrator); Clerk of the Board (2); Assessors Office (1); Health & Hospital Call Center staff; DOC Correctional Officers; Social Services Agency social workers
Core/State of Mind 5-day Training on the Principles: 5 per year for at least 10 years
Wisdom at Work: Monthly ½ day Topic Specific Training on the Principles - Did it for at least 10 years
Applications Class with Mark Howard: monthly 2 hours; did it for at least 11 years
Training of Trainers: average 2 year training; The Academy; Intern program; DADS Certified 50 people as having completed the TOT program

Various one-time trainings: DADS department customer service training; County Office of Education – Foster Care Program Staff; Alliance – residential mental health treatment program for schizophrenics, dual diagnoses, bi-polar

Research & Evaluation Studies: Mariposa Study; Alliance; Juvenile Hall – Santa Clara University Professor Brett Solomon; Center for Employment Training staff training

Special Training: Sydney Banks in the jails; With guest trainers: George and Linda Pransky, Bill and Linda Pettit, Elsie Spittle, Mavis Karn.

3 Principles Programs/classes in Santa Clara County non-affiliated with DADS: Domestic Violence Batterers Program provided by Before the After; Santa Clara County Human Resources sponsored by Human Resources; Children's Shelter; Barbara Towner, Outpatient medical clinic;

Present Day (as of this chronology—see *Note* above): Main Jail (1 weekly); Re-Entry Program (2 weekly); Mariposa (1 weekly); Evans Lane (Probation) 1 weekly; Blue House (Probation) 1 weekly; Domestic Victims group 1 weekly; Residential Treatment Center (3 weekly); Community Classes Drop-In class (3 weekly); Community Information Session (bi-monthly); County hospital (Fall, 2014).

PART III D

A MAJOR CORPORATION TAKES ON
THE THREE PRINCIPLES

written by Aaron Turner, Cheryl Bond, Dick Bozoian and senior executives in this corporation*

[*Note: The senior executives requested that they and the company remain anonymous.]

In 1998, Pransky and Associates began working with a high-tech electronics company in the Defense and Aerospace industry. This was the first large-scale corporate Three Principles application in a Fortune 50 (Fifty) corporation.

This effort was launched by training director Dick Bozoian when he contracted with George Pransky. The company's Organizational Development (OD) department developed and implemented the program along with Pransky & Associates, adjunct practitioners and senior executives who ultimately participated in teaching their employees. The program was supported by Cheryl Bond, the company's OD staff, many of the most senior executives at the company in various business units, and Pransky and Associates staff: Sandy Krot, Aaron Turner, Dicken Bettinger, Keith Blevens, Mara Gleason and their adjunct staff.

The following was written by Dick Bozoian:

One day a good friend and fellow worker and I were traveling in his car going between two different sites of the company. It was almost noon time and he asked me if I would mind stopping by the local library because he had to return a book. I had never been in this particular library and it seemed like a good chance to check it out. Once in the library I went to the section that deals with the disciplines of sociology and psychology. As it turned out I had read most of what they had to offer and the rest didn't really hit me as all that interesting. I started to work towards the front of the building when a little old lady crossed my path. She worked at the library and was pushing a cart loaded with books that she was returning to the shelves. As she went by I happened to notice a book on top of the pile in her cart which was entitled, *Sanity, Insanity and Common Sense.* I asked the lady if she would mind if I looked at this particular book and she said that it would be fine. As I looked at the book more closely I really started to get more and more interested. Finally I got my friend to borrow the book (I did not even have a library card for this particular library). I ended up reading the book several times and also got my friend to read it. The contents of the book really resonated with me and since part of my job was to arrange for Leadership training, as well as to help create a productive work environment in the company, the message of the book was, in my opinion, directly relevant to my work. At the end of the book there was a listing of tapes that covered a lot of what the book was pointing to, and I ended up ordering a number of these tapes and started to share them with a number of employees. The tapes were a hit! Out of the blue I got a call one day and it happened to be the person who had authored all of the tapes, George Pransky. He simply wanted to know who was ordering all the tapes and what I was doing with them. To make a long story a bit shorter, I got to know him very well on both a personal and professional basis. Through him, I got to meet Syd Banks, the person who discovered the Fundamental Principles that formed the basis for the book, as well as the tapes, and truly were the fundamental bedrock that underlies the human experience.

I will let others detail all the wonderful things that happened at our company as we introduced this understanding from the top of the organization on down through the ranks. The story is remarkable and it all started with an unplanned trip to a library that I had never previously visited and the chance meeting with the little old lady. Go figure....I guess there is something to what folks refer to as Serendipity!

The following was written by Aaron Turner, Cheryl Bond and contributions from senior company executives:

From 1998 to 2012 The Principles became the core foundation for leadership development and State of Mind (a Principle-based concept developed during this project). The company identified State of Mind (SOM) as a key cultural value and an important competitive discriminator in the marketplace.

During this period, over 250 senior executives, middle management leaders and other employees individually attended a four-day leadership Principles-based program at Pransky & Associates in La Conner, WA. Additionally, Pransky & Associates and the company's OD staff created and ran three of the company's seven Core Executive Institutes and based those courses on the SOM Principles. Personal Foundations for Optimal Leadership, the core Principles-based institute, had nearly a thousand graduates. Thousands of employees at all levels in the company received some training in The Principles, and in one business unit The Principles flowed down to over 5,000 employees. The formal training program in that unit, called 'State of Mind and Business Success', was a major driver in creating an enduring 'high-performance' culture and work environment in that business. As the name of the program implies, the purpose of the program was to enhance business success in the enterprise.

By every measure, business performance improved greatly year-over-year during over a decade-long period where SOM was the cornerstone of company's approach to leadership and accountability at all levels. In fact, improvement in all of the core performance metrics correlated perfectly with the number of employees trained in the Principles-based program. Scores on Customer Satisfaction surveys and Employee Opinion surveys improved greatly in this timeframe, and the SOM program was generally viewed as the catalyst for major improvements in: financial performance (sales, orders, profit), program performance (on-time deliveries, product quality & reliability, field performance) and the overall climate and work environment (leadership, teamwork, collaboration, camaraderie, conflict resolution, customer relations, organizational resilience).

Moreover, as indicated below, many of the employees often stated that they had experienced profound changes in their personal lives, their physical, emotional and mental health, and their personal relationships for which they credited their SOM understanding. Based on the success of the businesses that broadly implemented the program, variations of the SOM program spread organically to many other business units in this global corporation. Sydney Banks visited the company several times to meet with executives and scientists and conducted several retreats in the U.S. with company leaders.

The following was written by Cheryl Bond:

When I applied for an Organizational Development position at this company in the fall of 1997 I had no idea that my life would be changed forever. I had been commuting a very long way for work and, truth be told, I was most excited about a significantly shorter commute. It was the beginning of a fantastic 15-year journey.

In 1997 my boss, Dick Bozoian, had already connected with George Pransky and was in the initial stages of introducing the Three Principles to a Defense & Aerospace industry contractor composed primarily of engineers and scientists. The first class I attended was in an amphitheater of engineering directors and featured a soon-to-be-infamous imitation of "John Wayne in a lab coat" by Keith Blevens. (John Wayne in a lab coat was a way of describing how the engineers thought of themselves.) George Pransky, Dicken Bettinger, and Sandy Krot were the 3P faculty that day along with Keith. To say there were skeptics in the audience would be a gross understatement.

It was a privilege to participate in a culture change that eventually led to one Business Unit President requiring all of his thousands of employees to attend what we called State of Mind (SOM) training. Many of the employees participated in a curriculum of SOM Executive Institutes that included 4-day individual intensives at Pransky and Associates and week-long residential executive institutes on the campus of a major state university. All employees received some level of training. In 1999 I went to my first intensive in La Conner, Washington with Dicken Bettinger. I saw the world and myself from a whole new perspective and was flooded with insights that changed my marriage and my relationship with my family. I was hooked. I began attending every SOM training and offsite I could, and I gradually started facilitating and teaching rather than being a participant. Some of the best weeks of my life were spent up at the university working with the Pransky and Associates gang. We always had lots of laughs, and I almost always fought back the tears when the group shared what they had learned on Friday morning. Very often people literally looked different. Some of the highlights:

- A veteran who shared that he no longer suffered from PTSD.
- A woman whose Fibromyalgia symptoms visibly disappeared.
- A brilliant physicist whose improved interpersonal skills actually saved his life when a polygraph test required for security purposes showed a heart abnormality.
- A program director who saw that his driving, "take-no-prisoners" leadership style was not effective and was also ruining his home life.
- Hundreds and hundreds of people realized that they had terrible listening skills and were rarely engaged with anything or anyone in the moment – and that there was nothing *to do* to fix themselves; it was an awareness of how their minds worked that changed everything.

Encouraged by Dick Bozoian I went back to grad school to finish my doctorate. In a remarkable stroke of luck I found an advisor who was fascinated by the work we were doing at this corporation. I worked with a VP/GM who wanted to improve the climate of his division, and who wanted to measure the success of what we did. (I describe that work and more about the transformation at the company in my dissertation.) The most startling aspect of this particular work was that after *only* the leadership team learned about SOM, the climate surveys indicated significant improvement. Just 13 people who became better listeners, more open to new ideas, focused on solving problems rather than assigning blame, and aware that their emotions were not coming from their circumstances made a significant difference in the culture.

In 2013 I was able to interview a number of people who had been a part of the SOM programs in the company. Many of them had attended training nearly a decade ago, but they were very clear about the realizations that had stuck with them; such as, seeing their thinking causing their impatience, having faith in resilience and focusing only on the moment and task at hand, working more efficiently with greater clarity of thinking, but accomplishing the same and using less energy. People also admitted that they could still go down a "rat-hole" of thinking and feeling that wasn't helpful, but they didn't get stuck there. Their lives got a little easier.

Mine, too. I have my own business today doing coaching and training. I recently did a virtual talk called "It Always Comes Down to the Principles" for a 3P-based business in London. Whether I'm coaching a leader who needs to improve his or her relationship skills, helping a client see that her boss is not responsible for how she feels, or listening to a friend who is struggling with life's transitions, I always teach The Principles. I've been in training and development for almost 30 years. If I found a better way to help people be more productive at work and happier in their lives I would be teaching that instead of The Principles.

For more detailed information, see the two doctoral dissertations written about the Principles-based work at this company (see Publications: Roy 2007, and Bond 2007).

PART III E

National Resilience Resource Center of St. Paul, Minnesota

written by Kathy Marshall Emerson

"Trust the process!" Roger Mills, my first Health Realization teacher, drilled into my head in 1993. What I did not realize was that before I ever met him I must have trusted an invisible process in both my personal and professional life. There was no plan, no early goal to spend the rest of my life living and teaching the Principles. I came to the University of Minnesota in 1991 to accept a position as Director of the federally funded Midwest Regional Center (MRC) for Drug Free Schools Minneapolis Area Office serving three states. I had unexpectedly become the breadwinner for our family. I settled into the academic world charged with administering federal prevention training programs in three states. We were directed to focus on what was wrong with kids and communities and fix problems.

Halfway across the country my colleague Bonnie Benard was in an identical position working for the same federal funder. We represented regional educational laboratories that lived by the gold standard of research. We knew the emerging body of resilience research was delivering a more hopeful and appealing approach to prevention than the predominant evidence base of our funders. I was housed at the University of Minnesota, a global leader in resilience research. Bonnie was well known for synthesis of resilience research and its application to youth prevention. The day Bonnie called in 1993 and said I needed to come to a conference where Roger Mills was speaking was a turning point. We attended together.

My first impression was that, although Roger kept tugging at his sports coat, saying he was not as good at public speaking as one of his project's police officers, his message came through about his work in Modello and Oakland public housing. Bonnie and I knew we could bridge the gap between resilience research and Roger's promising community practice. The rest is history.

Yet the story is more involved than that. In retrospect I know with certainty that personal learning is prerequisite to professional application. If anyone had told me this before I heard Roger I would have refused to attend. I wanted to discover what could improve my work. I went on to attend various extended trainings with Roger, and then with George and Linda Pransky. I was on a work mission, but personal learning sneaked up on me. My husband and my employees noticed me changing way before I did. Thank goodness the change got out of control in a good way.

For me it was a rough road from 1995 to 1997. Amazingly, with some understanding of the Principles, I was able to navigate very difficult times with peace of mind, gratitude and understanding. In this period my spouse died suddenly, I organized hospice care for a dear family member, my last child left for college, all regional training centers' federal funding ended nationally; we were forced to relocate within the University and become totally self-supporting. The Dean allowed me to begin selling training services in order to keep the doors open month-by-month. The *National Resilience Resource Center* program name was born and I lived by budget printouts! Despite it all, by 1997 Bonnie and I published our own prevention framework grounded in resilience research and the Principles of Health Realization.

The National Resilience Resource Center (NRRC) is dedicated to fostering resilience and the understanding of Principles for realizing health globally. NRRC guides school, community, and organizational leaders in learning to tap natural, innate health and resilience in themselves and others. The goal is seeing all students, employees, residents, clients, or organizations as *at promise* rather than as *at risk*.

> *We believe every person has the capacity for natural resilience and that it can be tapped and brought forth. This requires both traditional supportive environmental protective factors identified in research, and activation of natural internal protective mechanisms emanating from an individual's thinking and understanding. These internal principles—an inside out*

process—play a critically important role in realizing resilience. Our services are built on this foundation.

This operating philosophy is grounded in resilience and complementary research spanning more than 60 years in a wide variety of disciplines. The foundation for all NRRC training, technical assistance, keynotes and long-term systems change projects is the Principles for realizing health (Health Realization, Three Principles, Psychology of Mind, Innate Health). New NRRC charitable services include a major website for dissemination of seminal resources and information, and limited training, writing and consultation. Since 2011 the private National Resilience Resource Center, LLC has continued the work that originated at the University of Minnesota 23 years ago.

Long-term Community Projects
Community projects have never been the whole of NRRC services, but they held the key to a sustainable future. We initially conducted many free federal MRC prevention trainings in St. Cloud, Minnesota. This allowed us to consistently weave resilience and Health Realization into the workshops. As the federal prevention funding ended nationally a miracle unfolded. Dr. Dick Holt, Director of St. Cloud Area School District's Student Services, stepped forward. He did not care that our trainings were no longer free. He contracted very generously for a full year of many trainings and technical assistance for educators; we focused on resilience and Health Realization. He too saw the vision; he was frustrated by the national special education focus on what was wrong with kids!

With temporary funding for continued services authorized by Dr. Holt we all kept our eyes peeled for possible grants. Shortly after my husband died we were thrust wildly into the flurry of chasing a real grant. With only a few days to submit we created a community coalition chaired by Dr. Holt and Stearns County Board Chairperson Mark Sakry, developed an evidence-based prevention plan, obtained the required County Board of Supervisors' endorsement, secured a fiscal agent and were awarded what became five and a half years of state government full funding. Trainings commenced with participants from a wide range of public education, health and human services agencies, and non-profits. An additional state grant expanded the effort.

The St. Cloud Partners in Hope coalition continued with an additional grant for ten years of new federal funding. Part way into that grant a companion four-year federal augmentation grant was also procured. This meant NRRC was providing publicly funded resilience and Health Realization training and technical assistance for two decades. Participation was always free. We wrote major government grant applications every year for 20 years. I conducted the bulk of those introductory and advanced trainings and was assisted in the very early days by Cindi Claypatch, then Gary Johnson, and much later by Mary White. Many of the nationally known Principles leaders made special presentations: Roger Mills, George and Linda Pransky, Bill Pettit, Joe Bailey, Mavis Karn, Jack Pransky and others.

Our St. Cloud funding successes depended on totally understanding specific state and federal grant application instructions, having solid needs assessment data from customized longitudinal local student surveys, and on the NRRC research-based prevention framework and our ability to operationalize it with Health Realization. We paid meticulous attention to grounding in the Principles, funded evaluation, and stayed current with emerging science. Equally important, community members had the contacts and relationships needed to mobilize and maintain the coalition. My experience developing and teaching the University of Minnesota graduate Principles course, *Spirituality and Resilience* continuously since 2002, greatly enhanced Principles learning in the community. In addition, we have always used Health Realization terms so two decades of participants can understand each other. We intentionally developed systems change common language. We simply integrated new Principles terms as they emerged. We were able to trust the process in our personal and professional lives. In retrospect, this gave the project a life of its own, free of crippling funding concerns.

A similar NRRC story played out simultaneously in Menomonie, Wisconsin. Cooperative Educational Service Agency (CESA) prevention coordinator, Bonnie Scheel, persuaded Menomonie School Social Worker and Alcohol Drug Prevention Coordinator Gary Johnson to attend an NRRC resilience and Health Realization training in Minneapolis. Bonnie Benard, Roger Mills and I were presenters. Gary realized there was "nothing to be fixed in kids" and felt a gigantic load lifted from his shoulders. Like Dr. Holt he called to contract for NRRC training and technical assistance. He had a small state prevention annual grant and could fund NRRC trainings. With the federal grant model from St. Cloud fresh in our minds, we collaboratively worked to successfully secure a similar ten-year grant and later the four-year augmentation award with School District of the Menomonie Area serving as fiscal agent.

Over time each community coalition was looking at direct and indirect funding totals in the seven digit range, which we could not have imagined at the beginning. These communities are in two different states, three hours apart. A few key leaders get together when possible. They share resources and speakers and learn from each other about everything from the Principles to strategic planning for sustainability. In both communities people who have learned the Principles are living with peace of mind, sharing the ups and downs of life and the joys of connections to others who live and treasure the Principles; adjusting to losses, health issues, retirement, and aging over two decades. They welcome new school and community administrators who come and go every two or three years, navigate federal and state program regulations that are anything but *inside out*, and gracefully carry the word to family members, neighbors and other communities. In both sites the commitment to resilience and Health Realization is the longest running program effort that anyone can remember, even though it is not perfect.

We have also been surprised at how global the reach of these Midwestern communities is at times. Susan Costello-Tennyson, a Menomonie educational psychologist working at a private international school in Cairo, Egypt, arranged for Gary and me to conduct staff and student trainings there in 2010. When St. Cloud school social worker Braden Hughs deployed to Iraq, we collaborated at a distance so he had the support, materials, and evaluation he needed to conduct Principles training for a small group of soldiers in combat. Retired Menomonie school nurse Lucy Weidner teaches the Principles to traveling senior citizens who annually return to an RV park half way across the country.

In both communities a modest NRRC transition plan has been implemented and does not require grant funding. A small cadre of local, official NRRC facilitators who are retired from or employed by school districts or community agencies deliver ongoing free NRRC trainings. Trainings have local administrative endorsement. As a charitable service NRRC provides oversight, guides facilitator development and assists with systemic sustainability strategic planning. An extensive NRRC website also makes training materials and relevant information readily accessible to facilitators and participants. Continuous systems change grounded in resilience and Principles for realizing health requires attention permanently.

Concluding Evidence
The NRRC goal is always to increase the *health of the helper*. In turn, participants pass their understanding to students, clients, colleagues, family members and others. For example, In 2012 I helped establish an in-house training cadre in St. Cloud at Stearns County Minnesota Department of Human Services, where DHS director Mark Sizer incorporated Health Realization into the work of 350 staffers, serving approximately 30,000 clients. While research was not feasible, NRRC's longitudinal outside evaluation is solid. Focus groups document *enhanced mental and physical well-being, enriched inner life and reflection, improved relationships with others and increased satisfaction with workplace or daily life*. The statistically significant pre/post introductory training survey with an *n* of 797 shows positive impact reducing stress and improving life quality, and producing a more secure state of mind essential to well-being and healthy living. Post survey means indicated there was statistically significant change in perception at .005 or .001 probability levels on 38 of 39 items. It

follows that these changes in perception would indicate significant changes in the behaviors that proceed from these perceptions or beliefs. An additional post-post survey with an *n* of 143 subjects tested from 10 months to six years with a mean of 3.1 years after initial training shows *long-term statistical significance* on 37 of the 39 items. "The overwhelming evidence is that the changes in perceptions, thinking, and behavior that were reported by participants following their training remain intact over time. The principles of resilience and Health Realization become internalized and continue to bear fruit and effect change long after the initial training is over." For complete qualitative and quantitative details see *Outcomes* at nationalresilienceresource.com.

PART III F

THE MICHIGAN STORY:
INGHAM REGIONAL MEDICAL CENTER

written by Milly Gilin and Lisa Davidson Laughman,
with an inserted personal reflection by Milly Gilin

In 1993 two hospitals in Lansing, Michigan (Ingham Medical Center and Lansing General Hospital) merged. Ingham Regional Medical Center (IRMC) posted a loss of $7.1 million in 1993, the first full year of the merger. By 1994 the Senior Management team was reduced from 23 to 8. Dennis Litos became the new CEO. Litos hired Senn Delaney, a consulting team from California, to begin working with the leadership of the organization. Retreats were held for management, board and physician leadership. Milly Gilin was hired as Director of Organizational Development and Education in 1995.

Marsha Madigan, M.D. wanted to learn more about who trained the trainers from Senn Delaney, discovered it was Pransky and Associates and reached out to them. Training then began by various trainers from the Pransky group for board members, physicians and the entire management team, both in La Conner, Washington and Michigan. Meanwhile, Chris Goeschel and Milly Gilin participated in a year-long training program with Roger Mills and Elsie Spittle.

Understanding of the Principles allowed people to begin to work with each other more productively and to bring the two cultures together. By the end of 1998 overall patient satisfaction increased to 92.8%, 82% of employees had high job satisfaction and Ingham Regional Medical Center had a net income of $11 million, up from a loss of $7.1 million in 1993.

While focusing on its own organizational development work, IRMC allowed some members of the community to attend the classes they were offering. Several key members of the Ingham County Health Department became curious about the Three Principles and sent a representative to the National Annual Conference in Minnesota. As a result of that experience "Health Realization" was written into a W.K. Kellogg Foundation Community Voices Grant by Doak Bloss. IRMC was a key stakeholder in that grant and was assigned the responsibility for disseminating Health Realization Training to local community organizers. Lisa Laughman was hired as the Health Realization Services Coordinator for this Grant, reporting to Milly Gilin.

Insert: Personal Reflection by Milly Gilin

When I first heard the Principles in 1995, I was curious. Something about what people were saying rang true to me. I had many opportunities to hear people talk about the Principles because of my position in the Healthcare System as Director of Organizational Development and Education. At first, I thought it was an interesting way to manage stress and I was interested in that topic both personally and professionally. Little did I know my life would change completely as a result of learning the Principles.

The context of my learning happened in an organization that was in the middle of two mergers. It was a very difficult time for many people and others seemed to thrive. Personally, I was focused on helping other people and the organization be as effective and creative as possible. I was so involved in the work that I did not realize that my personal understanding was growing. At the same time the upset in the organization was also growing. Some people in the organization felt that learning about the Principles was extremely helpful; others felt it was mandatory, a cult, and resented the money being spent on bringing people in to teach the Principles. People became polarized partially because they felt they were being judged and that hiring and firing decisions were being made based on who was "above the line" and who was "below the line," a concept taught then to explain the Principles.

The polarization was not helpful. We became increasingly concerned about this perception and when things in the organization changed enough so we could do things differently, we did. The classes and retreats became voluntary and we invited people from the community to join us. This allowed the understanding to reach many more people in the organization and in the community. The organization continued to change as a result of the mergers. The growth of the organization is documented in the history. This happened as a result of the work of many people in the organization and many people who were teaching the Principles to people in the organization.

Personally, after five years it became increasingly difficult for me to be part of the organization. As the merger continued and people began to feel more insecure, people's behavior changed including mine. What had once seemed easy became difficult for me.

After a 3P class, I was having lunch with Beverley Wilson and Lisa Laughman on a Friday and I asked Beverley what she thought I should do. Beverley wisely said, "I think you know what to do, and you are just not doing it." It was like someone hit me with a dart. Beverley has a way of bypassing your head and going right to your heart. In fact, I did know what to do and I was not doing it. After lunch, when I got into my car, I called the CEO's office and asked for an appointment. It was rare but he had one on Monday. Then I called my husband and told him I was going to resign. He said, "It's about time." The decision to leave a twenty-year career came in a moment when I was present and clear. I have never looked back.

I knew I wanted to teach the Principles but I did not want to ask Lisa Laughman to leave the organization. I had just hired her to manage the Kellogg Foundation grant that I was leading for the organization. When I called her over the weekend to tell her I was leaving, she said, "I know. I could see it on your face." She said, "How about we leave the organization together and form our own business and teach the Principles?" I said, "Great, let's do it!" and Lakeside Consulting was born. My soon-to-be former employer chose to have us represent them in the Kellogg grant and they were our first clients.

That was 15 years ago and we have had a great ride. Lisa and I have been able to teach the Principles to many people and at the same time I have been able to be a "Mema" to my six grandchildren, be with my Mom and my Aunt who are both 95, improve my physical health that was suffering from neglect, have more precious time with my husband and children, learn to paint and live a life that is meaningful to me and that flows from my deepest connection. I have learned to trust and to know that when we are open, our life will flow in the direction it is intended to flow in and that we will have everything we need to live it when we get there.

My understanding continues to deepen and I am very grateful to the leadership of the organization I served, to all the people who shared the Principles with me, and to Lisa Laughman for fifteen years of fun, support and learning as we have taught the Principles together, and who is one of the best teachers I know. A final note of thanks goes to Dicken Bettinger, who has been my mentor, friend and colleague for 20 years. His wisdom and patience have been a blessing in my life.

LAKESIDE CONSULTING
In September 1999 Milly Gilin and Lisa Laughman left Ingham Regional Medical Center to form Lakeside Consulting. Its mission was to share Health Realization (now the Three Principles) with as many people as possible: individuals, families and communities. Ingham Regional Medical Center contracted with Lakeside Consulting to represent them in the Community Voices Grant and to continue to provide courses for Ingham Regional Medical Center through the grant. The following is a representative list of the work Lakeside Consulting has done since 1999 through 2014.

COMMUNITY PARTNERSHIPS
Community Voices Grant Partner: Roger Mills came to Michigan to teach courses and to consult with the partners in the development of the Community Voices Grant. Lakeside Consulting, Inc. participated in this grant between 1999 and 2003. The grant was funded by the W.K.

Kellogg Foundation to improve the health status of Ingham County residents with particular emphasis on indigent, uninsured or underinsured individuals and families. Partners for the grant included: Ingham Regional Medical Center, Ingham County Health Department, City of Lansing, Public Sector Consulting and Lakeside Consulting. Lakeside participated in two ways: first as a community development builder and change agent in South Lansing, and second as Health Realization trainers (see below) for Ingham County. Trainers included Milly Gilin and Lisa Laughman* with the support of many others including: Bob Carr*, Marsha Madigan, Carol Fitzgerald, Sue Weiss, Janet Foreman, Deb Brinson, Joy Carr, Lisa Robinson, Connie Marin, Teresa Patterson, Damita Zweiback, Jennifer Novello*, Doak Bloss, Marilyn Sylvan Thompson*, Evonne Alhaddad, Melany Mack, Peter Houk, Susanne Hoekzema, Jami Witbeck, Jannine Sinno, Wendy Greene, Georgia Davidson, Mara Stein, Toni Stevenson, Pieternel Feeheley, Jon Novello*, Jan Kimble, Sylvia Hirschegger, Cindy Claypatch, Sandy Krot, Beverley Wilson, Cathy Casey, Kristen Mansheim, Mark Howard, Dicken Bettinger and Joe Bailey.

> * = individuals providing counseling in the Lansing area as of the date of this chronology

Summer Enrichment Project: Lakeside Consulting participated in Ingham County's groundbreaking Summer Enrichment Program. Implemented in the summer of 2000, Lakeside conducted training for men and women attempting to move from welfare to work. Lakeside conducted psycho-social assessments, linked clients to resources, and provided information back to Family Independence Agency (FIA) caseworkers. Lakeside also provided training for other staff involved in the project such as Black Child and Family Services, Capital Area Community Services, Refugee Services, Lansing School District and Highfields.

Community Access Program (CAP): Lakeside Consulting provided training and personal coaching for the staff, administrators, consumer advisory boards and providers who deliver healthcare services for the Ingham Health Plan. The CAP grant was awarded by the Health Resources and Services Administration of the U.S. Department of

Health and Human Services for the purpose of strengthening and expanding health care coverage strategies of uninsured persons residing in Ingham, Clinton and Eaton Counties.

TRAINING / PERSONAL COACHING / ORGANIZATIONAL DEVELOPMENT SERVICES: These services were provided for the following organizations: Lansing School District, Michigan State University, Ingham County, Ingham County Health Department, American Red Cross, Ingham Regional Medical Center, Refugee Services, Lansing Community College, The Peoples Church, and other organizations. Trainers included Milly Gilin, Lisa Laughman, Roger Mills, George Pransky, Paul Nakai, Dicken Bettinger, Judy Sedgeman and Bill Pettit, M.D.

TRAIN-THE-TRAINER PROGRAMS: TOTs were provided for over 30 people in the Lansing Community, and Lakeside coordinated and supervised 15 community based internship sites, which began to allow Health Realization to be taught in a wide array of community settings. Trainers included Lisa Laughman, Milly Gilin and Dicken Bettinger.

2-4 DAY COMMUNITY COURSES: These courses in the community were offered for individuals interested in learning more about Health Realization.

MICHIGAN STATE UNIVERSITY: In 2003, Lisa Laughman became the coordinator of the MSU Employee Assistance Program. She hired another Three Principles-oriented counselor, Jonathan Novello. Lisa collaborated with MSU Human Resource Development and in January of 2004 began offering 2-day Principle-based stress reduction courses. The University supported these courses by providing employees release time to attend and covering all of the costs associated with offering these classes, co-facilitated by Milly Gilin. The "Breaking Free from Stress" Course was offered for 10 years, with more than 1,000 employees benefiting from this 3 Principle-based education. Lisa also taught similar courses for specific departments and within the program structure of the MSU Health4U program where as of the date of this chronology she serves as an Emotional Wellness

Consultant. More recently, Dicken Bettinger returned to Michigan to work with several MSU departments.

Wisdom Heart Life: Lisa Laughman also teaches the 3 Principles as part of her facilitated community groups designed to help people live their day-to-day life, lined up with their deepest wisdom and their greatest sense of meaning and purpose.

APPENDIX

APPENDIX A

March, 1998. Psychology of Mind (POM) meeting. Issues discussed, as summarized by Jack Pransky, who served as note-taker for the meeting:

- The closer POM operates as a "formless structure" (a contradiction in terms), the closer it will be to the pure, and the better off it will be.
- The more the POM community operates in alignment with each other in terms of living and practicing what it teaches, the better off it will be.
- The more the POM community as a whole is in alignment with who plays what role within the organizational structure, the better off it will be.
- The fewer limitations of thinking on how POM should be taught, the more it will get out to the world.
- The more the public becomes aware of incredible POM results, the more it will spread out into the world.

Questions raised:

- Who, if anyone, should call the shots or provide direction?
- What types of direction are appropriate and inappropriate?
- If part of the POM community discovers a new level of understanding or teaching, how does it get disseminated throughout the POM community, and who decides whether it is worthwhile or not?
- How do people get training to teach POM, and who decides who is qualified to teach it?
- What gets put out in the name of POM, and who decides?
- How do POM materials get disseminated and should they be in the name of the POM "organization," instead of through a private business, or should the POM organization officially contract with a private organization for this purpose?
- What kind of financial flow is needed to maintain a POM organization, how is that determined, and how can the costs be respectful of both the POM community and the prevention, treatment and business communities?

- Who decides what official "centers" or "institutes" operate in the name of POM/HR?
- Are people willing to make a personal commitment to operating with high integrity with each other and to using the alignment model?
- The "founders" issue: It is Syd's decision whether he wants to be called the founder, but if he does not want to be, who decides? [If anyone besides George and Roger wants to claim they are one of the founders, they need to step forward and make that claim.]
- Should an official historical record of the development of POM be compiled, and who should do it?
- Is the name "Psychology of Mind" one of its own limitations?
- Will all POM/HR projects be willing to document the results?

APPENDIX B

July 15-18, 1998. Psychology of Mind Foundation Curriculum Development Committee meeting at West Virginia University, Department of Community Medicine in Morgantown, West Virginia, Summary of Issues to be discussed by Judith Sedgeman, Adjunct Assistant Professor at West Virginia University:

While POM is producing large numbers of increasingly healthy clients and excellent practitioners, there is a much smaller number of people who are undertaking to teach others to teach—to break down the training and education process behind producing instructors dedicated to educating future educators of POM...

Questions for the meeting:

- What is at the heart of the teaching process in POM?
- What do POM educators have to do to prevent POM for being taught as "good ideas" and learned and practiced as methodology and techniques?
- What are the fundamental qualities of a POM educator?
- What does POM education have in common with traditional educational practices and how does it differ?

Discussion of ideas central to issues at the heart of teaching others to teach POM:

- Who should appropriately have stewardship over the evolution teaching teachers? Who defines what POM training would look like...?
- What makes POM teaching easily received, non-contingent, offered in service, safe students, consistent with a sound understanding behind the feeling?
- How do we sustain well-being of teacher?
- How do we show people how to be responsive, in depth, and how to teach for insight, spontaneously, keeping content secondary and not be driven by the content—yet teaching a Curriculum?
- What do you look for in a POM teacher to see how to "let the light go on?"

- We know we have to awaken intuitive wisdom at the heart of the teaching process, but what are we looking for or measuring to see if it is there?
- How do we produce a Curriculum that is in depth, but not an intellectual document?
- What is the understanding behind teaching that keeps the Curriculum fresh?
- How do we keep defensiveness out of the feedback/learning process while we are developing this?
- We must respect differences in what and how teachers decide to teach and respect and nurture creativity within the Curriculum; we must always put the health of the teachers first. How do we find ways to communicate how natural the flow of good teaching is—that simplicity works and they both emerge naturally from health?
- How do we isolate the active ingredients attached to—the life behind the words that actually does the work?
- We need to generate teaching ideas to assist the discovery of the insight-learning process (versus information learning).
- Who should actually be responsible for the training of trainers, and who does it? What is the role of the Foundation versus private teachers and centers doing things their own way?
- How do we make the invisible visible without creating a form that takes on a life of its own?
- POM teaching is ordinary and real; we are all students in order to teach and work for freedom—how do we indicate that without creating a "system" or "form" that kills it?
- How do we demonstrate that even what you're learning is not what "it" is? POM is always evolving; it is understanding of that—not what it produces—that is at the heart of it.
- How do we build a growing network of colleagues who support and further each other?
- How do we keep trust alive?
- We need to answer the question of, "What do teachers know?"
- POM teaching is all grounding, claiming our innate health and working from it, but how is this communicated through the eyes of the teacher?

Final debriefing and summary:

- The only constant, universal Curriculum is the fundamentals: the Three Principles and the profundity of the idea and implications of Innate Health;
- Professional development should always lead in the direction of simplicity, of defining the obvious and keeping the presentation uncontaminated;
- The key to inspiring POM teachers and keeping them inspired is engagement in the process;
- Every teacher should feel free to produce materials that will be useful in his/her situation and the Foundation should take some responsibility for encouraging the production teaching materials and simple, straightforward texts for teachers' use;
- The Foundation should spearhead true scientific research, which will in itself generate professional interest in our teaching process and draw in the teachers.

APPENDIX C

August 1999. AEquanimitas Foundation meeting to establish Objectives for Foundations Courses. Summarized by Judy Sedgeman:

Objectives for Foundations I Course:

Participants will –

- explore the nature of a principle-based approach to human understanding and the effects of principles on a field of study;
- learn the three principles of Mind, Consciousness and Thought;
- learn how these principles provide an explanation of the full range of human behaviors and experience;
- learn the operation and relevance of these principles in people's lives and how they explain and predict people's moment to moment levels of psychological well-being, or distress, and behavioral options;
- learn how and why understanding these principles leads to improved psychological health, resiliency, stability and calm.

Objectives for Foundations II Course:

Participants will –

- deepen understanding of the three principles of Mind, Thought and Consciousness;
- learn the implications of this understanding for the development of deep listening and rapport;
- learn how this understanding helps to draw out the psychological health of others;
- discover how to share their own understanding of the principles in ways that bring the understanding alive for others.

Taken together, these are entry-level courses for individuals wishing to pursue this understanding, either for their own benefit or as a starting place to using the approach in their work.

APPENDIX D

*Stages of Early Three Principles Development
conceptualized by George Pransky*

Pre-Concept stage: 1976 to 1985

Objective:　　　To teach new psychology with "the feeling"
Critical skill:　　Health of the helper

Concept stage: 1985 to 1988

Objective:　　　To make accessible and professional
Critical skills:　Teaching concepts

Principle stage: 1989 - onward

Objective:　　　Profundity and scientific
Critical skills:　Understanding at a deeper level

Therapy Development Stage: 1990 -

Objective:　　　To make therapy teachable and supervisable.
Critical Skill:　Break down the therapy process.

Dissemination Stage: 1992-

Objective:　　　To get the Principles and therapy to the field
　　　　　　　　with integrity
Critical skills:　Rigor and conceptual integrity

- - - - -

*(This came after George's original depiction of the stages, and is gleaned
from his interview.)*

Distillation Stage:　present (as of the time of this chronology)

Objective:　　　To see and communicate that there is *nothing
　　　　　　　　else* but the Three Principles operating in
　　　　　　　　every moment
Critical skills:　Depth of understanding and grounding

APPENDIX E

**Sydney Banks Foundation
for
Inner Consciousness Development**
Box 869, Ganges, B.C.
Canada V0S 1E0

January 2, 1979

Dear friends:

I would like to take this opportunity to wish you all a very happy new year. I hope with all my heart to continue to grow towards the wisdom you seek in the coming year.

1978 held many beautiful experiences for me. I have seen many disturbed couples bring their lives together simply by finding a microscopic glimmer of the wisdom and love that lay deep within themselves. I have seen these same couples pass this inner knowledge to their children, curing them of mental and physical ailments. I have seen people physically change. They have reshaped their bodies. They have become youthful in both body and mind. Such is the power that lies within.

It is truly gratifying to know that many psychologists, therapists and people involved in mental health are starting to listen. With what they are learning and passing on, it is helping others.

When I first had the realization of what God really meant, I knew in my heart what I had found was so valuable I would have to share it with others.

I feel the best way to do this is by cassette tape because it is direct. Those who want to listen can listen in the silence of their home, not being disturbed by other people's opinions.

A special thanks goes to the members who assisted me in the running of the foundation last year. I regret that the treasurer has informed me that this year only 47 members have renewed. This naturally makes it impossible for the foundation to continue for very much longer. If the worst comes and the foundation does close I am sure the work will continue in another form.

All my love,

Syd